Instant INTERNET™ WITH WEBSURFER™

DAVID SACHS & HENRY STAIR

P T R Prentice Hall
Englewood Cliffs, NJ 07632

Library of Congress Cataloging in Publication Data

Editorial/production supervision: *Camille Trentacoste*
Interior graphic design: *Gail Cocker-Bogusz*
Cover design: *John Churchman and Anthony Gemmellaro*
Manufacturing manager: *Alexis R. Heydt*
Acquisitions editor: *Mary Franz*
Editorial Assistant: *Noreen Regina*

Prentice-Hall, Inc.
A Simon & Schuster Company
Englewood Cliffs, New Jersey 07632

The publisher offers discounts on this book when ordered in bulk quantities. For more information, contact: Corporate Sales Department, Prentice Hall PTR, 113 Sylvan Avenue, Englewood Cliffs, NJ 07632, Phone: 800-382-3419 Fax: 201-592-2249, E-mail: dan_rush@prenhall.com

Printed in the United States of America
10 9 8 7 6 5 4 3 2 1

ISBN 0-13-210675-2

Prentice-Hall International (UK) Limited, *London*
Prentice-Hall of Australia Pty. Limited, *Sydney*
Prentice-Hall Canada Inc., *Toronto*
Prentice-Hall Hispanoamericana, S.A., *Mexico*
Prentice-Hall of India Private Limited, *New Delhi*
Prentice-Hall of Japan, Inc., *Tokyo*
Simon & Schuster Asia Pte. Ltd., *Singapore*
Editora Prentice-Hall do Brasil, Ltda., *Rio de Janeiro*

Dedication

Instant Internet with WebSurfer is dedicated to my wonderful wife Linda, and to our dear friends Jeff and Deane, Barbara and Arnold, and Jeff and Caroline, who have participated in more conversations about the Internet and the World-Wide Web during this past year than anyone would have thought possible. Thanks for all of the help, support, and understanding. Who knows what 1995 will bring?

—David Sachs

Instant Internet with WebSurfer is dedicated with love to the five constant Stairs in my life: my wife Lorrine, and our scattered yet still telelinked family, Sharon, Craig, Diane, and Carol.

Imagine a universe…

—Henry Stair

About the Authors

David Sachs is Professor of Office Information Systems and Assistant Dean in Pace University's School of Computer Science and Information Systems. He has been actively involved in the development and teaching of computer science and telecommunications courses since 1984. He has co-authored *Discovering Microsoft Works, Mastering Microsoft Works, Hands-On Internet,* and *Hands-On Mosaic.* Dr. Sachs is particularly interested in the field of telecommunications and its impact upon our world. His interests include racquetball and downhill skiing.

Henry (Pete) Stair is a senior consultant with Mycroft Information in New Canaan, Connecticut, where he specializes in high-performance global telecommunications and computer networking. He co-authored the post-graduate textbook *Megabit Data Communications,* as well as *Hands-On Internet* and *Hands-On Mosaic.* He is a registered professional engineer (CA) and a member of the IEEE and the Internet Society. His interests include demystifying technology, cross-country skiing, consciousness research, and classical music.

Contents

Session 6: File Transfer Protocol 73

Session 7: Exploring GopherSpace 93

Part 3: WebSurfer

Acknowledgments

Instant Internet with WebSurfer is the product of many hands. Our gratitude goes out to all who have been so supportive and encouraging. There are several individuals who deserve special thanks.

At PTR Prentice Hall, our acquisitions editor, Mary Franz, continues to be our guiding light and wonderful support. Once again, Mary showed up with just the right software at just the right time, as if by magic. Camille Trentacoste, production editor, has done a wonderful job of turning our prose and figures into the book you now hold in your hands, in record time. Gail Cocker-Bogusz has enhanced the quality of *Instant Internet with WebSurfer* with her skilled graphics design.

Our copy editor, Martha Williams, has added many useful suggestions to our writing. Martha's attention to detail is wonderful, and her caring suggestions about how to improve the clarity of the writing have been gratefully accepted.

The technical review of *Instant Internet with WebSurfer* has been provided by Bob Williams from NetManage, Inc. Bob knows Internet Chameleon by heart, and has provided us with careful, thoughtful, and wonderfully quick feedback throughout the past few months.

We are grateful for all of the help and support we have received while writing *Instant Internet with WebSurfer*. Even with all of this help, we and we alone, are responsible for any remaining goofs, glitches, and gaps.

—David Sachs and Henry Stair

Introduction

Once upon a time there was a jungle called the Internet. It was a dark and forbidding place explored only by those with a taste for complexity, confusion and computer commands. Hardy souls ventured there because the Internet held riches of information akin to the fabled seven cities. They spoke an arcane tongue with words like *grep*, *ping*, *telnet* and *ftp*.

But suddenly..., quite suddenly, things began to change.

In an amazingly short time, new maps to explore the jungle emerged and came within reach of anyone with a computer and a modem. Citizens of America Online®, CompuServe®, Delphi®, and Prodigy® began to penetrate the edges. People found friendlier ways to enter the jungle and come out alive. New comfortable words like Gopher and browser began to appear.

News magazines, newspapers and television discovered the Internet. Now the Internet was not only friendlier, but it was also hip! People and businesses talked about the Internet, but few could actually see what all the excitement was actually about as some of the old complexity remained.

Then came Instant Internet with WebSurfer!™

Now you can explore the riches of the Internet with only a mouse as your guide. You can see what the natives see and hear what the natives hear. Instant Internet with WebSurfer has taken all the hard and complex tasks and hidden them away. Instant Internet with WebSurfer will

permit you to sign on to the Internet automatically with your choice from among many major, well-known Internet providers.

Literally within minutes, you will be exploring the Internet's world-wide resources. Instant Internet with WebSurfer will show you the maps and paths and wonders of the incredible jungle. You will return alive and amazed.

Introduction to the Internet

It's been called the world's only functioning anarchy, but many heads of state can be reached there. No one is really in charge, yet most U.S. government agencies are there. Millions of people are already trading electronic mail with each other. Thousands of discussion groups are active, and mailing lists keep people in touch with their shared, very special interests. Tools such as Gopher "go-fer" information from around the world. And then there's the World-Wide Web!

The World-Wide Web and the windowslike graphic browsers such as WebSurfer are creating revolutions in education, business and government. Now anyone can reach businesses, schools and governmental agencies without waiting. No "Press 6 for..."; no "Please leave a message at the tone"; no "We'll have someone get back to you." Just point and click and you're there.

Businesses, cities, counties and individuals are hanging out shingles on what is quickly becoming the "Information Highway." It's not a superhighway just yet, but you can get there from here and you're in control.

So what *Is* the Internet?

It's a loose but effective collection of everyone who wants to have their computers on this "network of networks." It's people and schools and governments and telephone companies and businesses all hooked together and all able to communicate with each other. Each controls their own information and computers, and they are all connected.

No one really owns it or runs it. Lots of people contribute to their corner of the Internet and many people volunteer to make it faster and better. But there is no chief or president or emperor of the Internet. It's just people working together to keep it running and to build it bigger and faster. And you can join them as a full partner. Your computer will be an equal "host" with all the connected computers in the world.

Join us now, as we venture out upon the Internet!

Why Have We Written This Book For The Windows PC User?

Users of Microsoft® Windows™ are accustomed to having a friendly, powerful interface for their software. Many commands can often be invoked by pointing and clicking at them. Until now, this has not been true for most Windows PC users who have been Internet users as well. If you have been using what is known as terminal access, then the interface you have had to use is one filled with many UNIX commands, a command-line interface, and no ability to have color, sound or graphics. Using Internet Chameleon™ and WebSurfer as your multimedia Internet navigators will change all that.

We believe that Internet Chameleon is an extremely powerful tool with which Windows users can navigate the Internet. Internet Chameleon contains Instant Internet, which will provide you with immediate connectivity to an Internet service provider. In addition, Internet Chameleon includes software that will permit you to communicate with others using e-mail, to remotely access other computers on the Internet, to upload and download files easily, and to search for information with powerful tools such as Gopher and Archie. And, perhaps most importantly, Internet Chameleon contains WebSurfer, an extremely powerful, easy-to-use Internet browser. We have written this book to show you how you can have access to the global Internet on your Windows PC.

Introduction

Welcome to *Instant Internet with WebSurfer.* This book contains everything that you need to explore the world's greatest network of networks—the Internet. In a series of online sessions, you learn how to

1. install the special type of software (included with this book) that is needed to use WebSurfer
2. establish the special type of connection that is needed for your computer to be directly on the Internet
3. use many of the traditional Internet tools such as E-mail, telnet, ftp, and gopher
4. use WebSurfer to navigate the multimedia Internet

All of the software and instructions you will need to do this are included in this book.

For Whom Is This Book Intended?

Beginning Internet Users

This book has been written with the beginning Internet user in mind. If you are comfortable using your computer and are familiar with the Windows environment, you should enjoy learning about the Internet as you work through *Instant Internet with WebSurfer*. This book will provide you with a very supportive environment in which to explore the Internet. You will learn all of the fundamental Internet skills, as well as the more advanced capabilities provided by the World-Wide Web and WebSurfer.

Internet Users with Terminal Accounts

If you have been using the Internet for some time, using a terminal account, and a traditional UNIX environment but have been wishing for more ease-of-use and power, this book is definitely for you.

Instant Internet with WebSurfer will teach you about the special type of Internet service provider connection you need to use WebSurfer. We help you install the special type of software that is required to run a Web browser like WebSurfer. Finally, we teach you all about the many powerful opportunities Internet Chameleon and WebSurfer can provide. All of these will enable you to learn how to access the Internet using a Windows environment. In addition, you will have the ability to quickly and efficiently download and use multimedia files of all shapes and sizes.

Experienced Internet Users

If you are an experienced Internet user who would like to significantly upgrade your Internet capabilities, *Instant Internet with WebSurfer* is for you as well. As soon as you change your terminal account to a SLIP or PPP and install Internet Chameleon, you will be able to do all of the usual Internet activities (E-mail, ftp, and telnet) far more easily. In addition, you will then find that you have access to a whole array of multimedia resources that were previously unavailable.

NOTE: If you have an existing account with one of the preconfigured Internet service providers included with Internet Chameleon, then be sure to read the special directions in Session Two.

How Is This Book Organized?

In the text and graphics that follow, we will guide you hands-on through three parts: "Instant Internet," "Basic Internet Tools," and "WebSurfer."

Part 1: Instant Internet

To use Web browsers such as WebSurfer or other Internet browsers such as Mosaic™, two preliminary conditions must be met. First of all, you must have installed a TCP/IP stack of software. And second, your computer must have a SLIP or PPP connection that provides you with a direct connection to the Internet. We teach you how to do both of these in "Instant Internet."

First, we teach you how to install NetManage's Internet Chameleon, which contains the TCP/IP stack of software. This is an easy process, which should only take a few minutes.

Second, we help you to find an Internet service provider that can provide you with SLIP or PPP access. Internet Chameleon comes preconfigured with Instant Internet. As the name implies, you will be able to instantly sign up with any one of the national service providers without having to learn any complicated computer commands at all. It is possible to do this whole operation in less than five minutes!

Part 2: Basic Internet Tools

In "Basic Internet Tools," we use Internet Chameleon to explore a variety of Internet activities. With Internet Chameleon, you will be able to

1. use telnet to log in to computers around the world
2. use electronic mail to communicate with others on the Internet
3. use ftp to download file compression and virus protection software
4. use gopher to explore the many wonderful resources located in GopherSpace

Part 3: WebSurfer

In "WebSurfer" we lead you through many hands-on sessions as we explore the multimedia World-Wide Web using WebSurfer. We introduce you to concepts such as hypertext and hypermedia, which are exciting new English language ways to navigate the Internet. Finally, we show you how to use WebSurfer to find your own treasures. Not only will be you able to find text files, but you will also be able to find

an enormous array of multimedia software, including art work, maps, satellite photos, voices, and music!

Conventions Used throughout the Book

Sessions—There are twelve sessions in this book, each of which is intended to be done online and hands-on, so you can work along with us as you first install your own copy of Internet Chameleon (which includes WebSurfer) and then put your Windows PC directly onto the Internet.

Overview—As you will see, once you have WebSurfer up and running, these pages will provide you with an overview of the options awaiting you each step of the way.

Instant Activities—In each session, you will find many hands-on activities in which we lead you carefully through the steps that are necessary to complete each activity successfully.

Pointers—From time to time, there are suggestions about ways to make particular activities flow more smoothly.

HeadsUp!—There are times when what you are about to do will be somewhat complicated, or more technical, than you may have experienced previously. We would like you to be fresh, alter, and paying close attention when we get to these activities.

Tips—Sometimes we provide some commentary about what may have just happened.

What Will You Need?

1. First, you need an IBM personal computer or compatible capable of running Microsoft Windows 3.1 (or higher) in enhanced mode. That is, you need what is known as an 80386 (or higher) processor and 640 kilobytes of conventional memory, plus at least 4 megabytes of extended memory.
2. In addition, you need a 3 1/2″ floppy disk drive and a minimum of 4 megabytes of free hard-disk space for the Internet Chameleon diskettes that are provided with *Instant Internet with WebSurfer.*
3. We suggest you have at least 6 megabytes of free disk space for the information you will be receiving from your travels with us about the Internet.
4. To communicate with an Internet service provider, you need a modem and a telephone line connected to your computer. We strongly recommend a high-speed modem (14,400 bits per sec-

ond or higher) due to the amount of multimedia information you will be receiving once you are using WebSurfer. (The faster your modem, the more quickly the information will be transferred to your computer.)

You do not need any other software. The Internet Chameleon diskettes included with this book are all that you need to establish a direct Internet connection so you can use all of the traditional tools such as E-mail, telnet, ftp, and gopher, as well as "surf the Internet" using WebSurfer.

Let's get started!

Instant Internet will help you prepare your Windows PC to be on the Internet and to run WebSurfer. To do so, you will need to learn about the special Internet connections that are required, as well as about the special software (included with *Instant Internet With WebSurfer*) that must be installed.

In **Session One**, you will learn how to install Internet Chameleon on your PC.

In **Session Two**, you will learn how to sign up with an Internet Service Provider. If need be, you will learn how to configure Internet Chameleon to work with an existing account.

In **Session Three**, you will learn how to connect to (and disconnect from) the Internet using Internet Chameleon. In addition, you will Ping several Internet hosts.

By the end of ***Instant Internet***, you will be ready to explore all the features that the Internet has to offer.

PART 1

INSTANT INTERNET

BASIC INTERNET TOOLS

WEB SURFER

SESSION 1

Installing Internet Chameleon

Installing Internet Chameleon

Session Overview

Welcome to Instant Internet!

Installing Internet Chameleon consists of two very quick and simple steps:

1. Installing and signing up with an Internet service provider. This is done with a secure 800-number telephone call so that your credit card will not appear on the Internet.

2. Connecting to the Internet on a second telephone call to your selected Internet service provider.

We will have you on the Internet and surfing the web so fast, you will be dazzled. If you're not sure what the web is, we will show you step by step. Just follow along as we install Internet Chameleon.

To begin, we will install the Instant Internet programs onto your Windows PC. Before we start, check your PC configuration and make sure that you have everything needed to make the programs work correctly. Here is the *Must Have* list.

1. You *must have* an IBM personal computer or compatible PC running Microsoft Windows 3.1 in enhanced mode. That is, you will need what is known as an 80386 (or higher) processor and 640 kilobytes of conventional memory, plus at least 4 megabytes of extended memory.

2. In addition, you *must have* a 3.5″ floppy disk drive and a minimum of 10 megabytes of free hard-disk space for files from the Instant Internet diskettes.
3. You *must have* a modem and a telephone line connected to your computer.
4. You *must have* a valid credit card (American Express, Discover, Master Card, or Visa) to sign up with an Internet service provider.

In addition to these *must haves*, we strongly recommend that you consider the following. While not absolutely necessary, they will make your use of the Internet and WebSurfer a much happier experience.

1. We *recommend* that you have at least 15 megabytes of free disk space on your PC for the information you will be receiving from your travels with us about the Internet.
2. We also strongly *recommend* that your modem be high speed. A high-speed modem runs at 14,400 bits per second or higher. The faster your modem, the quicker the information will be transferred to your computer. The fastest modems now on the market can be identified by having "True ITU V.34." You will see this term used in advertising, as well as on the modem packaging. This jargon means that the modem can run as fast as 28,800 bits per second and actually a lot faster with the compression features that most modems have built into them.

If you have the PC and Windows 3.1 ready to go, let's begin to install your copy of the Internet Chameleon.

Installing Internet Chameleon

1. Turn on your PC and start Windows.
2. Insert Internet Chameleon Disk #1 into your diskette drive.
3. From the menu bar at the top, click on **File**
4. From the drop-down menu, click on **Run**
5. In the Run Command Line box, type `A:\setup` (or `B:\setup`)

This is illustrated in Figure 1-1.

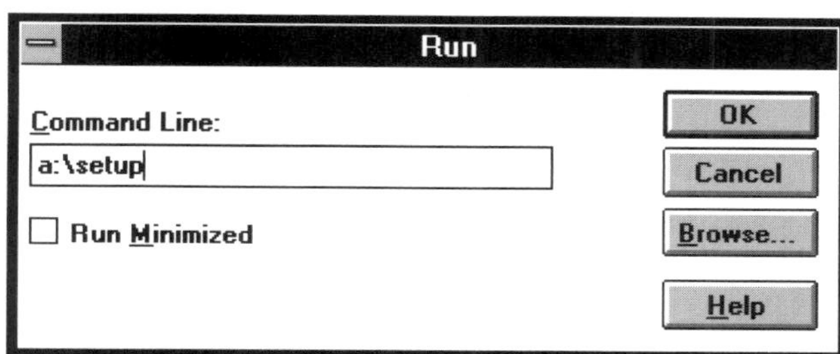

Figure 1-1
File, Run

Internet Chameleon's automatic Setup process will ask you what directory to use. We recommend that you accept the program's suggestion of C:\NETMANAG as shown in Figure 1-2.

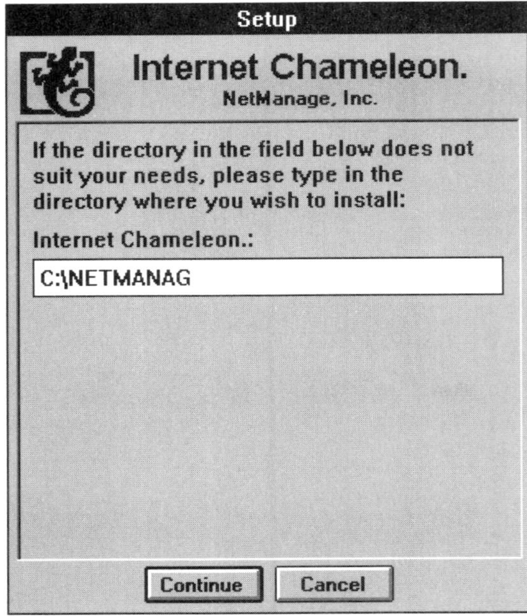

Figure 1-2
Installation Directory

Internet Chameleon will display information in the Setup box while the files from the first diskette are being transferred to your PC, as shown in Figure 1-3.

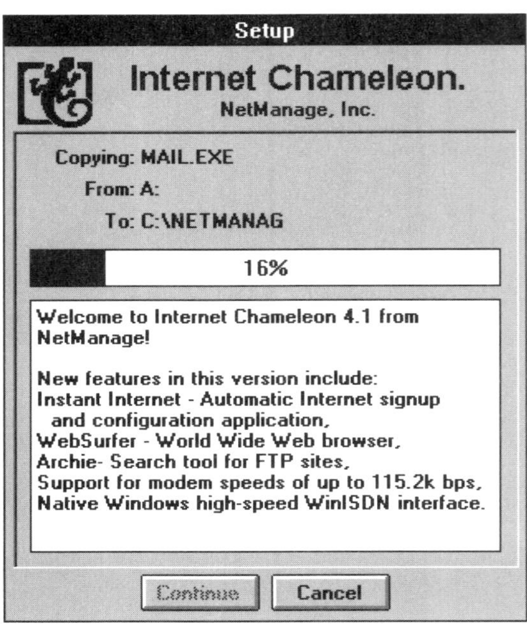

Figure 1-3
NetManage Welcome

6. When prompted by Setup, remove Internet Chameleon Disk #1 and insert Internet Chameleon Disk #2 as illustrated in Figure 1-4.

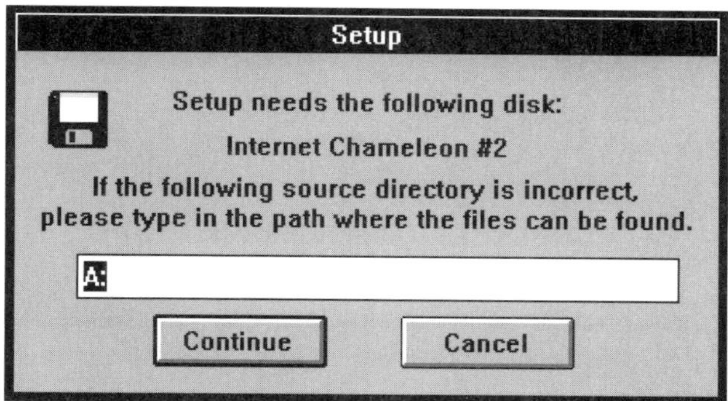

Figure 1-4
Insert Internet Chameleon Disk #2

While the files from the second diskette are loading, additional information about NetManage's other products will be listed on the screen, as shown in Figure 1-5.

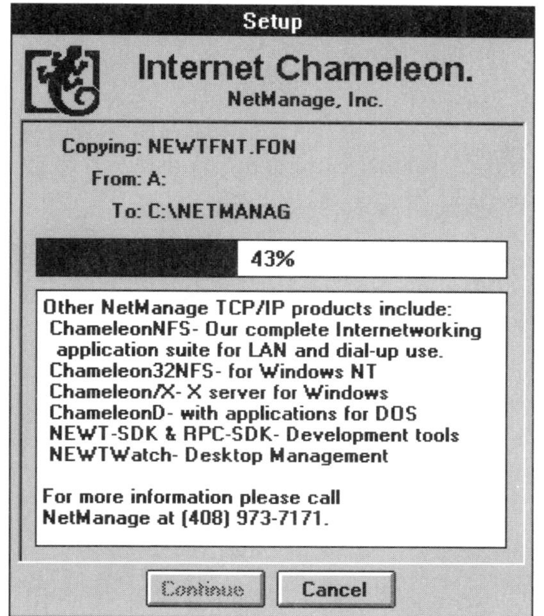

Figure 1-5
NetManage Products

7. When prompted by Setup, remove Internet Chameleon Disk #2 and insert Internet Chameleon Disk #3, as seen in Figure 1-6.

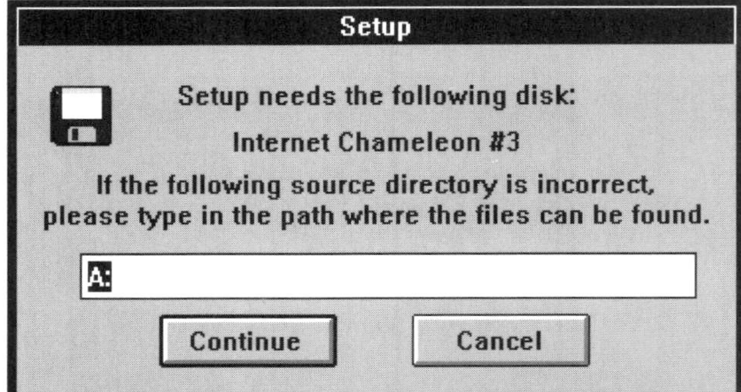

Figure 1-6
Insert Internet Chameleon Disk #3

While the third and last set of files is being transferred to your PC, the last installation message box will appear, as shown in Figure 1-7.

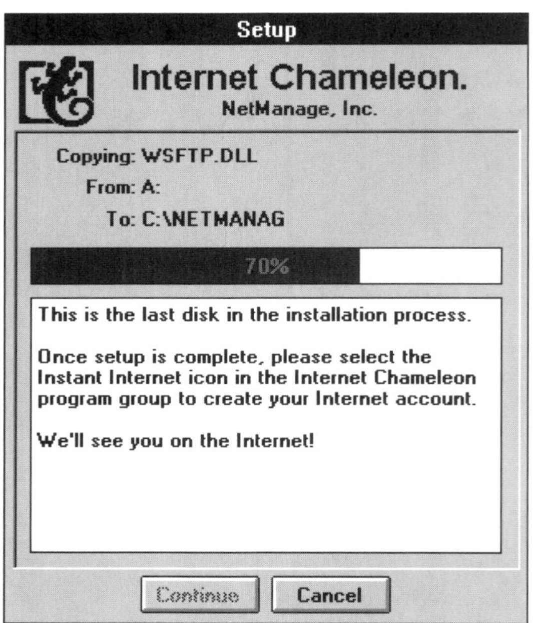

Figure 1-7
Last Disk Message

8. When you see the Installation Complete box, as shown in Figure 1- 8, click on **OK**

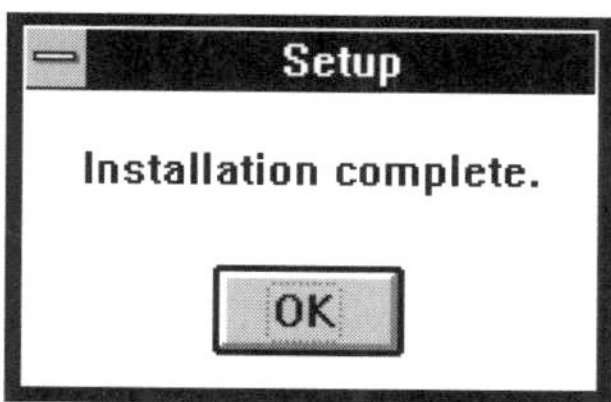

Figure 1-8
Installation Complete

When you click on the OK button or press Enter, everything will shrink to icons, including your Windows Program Manager. You will be left with your Windows background pattern. Not to worry; this is a normal part of the installation.

9. Move your mouse to the Program Manager Icon and double-click on it.

You will be back to your normal Windows screen with an addition. The addition on your screen is the new Internet Chameleon Group.

10. Double-click on this **Group Icon**. The Internet Chameleon window, as illustrated in Figure 1-9, should appear on your screen.

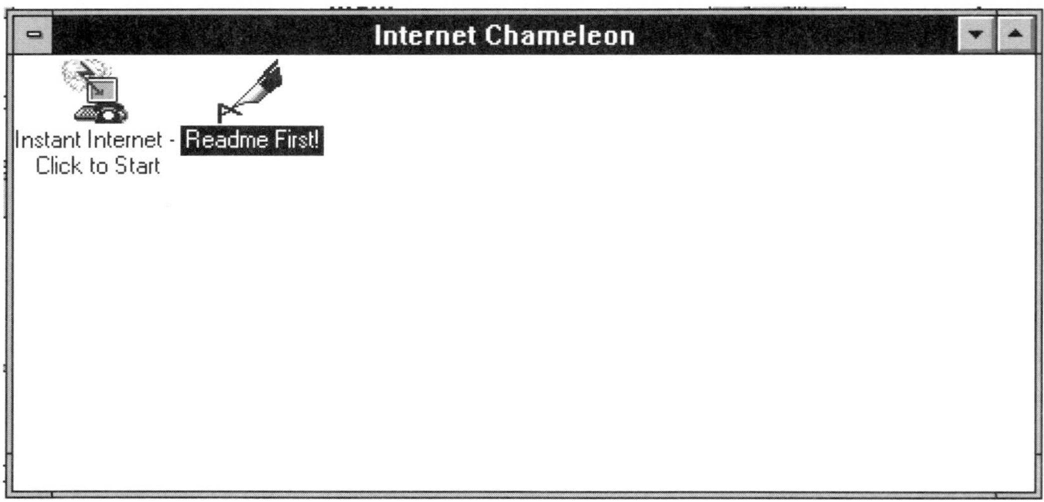

Figure 1-9
Internet Chameleon

This completes the installation of Internet Chameleon. You may want to double-click on the Readme First! Icon to get more information about Internet Chameleon. A sample of what you will see is shown in Figure 1-10.

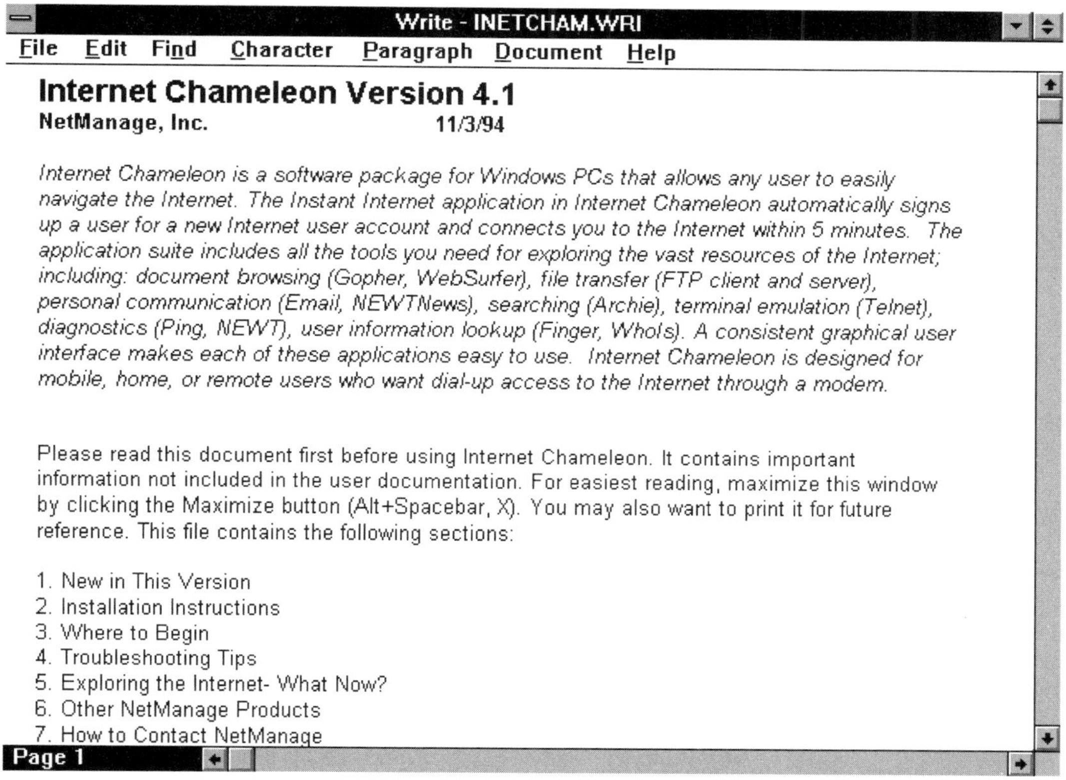

Write - INETCHAM.WRI

File Edit Find Character Paragraph Document Help

Internet Chameleon Version 4.1
NetManage, Inc. 11/3/94

Internet Chameleon is a software package for Windows PCs that allows any user to easily navigate the Internet. The Instant Internet application in Internet Chameleon automatically signs up a user for a new Internet user account and connects you to the Internet within 5 minutes. The application suite includes all the tools you need for exploring the vast resources of the Internet; including: document browsing (Gopher, WebSurfer), file transfer (FTP client and server), personal communication (Email, NEWTNews), searching (Archie), terminal emulation (Telnet), diagnostics (Ping, NEWT), user information lookup (Finger, WhoIs). A consistent graphical user interface makes each of these applications easy to use. Internet Chameleon is designed for mobile, home, or remote users who want dial-up access to the Internet through a modem.

Please read this document first before using Internet Chameleon. It contains important information not included in the user documentation. For easiest reading, maximize this window by clicking the Maximize button (Alt+Spacebar, X). You may also want to print it for future reference. This file contains the following sections:

1. New in This Version
2. Installation Instructions
3. Where to Begin
4. Troubleshooting Tips
5. Exploring the Internet- What Now?
6. Other NetManage Products
7. How to Contact NetManage

Page 1

Figure 1-10
Internet Chameleon Version 4.1

Session Summary

If you have completed the activities in this session, you have successfully installed Internet Chameleon on your PC. In the next session, you will select an Internet service provider, sign-up, and be on the Internet!!

SESSION 2

Signing Up with an Internet Service Provider

Configuring Internet Chameleon for an Existing Account

Signing Up with a Provider

Session Overview

In this session, we will help you to choose an Internet service provider so you will be ready to begin your Internet travels. The whole process should take no longer than five minutes from start to finish. Here is how to do this.

Signing Up with an Internet Service Provider

ONE

If you have the Internet Chameleon Group already open in Windows, find and double-click on **Instant Internet** (it also says **Click Here to Start**). You will see the Instant Internet Account Sign-up & Software Configuration screen as shown in Figure 2-1.

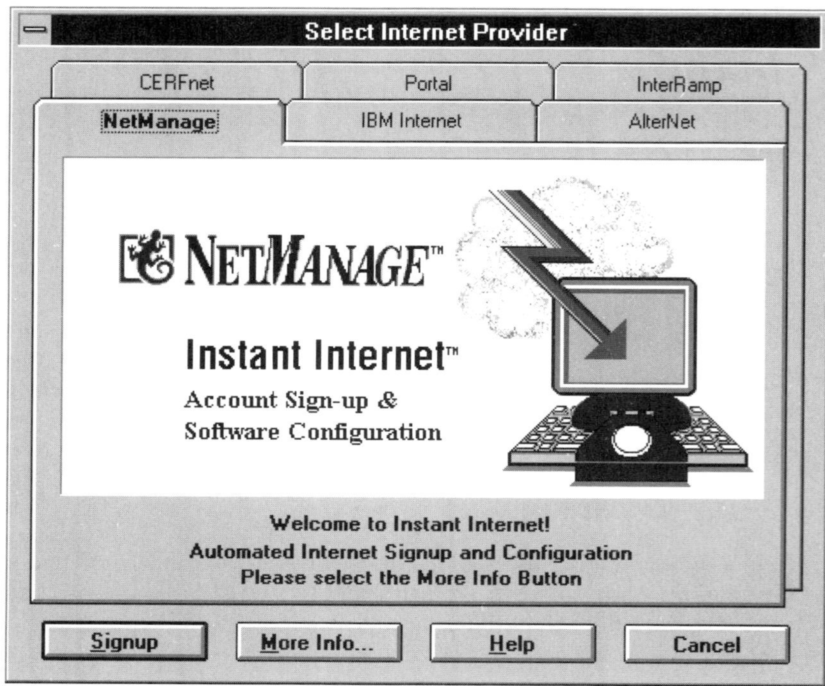

Figure 2-1
Account Signup

Notice the file folder tabs at the top of the window. A number of well-known providers have joined with NetManage to offer you Internet services. Each Internet provider has its own tab. By clicking on the appropriate tab, you will be able to read that provider's information and can signup with them.

NetManage also offers you another option. You can signup via the NetManage registration server to use Internet Chameleon with an existing Internet account that you may have already acquired.

Most of the providers and NetManage offer both Demonstration and Regular accounts. The demonstration accounts permit you to try out Internet services for a limited time period, usually from 7 to 30 days. You may ask for a demonstration or a regular account. Be aware that the demonstration accounts will expire automatically. Once this has happened, you will need to redo the account sign-up process with Instant Internet if you wish to have a regular account.

If you already have an existing Internet account, skip ahead to the Configuring Chameleon for an Existing Account activity at the end of this session.

Each of the provider's screens has a similar look and feel. Each has a More Info... button that will give you exactly that; more information about the options and services offered by that provider. Figure 2-2 provides an illustration of the NetManage More Information... screen.

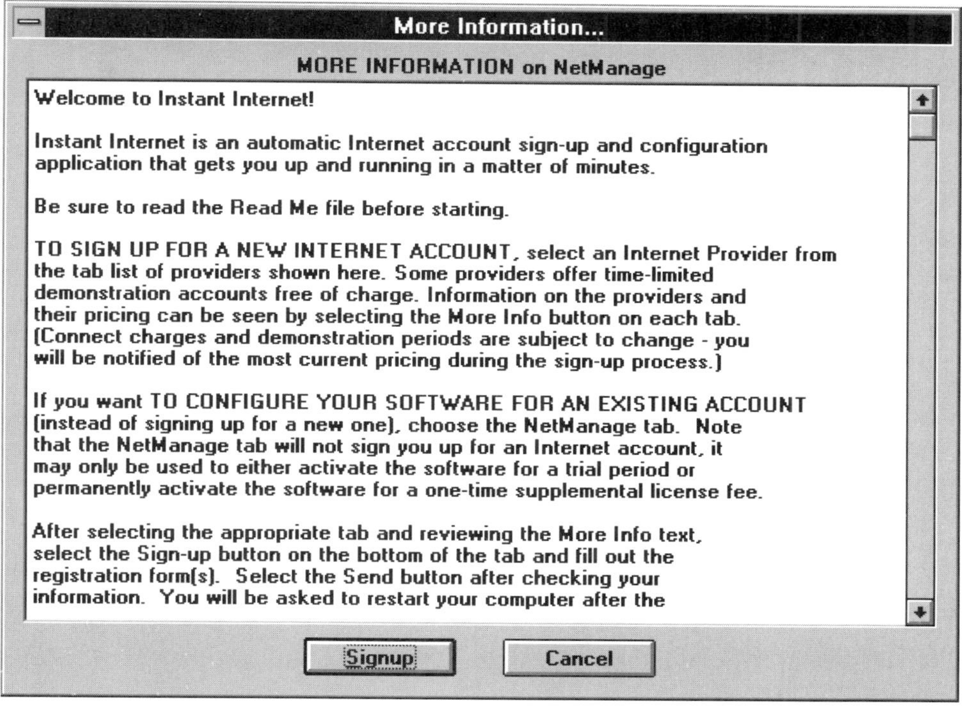

Figure 2-2
NetManage
More Information...

If you already know which provider you would like to use, click now on their tab and begin to fill out the electronic forms.

Here is what each provider's main screen looks like.

The IBM Internet Connection is illustrated in Figure 2-3.

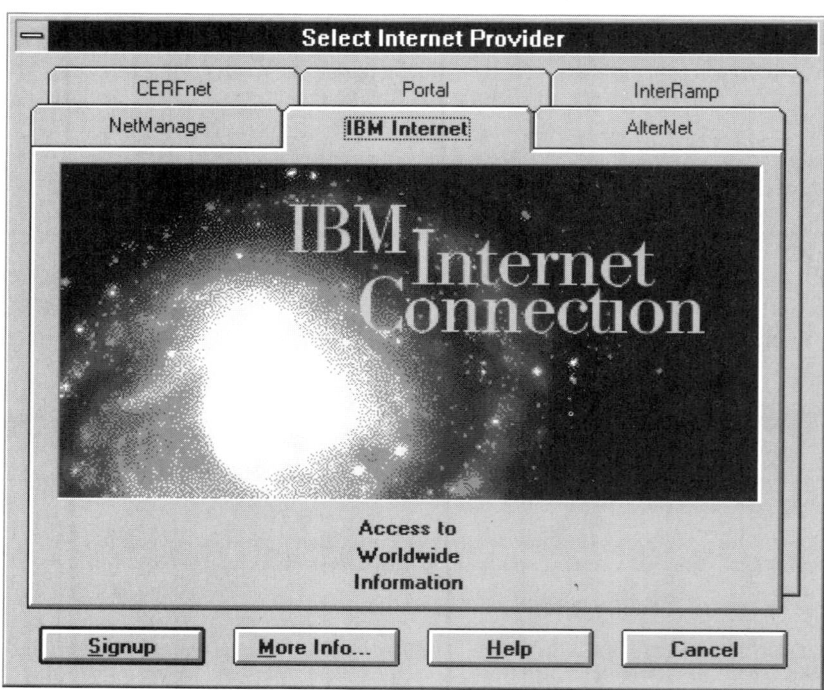

Figure 2-3 IBM Internet Connection

AlterNet's opening screen is shown in Figure 2-4.

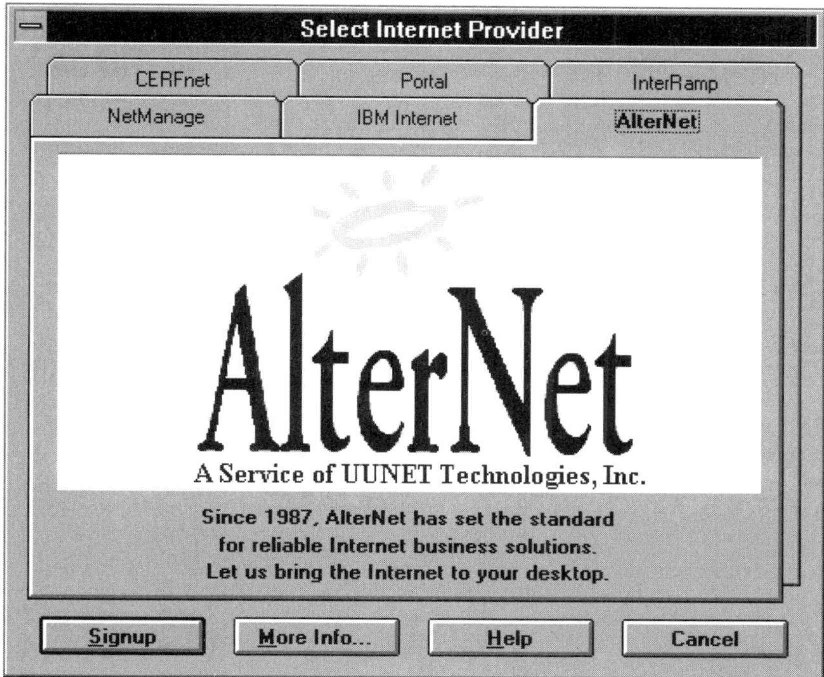

Figure 2-4
AlterNet

Figure 2-5 provides a view of CERFnet's opening screen.

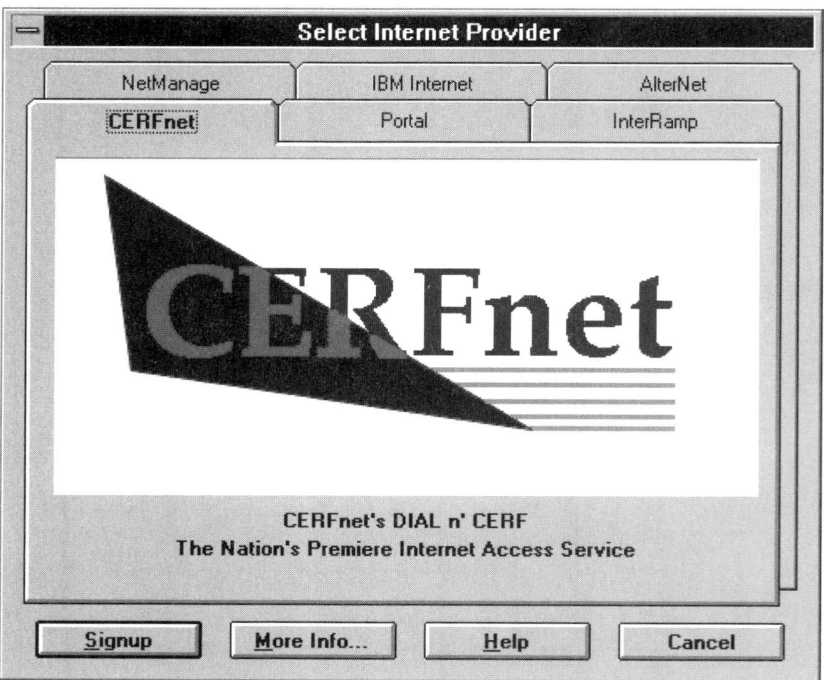

Figure 2-5
CERFnet

The opening screen for The Portal Information Network is shown in Figure 2-6.

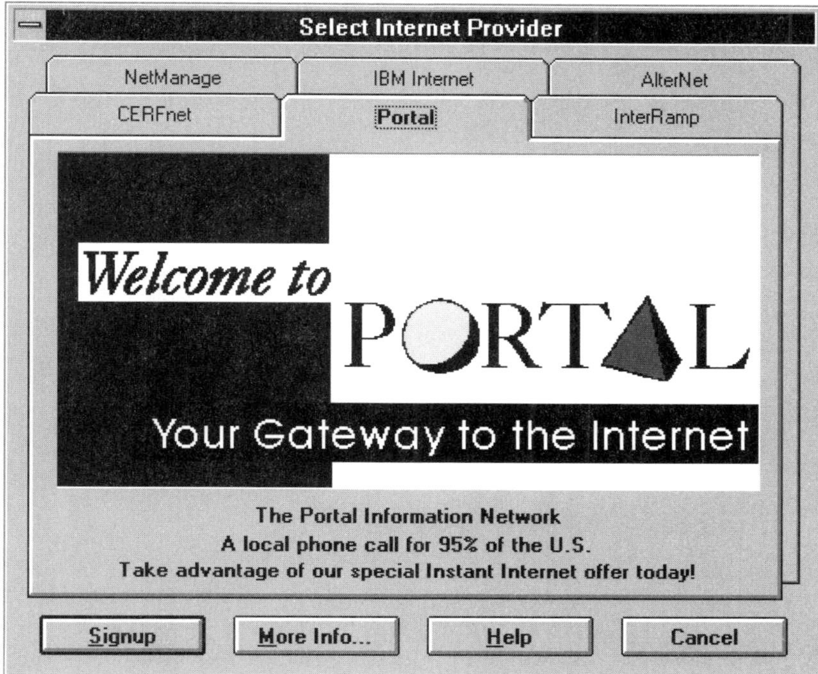

Figure 2-6
Portal

Finally, PSI InterRamp is shown in Figure 2-7.

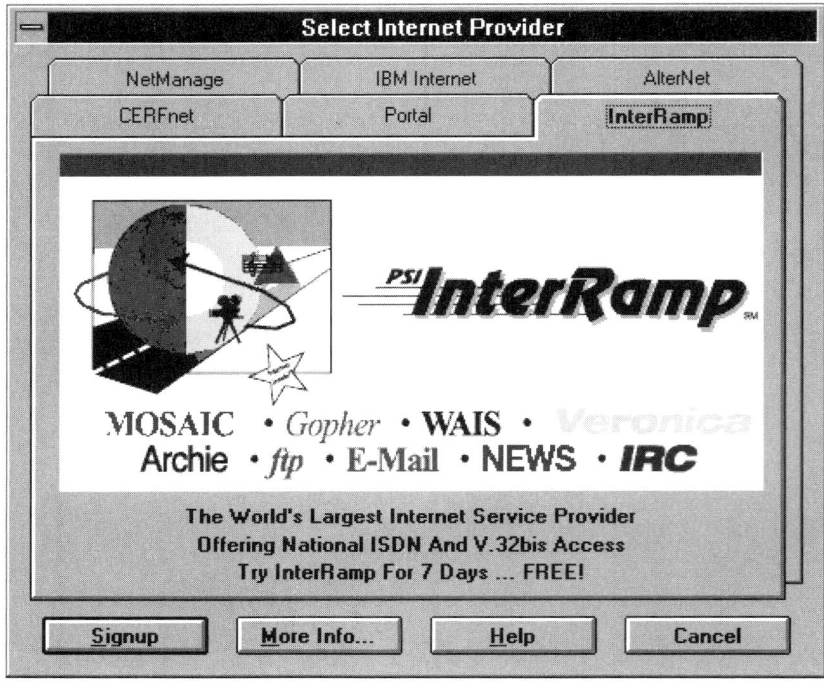

Figure 2-7
InterRamp

If you are not sure which provider you would like to select, click on each provider's tab and then click on their **More Info... button**. This will help you to choose among them. Remember that you can change your mind later and select another provider. Some of the providers offer trial periods and special rates. Read through all the information until you are able to select one. Then click on their **Signup button**. Up-to-date information on pricing and demonstration periods will be presented when you contact each provider's registration server.

It's also important to note that you will always be given the opportunity to cancel the registration process at any point if you so wish.

Although each provider's signup form differs, they share many common parts. Figure 2-8 provides a sample Instant Internet Account Signup screen to illustrate what you will see. Read each form thoroughly and fill it out carefully and completely. Not all providers take all credit cards, so check to see if the provider you have chosen will take your card.

Figure 2-8
Account Sign-Up

Now fill in the form of your chosen service provider.

1. First fill in the blanks with your name, address, and so on.
2. Next, click on your credit card type.
3. Finally, fill in your complete credit card number and expiration date.

Your credit card number will *not* be traveling over the Internet. Each provider has set up a special 1-800 number just to register you and your account.

Some providers have more than one signup screen. Check for tabs at the top of the window saying "Fill this additional form out as well." A sample of one of these screens is shown in Figure 2-9.

Instant Internet Account Sign-Up

Please fill out this registration form | Fill this additional form out as well

Additional Information:

Name as it appears on credit card:

Hostname (1st choice):

Hostname (2nd choice):

Send | Phone List... | Advanced... | Help | Cancel

Figure 2-9
Additional Information

This "additional information" form will differ from provider to provider; be sure you read and fill it in carefully. Some providers will ask you for a hostname. By hostname, they mean the name your computer will have on the Internet. Other providers will assign you a hostname. If you are asked to choose a hostname, pick one that appeals to you, as you may be receiving electronic mail there.

4. When you have finished with the form(s), click on the **Send button**.

Now watch the small traffic lights at the bottom of your signup screen. The first one will turn green when your computer checks the form and finds that it is complete. Next, Instant Internet tries to find your modem.

If you get a message that your modem may not be turned on, click on the **Advanced button** and select the correct COM port (COM1, COM2, etc.) for your modem. If you are not sure which one is correct, try each one and go back to the Send button.

When your modem has been found, the second traffic light will turn green and you may hear your modem dialing the provider. You will see messages in the small window below the traffic lights.

When the call has been connected, the middle traffic light becomes green. Next, the provider's modem answers and its traffic light turns green. Finally, the provider's serving computer begins to register your application.

This light will continue to flash yellow as the computer checks your data and credit card. With amazing speed, your account is usually approved and the data is automatically sent back to your PC.

While each provider handles your signup differently, you will probably receive back a screen of important information. Be sure to record this information and keep it in a safe place. Figure 2-10 is a sample of such a screen.

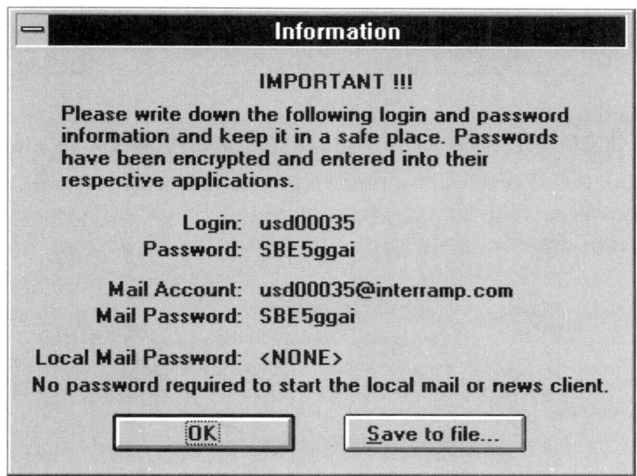

Figure 2-10
Information

When the signup process is finished, you will be told that the registration is complete, as illustrated in Figure 2-11. Account Registration Complete means that you are now registered with the provider.

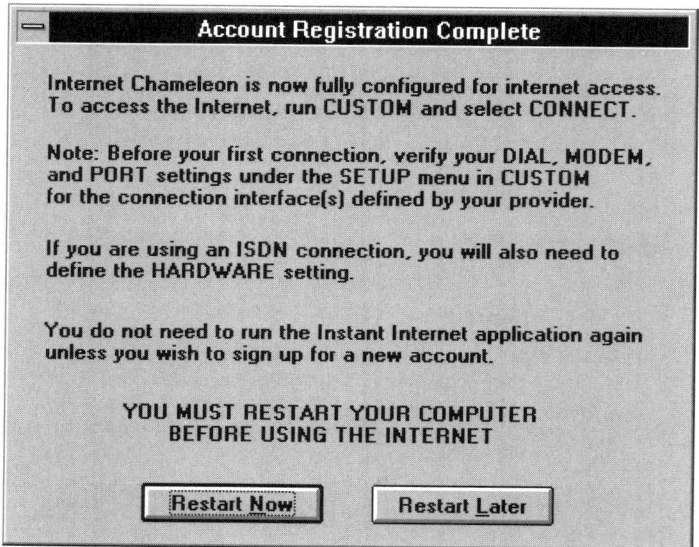

Figure 2-11
Account Registration Complete

5. Click on the **Restart Now button** to complete the process.

When your PC has restarted and returned to Windows, you will see a whole new array of icons in your Internet Chameleon Group. Figure 2-12 shows what the group should look like.

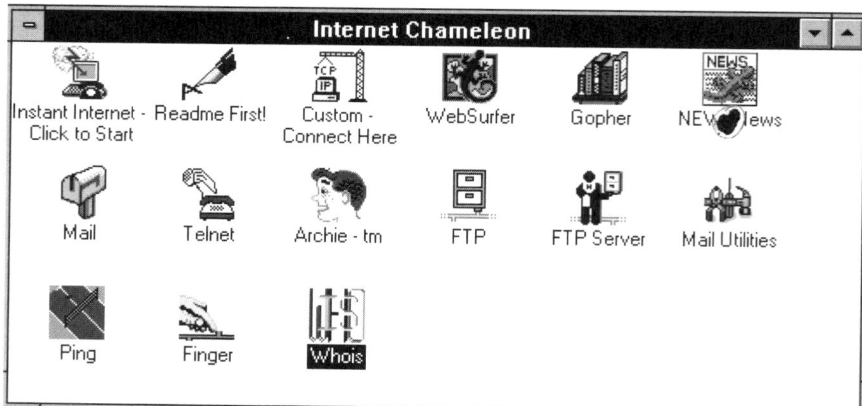

Figure 2-12
Internet Chameleon

Most providers, including NetManage, offer both demonstration and regular accounts. If you sign up for a demonstration account, Internet Chameleon will stop working after the demonstration period is over. If this happens, you will see the screen which is illustrated in Figure 2-13. Once this occurs, you will need to redo your account signup with the Instant Internet Icon and establish a regular account with one of the Internet providers or with NetManage. Once you have tried one demonstration account, you may be restricted from trying another.

Figure 2-13
Your DEMO version has expired

When you sign up for a demonstration account with one of the Internet Service Providers (or a demonstration license with NetManage for another provider) your Internet Chameleon will have a demonstration serial number. Although the trial periods may differ, when a trial period expires, you must obtain a permanent license serial number. You can click on the Instant Internet Icon to get a permanent license with any of the providers or with NetManage.

If you experience any difficulties with this process, contact your Internet Service Provider. You will find their telephone numbers listed in the screens behind the More Info... button of the Instant Internet Icon.

Usually, when you switch from a demonstration account to a regular one, you will be given new account information and a new password. Remember to write these down and to keep them in a safe place. The provider (or NetManage) will automatically reconfigure your copy of Internet Chameleon with a new permanent serial number.

Once you have a regular account, you may still change to another Internet Service Provider at the end of any billing period. Refer to the More Info... button for each provider to see their account terms. Alternatively, you may contact them by phone.

The following section is only for those installing Internet Chameleon who already have an existing Internet account. Note that this account must be either a SLIP, CSLIP, or PPP account.

TWO

Configuring Internet Chameleon for an Existing Account

1. Choose the NetManage registration folder tab.
2. Fill out the two registration forms as completely as possible.

   Ask your provider for the provider identification number. If they do not have one, leave this blank.

   If your provider uses dynamic IP assignment (e.g. you get a different IP address assigned to you each time you connect), fill the IP address field in with '`1.1.1.1`'
3. Click on the **Send button**

   Instant Internet will configure your Internet connection with the information you provided in the registration form.
4. When prompted, restart your computer to save the settings.
5. Click on the **Custom Icon** and complete the configuration. Do this by filling in, correcting, or verifying the Domain Name and Dial (access phone number) in the Setup Menu, and the Domain Servers in the Services Menu. Click on **Save** in the File Menu, exit Custom, and restart Windows and Internet Chameleon.
6. Use Window's Notepad to edit the SLIP.INI file in your NETMANAG directory to assure that your provider's script is correct. If you have not done this before or your provider is not on the list, you will want to contact your provider for assistance.

Here are the some of the names already in the SLIP.INI file. If you see your provider here, use File Open to bring in that provider's configuration file. Then use the Custom and Setup menus to complete or verify your provider's information. You will see that much of the information is already there.

The SLIP.INI file is already configured for these providers. If your provider is not listed here, you will need to obtain the information listed in the Provider Information section from your provider.

AlterNet	JVNCnet
ANSRemote	MRnet
CERFnet	NetCom
CICNet	NWNexus
ClarkNet	Olympus
CRL	OnRamp
CTS	Panix
Cybergate	PICnet
Digex	Portal
Hookup	PSINet
Iglou	TIAC
InterAcc	WLN

Provider Information

If you do not already have the following information from your provider, here is what you will need to get from them:

A telephone number to dial

An Internet protocol (IP) address for your PC

The domain name for your PC given to you by your provider

The IP address(es) of a domain nameserver or -servers (DNS)

Your login name and password

Telephone Number The telephone number is pretty obvious, but you should be aware that some providers add extra digits to be dialed. We'll show you what to do when that happens. Most providers, however, just give you an ordinary phone number to dial.

Internet Protocol (IP) Address Most providers give you one of your own, but several give them out each time you connect. They do this to conserve IP addresses.

Domain Name The domain name of the provider will let you send and receive E-mail by name.

Nameserver Your PC has to know how to reach them for almost every thing you would wish to do.

Login Name and Password You will need to have your personal login name and password, so that you can sign on correctly.

The SLIP.INI File

There must be an entry in the SLIP.INI file for each service provider that you use. This file tells your PC how to set up your session with the Internet service provider. Since this activity really consists of two computers trying to talk to each other, it has to be done correctly.

Here's a sample entry in SLIP.INI for AlterNet.

```
[AlterNet]
SCRIPT=Login: $u$r word: $p$r enabled $2$r
TYPE=PPP
```

Here's what it is actually saying:

It tells the PC to follow the SCRIPT after the modems have connected with each other.

First, the PC is to wait for a phrase that ends in "login:" such as "Enter your login:"

Then, the PC is to answer with your login name and an Enter (ur)

Next, the PC waits for a phrase ending in "word:" such as "Enter your Password:"

The PC is to answer with your password and an Enter (pr)

Then, the PC is to wait for a phrase ending in "enabled"

After 2 seconds, the PC sends a return.

This series of handshakes or interchanges is controlled by a set of commands. There are two types of commands: <expects> and <sends>.

The commands for Internet Chameleon's <sends> are

Commands for Internet Chameleon's <sends>

<send>	Command
`$n`	send a new line
`$r`	send a carriage return
`$s`	send a space
`$b`	cause a short "break" on the line
`$t`	send a tab
`$1 - $9`	pause the indicated number of seconds

Commands for Internet Chameleon's <sends> (Continued)

<send>	Command
`$xXX`	send the character with HEX code XX
`$u`	send the user id
`$p`	send the password
`$c`	send the SLIP COMMAND
`$d`	send the phone number
`$$`	send a "$" character
`$f`	define a prompt

The commands for Internet Chameleon's <expects> are similar to the <sends>. In addition, within an <expect> string you can include the following escapes:

Commands for Internet Chameleon's <expects>

<expect>	Command
`--`	expect "-"
`-n`	skip an expect
`-i`	expect IP address (to replace your own or the 1.1.1.1 dummy address)

You can use Window's Notepad Editor to edit the SLIP.INI file. (The Notepad Editor can usually be found in Window's Accessories Group.) You should have obtained the SLIP.INI information from your Internet service provider. Put that information in your SLIP.INI file now.

If you experience any difficulties, contact your Internet service provider and tell them you are using NetManage's Internet Chameleon 4.1. They will assist you in configuring your system.

Session Summary

At this point, you have installed your Internet Chameleon software and have registered with an Internet service provider. In the next session, we will check your key settings and begin your exploration of the Internet.

Session 3

Getting Started

Pinging around the World

Disconnecting from Your Internet Service Provider

Custom, Connect, and Ping

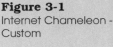

Session Overview

Custom, Connect, and Ping is not a law firm. It is what you will do on your first trip on the Internet with Instant Internet. Before taking off, we will go over a very short checklist to make sure that all will go well.

First, we will check the tool you will use to connect to your service provider each time you connect. The tool is called Custom and it is the icon with the construction crane. It also says Connect Here, as shown in Figure 3-1.

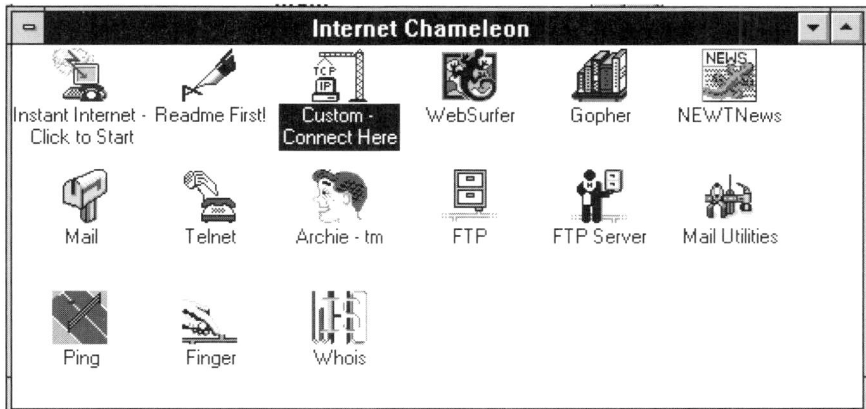

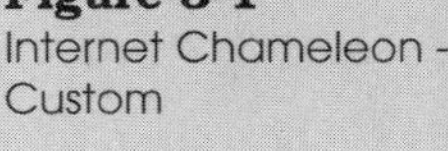
Figure 3-1
Internet Chameleon - Custom

Then we will use a tool called Ping to verify that we really are on the Internet.

ONE

Getting Started

Your Provider Account

Your account information is important, in the same way that your address and telephone number are important. If you give someone the wrong address or telephone number, they will not be able to reach you. Similarly, your account information must be correct if everything is to work well on the Internet.

A quick reminder is also in order about security. Your account has a user name (or login name) and a password. Together these allow access to your account. You will want to be sure that you protect them, particularly the password. This is because your user name or login name is or may be close to your real name and could be guessed. The only real protection that you have is your password. Treat it as you would treat your ATM personal identification number or PIN. Internet Chameleon stores your password in an encrypted form so that it is protected on your computer.

We now begin our connection to, and exploration of, the Internet.

1. Double-click on the **Internet Chameleon Group** if it is not already up.
2. Double-click on **Custom**

Watch the lower-left corner of your screen. A little green NEWT will appear as part of this process. NEWT is an acronym for the NetManage Enhanced Windows TCP/IP program and the icon indicates that the TCP/IP application has been started. (More about TCP/IP at the end of this session.) NEWT is also a measuring tool that can help you when you are having trouble with the provider's host or the telephone line. The Custom Connect screen is shown in Figure 3-2.

Custom - C:\NETMANAG\TCPIP.CFG

File Interface Setup Services Connect Help

Interface:	InterRamp2 - COM1, 19200 baud
Dial:	(617)450-5700
IP Address:	
Subnet Mask:	
Host Name:	
Domain Name:	interramp.com

Name	Type	IP	Domain
InterRamp1	ISDN	0.0.0.0	interramp.com
InterRamp2	PPP	0.0.0.0	interramp.com

Figure 3-2
Custom Connect

Some Internet service providers offer a type of dial-up service called ISDN which stands for Integrated Services Digital Networks. It offers higher speeds than can usually be obtained from regular telephone lines. If you have the ability to use ISDN, you should investigate this option. You will need a different kind of modem or ISDN card in your PC. If you are interested, you should contact your local telephone company to get costs and availabilities in your area.

Look carefully at the Custom screen. While it should resemble Figure 3-2, in all likelihood all of the data will be different. You usually don't need to know what the entries mean, but there is one thing you *must* check. (Later, you *may* want to check the port setup to speed up your connection.)

Look at the line that says "Dial:". The Instant Internet process can do almost everything necessary to get you connected instantly to the Internet, but it can't tell you a particular number to dial on your telephone.

If the number provided is a local number for your dialing area, check to see that it is correct. The easiest way to do this is to write it down and call it with your regular telephone. If you get a recording saying that you need to dial a "1" or don't need to dial a "1" or that you need an area code, write that down too.

When you have the number the way it should be, you should dial it on your telephone. You should hear the high-pitched tone of a modem answering. That's the number Custom should be calling.

Now look at the screen again. If the number is OK as is, jump ahead to step number 7.

If the number is not correct, follow these steps:

3. Click on **Setup** and then on **Dial:**

4. Enter the correct telephone number

5. Click on **OK** to return to the Setup screen.

6. Click on **File** and **Save** to keep the information

Now we are ready to connect to the Internet through your service provider.

7. Click on **Connect**

The Log window appears. At this stage, we will use the Log window to check on our connection's progress. (You cannot type in this window.)

You will see a pop-up Connect window and you should hear your modem beginning to dial. The Log window will display what is happening. Log will scroll down as the connection progresses. The Connect pop-up window will continue to appear until the connection with your provider has been completed.

Once the connection has been completed, your Connect pop-up window will disappear, and the word Connect on the menu bar will change to Disconnect. This may take a number of seconds after the last action in the Log window, as there is often a software "handshaking" going on.

When the Custom Menu Bar word Connect has changed to Disconnect, you are on the Internet! Congratulations! Your screen should resemble the one shown in Figure 3-3.

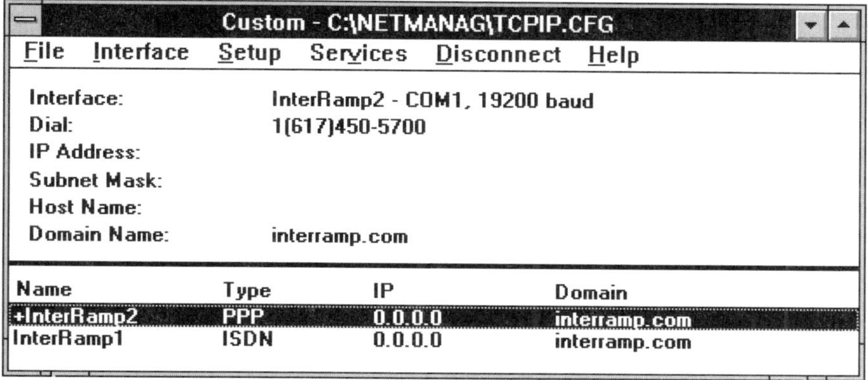

Figure 3-3
Custom Disconnect

You may want to get the Custom window out of the way. You can do this by clicking on the upper-right **minimize** (down-pointing) **arrow**. This will reveal the Internet Chameleon window.

Pinging around the World

Now we will check to see if you really are on the Internet. We will do this with a well-known tool called Ping. Notice the Ping-Pong Table Icon in the Internet Chameleon group. Ping is a way of sending a short "are you alive?" message across the Internet. It verifies that another host is up and running and can be reached from your host (your PC).

1. Double-click on **Ping** and the Ping window shown in Figure 3-4 will appear.

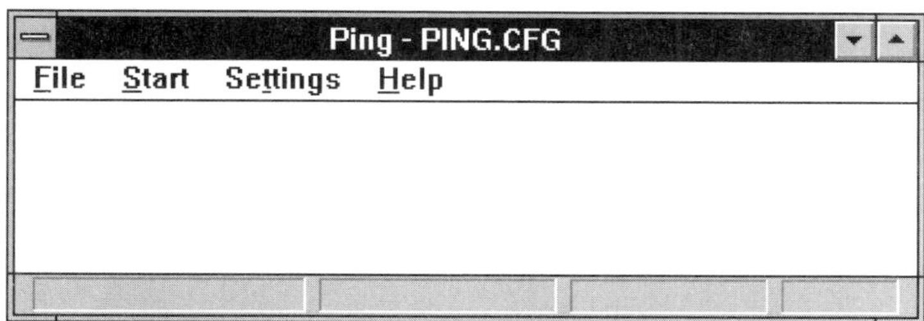

Figure 3-4
Ping

2. Click on **Settings** and then on **Preferences** Under Iteration, increase the number to 3 or more. This will allow you to see more interactions with the distant host. Click on **OK**

3. Click on **Start** and you will be presented with the Host box that is shown in Figure 3-5. We're going to type the first destination here as has already been done in Figure 3-5.

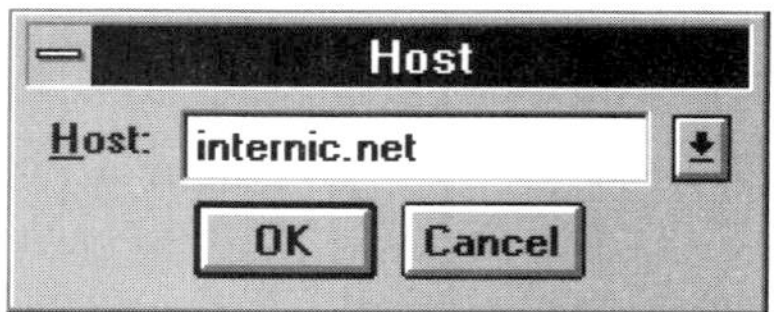

Figure 3-5
Ping Host

4. Type `internic.net` in the box and click on **OK**

If you are *really* connected to the Internet, you will immediately see the response. We captured a sample response in Figure 3-6.

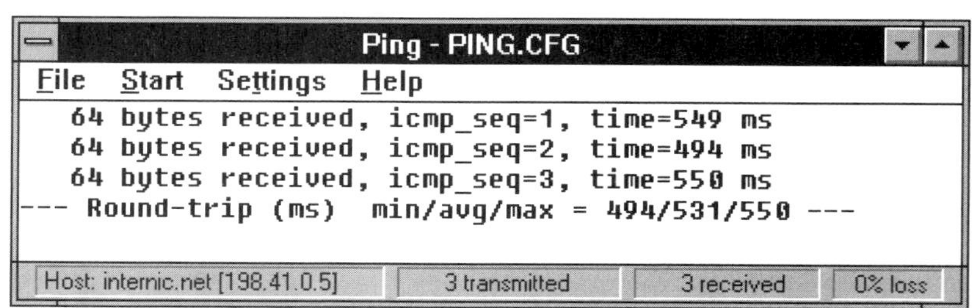

Figure 3-6
Ping Response

Notice several things in the Ping window:

a. Three messages of 64 bytes have been received; that is, they have gone to the InterNIC and returned. (InterNIC is an abbreviation for Internet Network Information Center.)

b. At the end of the line is the time (in ms or milliseconds or thousandths of a second) that it took each message to go round trip. The last line shows the minimum, maximum, and average times.

c. At the bottom of the Ping window, look for the Host: name and the actual IP address of the InterNIC. This tells you that your Internet service provider's nameserver was able to find an IP address for the hostname you typed. (More about IP addresses at the end of this session.)

d. Finally, the number of packets transmitted (meaning sent by your computer), received, and lost is shown. This gives you an idea of how well the network is working to that host destination.

You can see that Ping is a very handy tool to use. Should you ever have problems trying to reach another host on the Internet, you can use Ping to see if your destination host is reachable.

Close Ping by double-clicking on the file drawer handle in the upper-left corner. As shown in Figure 3-7, you will be asked if you want to save the changes to your PING.CFG file. Click on Yes to keep your preference changes.

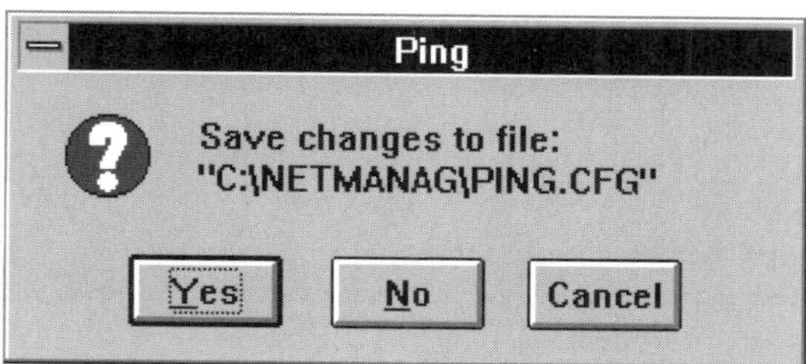

Figure 3-7
Ping Changes?

Disconnecting from Your Internet Service Provider

THREE

Finally, we want to disconnect from our service provider. You may not want to do this now, but here is how it is done.

1. Double-click on the **Custom Icon**
2. Click on the word **Disconnect** on the Internet Chameleon Menu Bar

Immediately you will see a pop-up box as shown in Figure 3-8.

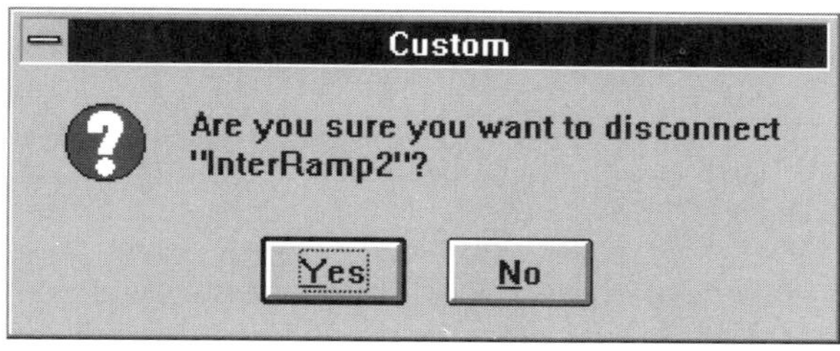

Figure 3-8
Disconnect?

3. Click on **Yes**

You can then watch the Log-CUSTOM box while the modem is instructed to hang up the line. That's the significance of +++ATH that is illustrated in the Figure 3-9. You will also see the Windows hourglass telling you that an action (hang-up) is in progress. When the hourglass disappears, you are disconnected.

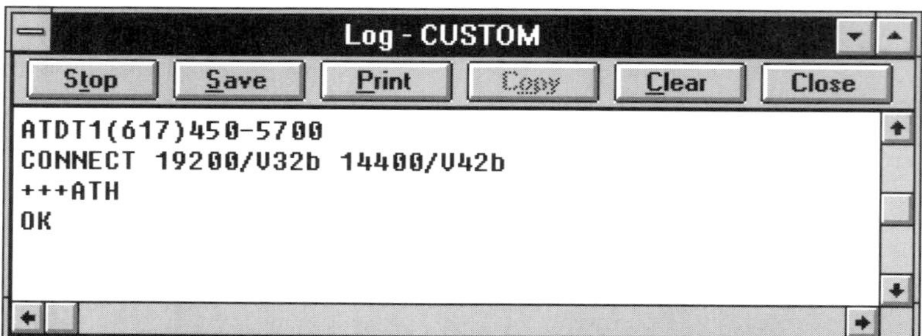

Figure 3-9
Log - CUSTOM

If all worked well, you may be able to increase your speed significantly by going back to Custom, Setup, Port. If you have a 14,400 bit per second modem, you may click on 19200, 38400, or 57600. If you have a 28,800 modem, you may try 115200. Not all providers support these speeds as yet, but they will in the future. If none of these works for you, you can use Setup to return to your original speed.

In our next session we will begin to use the other tools in the Internet Chameleon group.

Session Three Supplement

This supplement includes information about the Internet and TCP/IP. While you do not absolutely need to know this, it may help you to understand the territory better. This information will, of necessity, be brief. There are many books on the market that provide a wealth of detail on these subjects and you will find much online on the Internet itself. In Session Seven we will lead you to the InterNIC or Internet Network Information Center by Gopher. The InterNIC has a wondrous trove of data available.

The Internet may be described as all the computers in the world that can communicate electronically. A communications program called TCP/IP runs on every computer on the Internet. Actually, the Internet is made up of all of the interconnected computers running some version of this program. It's really a whole set of programs that goes by the name TCP/IP.

TCP/IP is an acronym that stands for Transmission Control Protocol/Internet Protocol. A protocol can be thought of as a way of reaching agreement. TCP/IP does just that. It lets all of the interconnected computers in the world talk to each other. We call that group of computers the Internet.

Think of TCP/IP as being similar to what is often referred to as "business English." Most business people in the world speak just enough English to communicate with each other. They know a limited set of words that permits them to work together. The basic set of words allows people of many different languages to talk. That's what TCP/IP does for all different kinds of interconnected computers.

We don't know why TCP/IP came to be the common tongue, any more than we know why English became the common business language. Partisans for each claim many reasons, but for our purposes it is sufficient to know that they both function similarly. If you know business English, you can conduct business all over the world, and if your computer knows TCP/IP, it can communicate with all of the other computers on the Internet.

There are lots of TCP/IP programs. Some can work on the big mainframe computers behind the glass walls. Some run on supercomputers and high-power workstations. Our Internet Chameleon TCP/IP program runs on PCs running Microsoft Windows.

TCP/IP is more than just a communications program; it also includes a number of applications (programs) and tools. The Internet Chameleon that is included with this book contains a number of these programs.

What TCP Does

TCP (Transmission Control Protocol) makes sure, to the best of its ability, that your information passes through the Internet complete and undamaged. TCP sets up sessions with other TCP programs across the Internet. This is very similar to a telephone call. Typically, you call another party, and when the connection is made, you talk. TCP does this with your data.

The TCP programs on two different connected computers work to assure you of good communications. TCP tries to keep your information clean from telephone-line errors and makes sure that all of the information is there.

What IP Does

IP (Internet Protocol) takes information from TCP and tries to get it across the Internet. Unlike TCP, IP just sends its datagrams into the network and hopes that they will arrive. This is like a postal system. You put the letter in the postal box and hope that it gets to its destination. If the datagram gets lost, IP doesn't worry; it has tried its best.

This may seem risky, but it works amazingly well. IP may lose an occasional datagram, but TCP assures you that the information will get through. TCP does this by getting a return receipt for all of its data. If IP loses some data, TCP will send it again. This means that if a line breaks or a computer in the network fails, that data will still get through. It's a lovely combination.

Internet Addresses

Once you are running TCP/IP, there has to be a way to make your PC unique in the Internet world. As humans, we have learned how to find individuals by a complex system of names, addresses, and telephone numbers. This works, most of the time, because there are a lot of people to ask.

However, with computers, it's more difficult because computers don't really know how (or whom) to ask. The solution is for each computer on the Internet to have a consistent, worldwide computer address. The address is called the Internet Protocol address or IP address. Once a computer has been given an IP address, it should be unique in the world. This means that no other computer should have that address.

Another convention we will use is to refer to the Internet computers as hosts. It's just a convention. The computer can be any size from the mainframes to your PC, but we call them all hosts. This means that the IP address is also referred to as the host address.

The IP address is really just a binary number made up of ones and zeros. This system makes it easy for the host (computer) but tough on humans. To simplify the problem for humans, we have a special way of talking about the addresses. We do this by converting the ones and zeros into four sets of numbers. Then, we can just say four numbers, and that's the IP address.

So when humans talk about IP addresses, they say

"One-ninety-two dot sixteen dot forty-one dot twelve"

after they have read "192.16.41.12".

The numbers that are used for each of the sets of numbers that make up the IP addresses can range from zero (0) to two-fifty-five (255).

This means that the lowest number we will use is 0.0.0.0 and the largest number we use is 255.255.255.255

IP addresses will continue to look like this for at least the next few years, and we will continue to say them this way.

Internet Names

While the hosts use IP addresses to find each other, this convention is often hard for humans. To make it easier, each host also has a name. Here's how the Internet uses names:

1. Your host (your own PC) can have any name that is acceptable to your Internet service provider.
2. That hostname then becomes part of what is called a subdomain and a topdomain (sort of like a family tree). There can be one or several parts to the whole name.

Let's look at some sample names to understand how it's done.

- **a.** netmanage.com
- **b.** ibm.net
- **c.** ncsa.uiuc.edu
- **d.** microsoft.com
- **e.** internic.net

If we examine each of these, we can see that they are (almost) self-explanatory.

- **a.** *netmanage.com* is the host address of NetManage, the company that makes Internet Chameleon. The *.com* tells us that the address is a commercial enterprise.
- **b.** *ibm.net* is easy, as it tells us that IBM Corp. is providing an Internet network. Like NetManage, it is commercial.
- **c.** *ncsa.uiuc.edu* is a host at UIUC that is used by the National Center for Supercomputer Applications (NCSA). NCSA is the developer of NCSA Mosaic and is an educational institution.

d. *microsoft.com* should be pretty easy to decode. Microsoft is a commercial (*.com*) company, so that extension is pretty obvious.

e. *internic.net* refers to the InterNIC, which is a shorthand name for the Internet Network Information Center (NIC). It has a number of functions, including giving out IP addresses and registering names, so it's part of a network (*.net*).

The last part of each name (*.gov* or *.edu* or *.com*) is called the *highest level domain*. When the entire hostname is used, it is called the *fully qualified domain name* (FQDN).

The final thing to notice about names is that we have printed them all in lowercase with no spaces. This is the usual convention in the Internet community, as many of the hosts treat upper- and lowercase letters differently. Although your PC treats upper- and lowercase letters the same, many hosts do not. So, you will find that many addresses use only lowercase.

If you have been using America Online or CompuServe or Prodigy for E-mail, you will recognize the following name forms:

aol.com

compuserve.com

prodigy.com

At this point, you may be asking how the Internet name and the Internet address relate to each other. That's a very good question. The answer is important and you will need to know it in the next session. Here's how it works.

Domain Nameservers

There are some special hosts all around the Internet called Nameservers. Their function is to know the current IP address of each name. This function is often called DNS.

DNS allows people to specify Internet names, which are easier for people to use and remember. And it allows hosts to use Internet addresses, which are faster for host computers to use.

This is a pretty quick (and superficial) overview of the Internet and how it works. We recommend that you go on to discover more information on your own from a multitude of sources.

Session Summary

In this session, you were able to use the Custom feature of Internet Chameleon so you could connect to your Internet service provider. In addition, you were able to use the Ping tool to enable you to connect to another host computer on the Internet. All of this is intended to ensure that you are correctly connected to your Internet service provider, and that you are, indeed, on the Internet. In the next four sessions, you will learn how to use telnet, E-mail, ftp, and gopher, the four primary tools for many Internet users. If you are impatient to begin using WebSurfer, a browser very much like Mosaic, you should skip ahead to Session Eight.

Basic Internet Tools will introduce you to the four primary tools that are used by most Internet users on a regular basis.

In **Session Four**, you will learn about the Telnet capabilities of Internet Chameleon. You will have a chance to explore a number of well-known Telnet sites, and to learn about a particularly helpful program known as Hytelnet.

Session Five explains the E-mail capabilities of Internet Chameleon.

In **Session Six**, you will use the FTP capabilities of Internet Chameleon to learn about file compression and virus protection. You will download copies of PKZIP and PKUNZIP, as well as a copy of SCAN. You will learn how to prepare all this software for use, so that you will be ready to take advantage of the full capabilities of WebSurfer.

In **Session Seven**, you will have a chance to explore Gopherspace, using the Gopher software included with Internet Chameleon. There are many wonderful resources available on the Internet. Gopher has been designed to help you find them quickly and easily.

PART 2

BASIC INTERNET TOOLS

INSTANT INTERNET

WEB SURFER

SESSION 4

Telnet to the InterNIC

Telnet to the University of Michigan WEATHER UNDERGROUND

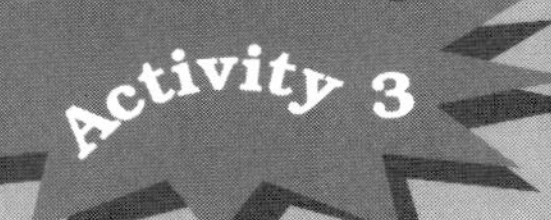

Telnet to NASA SPACELINK

Using Hytelnet

Telnet Around the World

Session Overview

This session will introduce you to some of the many resources that exist (legally) on computers other than your own. You will have a chance to get a feel for where these computers are located, how to sign on to them, and what happens once you have done so. The primary new vocabulary word for this session is **Telnet**; this is the word that you will use whenever you want to log in remotely to another computer.

For each of the Telnet activities in this session, we have provided actual screen shots, so you will have a better idea of what should be happening on your computer. However, since there are so many choices available once you have established a Telnet connection, it is possible that your actual computer screen may look somewhat different from the examples that are shown.

Now, let's get started.

Telnet to the InterNIC

ONE

Instant Activity

1. Double-click on Telnet and the Telnet window will open
2. Click on the **Connect** menu item and you will see the Connect To box
3. In the Host Name: box, type `ds.internic.net` and then click on **OK**

```
Telnet - ds.internic.net
File  Edit  Disconnect  Settings  Script  Network  Help
with the National Science Foundation.

First time users may login as guest with no password to receive help.

Your comments and suggestions for improvement are welcome, and can be
mailed to admin@ds.internic.net.

AT&T MAKES NO WARRANTY OR GUARANTEE, OR PROMISE, EXPRESS OR IMPLIED,
CONCERNING THE  CONTENT OR  ACCURACY OF THE  DIRECTORY  ENTRIES AND
DATABASE  FILES  STORED  AND  MAINTAINED  BY  AT&T.  AT&T EXPRESSLY
DISCLAIMS AND EXCLUDES ALL EXPRESS WARANTIES AND IMPLIED WARRANTIES
OF MERCHANTABILITY AND FITNESS FOR A PARTICULAR PURPOSE.


 ********************************************************
DSO will be rebooted every Monday morning between 8:00AM and 8:30AM




SunOS UNIX (ds)

login:

Ready                                    VT100            24, 8
```

Figure 4-1
The InterNIC Welcome

NOTE: You should see a screen similar to Figure 4-1. Notice that Connect on the menu bar has changed to Disconnect. If you get hung up or stalled while using Telnet, just click on Disconnect to break the remote host session.

4. At the login: prompt, type `guest` and press **Enter**
5. You will be asked to make several choices. Just press **Enter** each time. This will bring you to the InterNIC's Main Menu screen. It may look similar to Figure 4-2.

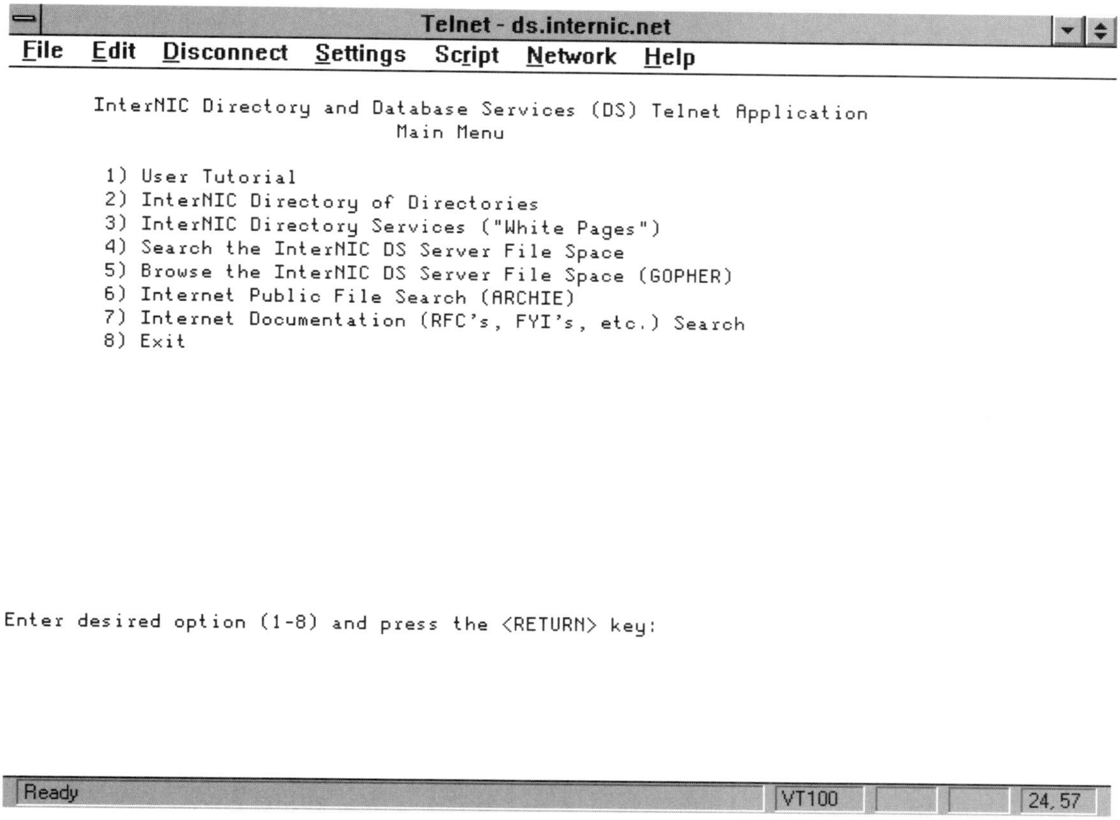

```
Telnet - ds.internic.net
File  Edit  Disconnect  Settings  Script  Network  Help

      InterNIC Directory and Database Services (DS) Telnet Application
                              Main Menu

       1) User Tutorial
       2) InterNIC Directory of Directories
       3) InterNIC Directory Services ("White Pages")
       4) Search the InterNIC DS Server File Space
       5) Browse the InterNIC DS Server File Space (GOPHER)
       6) Internet Public File Search (ARCHIE)
       7) Internet Documentation (RFC's, FYI's, etc.) Search
       8) Exit

Enter desired option (1-8) and press the <RETURN> key:

Ready                                              VT100              24, 57
```

Figure 4-2
The InterNIC Main Menu

You can make a number of choices. We recommend that you begin with choice 5 Browse the InterNIC DS Server File Space (GOPHER) that leads to a menu of information. Since these menus change frequently, it may or may not look like Figure 4-3, but there will be helpful choices for you on the menu.

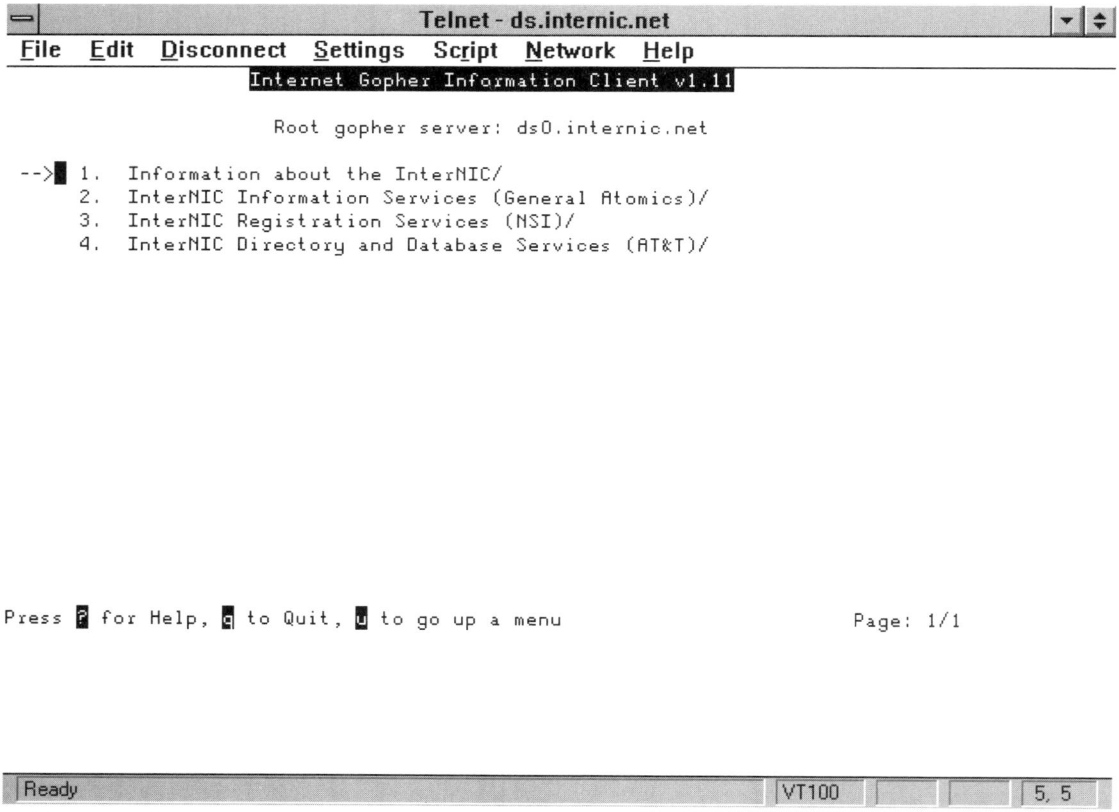

Telnet - ds.internic.net
File Edit Disconnect Settings Script Network Help

```
                    Internet Gopher Information Client v1.11

                      Root gopher server: ds0.internic.net

 -->  1.  Information about the InterNIC/
      2.  InterNIC Information Services (General Atomics)/
      3.  InterNIC Registration Services (NSI)/
      4.  InterNIC Directory and Database Services (AT&T)/

Press ? for Help, q to Quit, u to go up a menu                Page: 1/1
```

Ready | VT100 | 5, 5

Figure 4-3
The InterNIC Gopher

The menus offer you a number of options and ways of moving around. Many of the screens will offer help screens or tutorials. When you have finished your visit to the InterNIC, return to the main menu and select Exit.

6. Now, click on **Disconnect** on Telnet's menu bar to close the Telnet connection.

7. Double-click on the **down-arrow** in the upper-right-hand corner of the Telnet screen. This should reduce Telnet to an icon and return you to the Program Manager - [Internet Chameleon] screen.

IMPORTANT: Remember, you are still connected to your service provider.

Telnet to the University of Michigan WEATHER UNDERGROUND

1. Double-click on **Telnet** and the Telnet window will open.
2. Click on the **Connect** menu item and you will see the Connect To box.
3. In the Host Name: box, type `madlab.sprl.umich.edu`
4. Tab to the Port: box, type `3000`, and then click on **OK**

NOTE: You should see a screen similar to Figure 4-4. Notice that Connect on the menu bar has changed to Disconnect. If you get hung up or stalled while using Telnet, just click on Disconnect to break the remote host session.

Figure 4-4
University of Michigan WEATHER UNDERGROUND

```
Telnet - madlab.sprl.umich.edu
File  Edit  Disconnect  Settings  Script  Network  Help
------------------------------------------------------------------------------
*                          University of Michigan                            *
*                           WEATHER UNDERGROUND                              *
------------------------------------------------------------------------------
*                                                                            *
*             College of Engineering, University of Michigan                 *
*             Department of Atmospheric, Oceanic, and Space Sciences         *
*             Ann Arbor, Michigan  48109-2143                                *
*             comments: sdm@madlab.sprl.umich.edu                            *
*                                                                            *
* With Help from:  The National Science Foundation supported Unidata Project *
*                  University Corporation for Atmospheric Research           *
*                  Boulder, Colorado  80307-3000                             *
*                                                                            *
*        This service is for educational and research purposes only.         *
*        Commercial users should contact our data provider, Alden            *
*        Electronics, 508-366-8851 to acquire their own data feed.           *
*                                                                            *
------------------------------------------------------------------------------
*   NOTE:----------> New users, please select option "H" on the main menu:   *
*                    H) Help and information for new users                   *
------------------------------------------------------------------------------

Press Return for menu, or enter 3 letter forecast city code:

Ready                                                      VT100        24, 61
```

5. Press Return for a menu.

You will be presented with the following response:

```
WEATHER UNDERGROUND MAIN MENU
*****************************
 1) U.S. forecasts and climate data
 2) Canadian forecasts
 3) Current weather observations
 4) Ski conditions
 5) Long-range forecasts
 6) Latest earthquake reports
 7) Severe weather
 8) Hurricane advisories
 9) National Weather Summary
 10) International data
 11) Marine forecasts and observations
 X) Exit program
 C) Change scrolling to screen
 H) Help and information for new users
 ?) Answers to all your questions
 Selection:h
```

NOTE: We have selected option H which provides help for new users. Once you have read through the help, feel free to explore the many options which are presented by the Weather Underground. When you have finished exploring the Weather Underground, type X to exit the program.

```
INFORMATION FOR NEW USERS OF THE WEATHER UNDERGROUND
----------------------------------------------------
Welcome to the Weather Underground! Through our host computer in Ann Arbor,
Michigan, we provide a variety of weather information through this menu-
driven, interactive program. Use of this service is free, as long as the
information is for personal or educational use. Feel free to access the
service as much as you like, but be aware that during major weather events
usage gets quite heavy, and you may receive the following message:
The Weather Underground is fully loaded. Try again later.
The Weather Underground is limited to 100 simultaneous users, so you will
have to wait until someone else signs off before you can get on. Once you
do get on, please limit the duration of your session so that others may sign
on.
```

```
BYPASSING THE MAIN MENU
-----------------------
When first entering the Weather Underground, you will get the following
prompt:
Press Return for menu, or enter 3 letter forecast city code:
At this point, you can either hit <Return> to get the main menu, or enter a
special code that will immediately give you a forecast or observation. The
special codes are explained under the various options available on the main
menu. You may enter any of the following codes at the initial prompt:
1) A 3-letter code for a U.S. city forecast. For example, entering DTW will
give the forecast, plus any warnings or special weather statements for
Detroit.
2) A 2-letter state or province code, to get current observations for the
U.S. or Canada. For example, entering MI will give the current observations
for Michigan.
3) A number between 1 and 20, to get the current forecast for a Canadian
Province. For example, entering 18 will give the forecast for the Yukon.
Note that as a special feature for users who access the Weather Underground
non-interactively through special "script" programs, an extra character can
be entered after any of the 3 options described above to set unlimited
scrolling. For example, entering "DTWF" will give the Detroit forecast only
(no special weather statements or 3-5 day forecast included) with unlimited
scrolling. For more information on these options, plus much more information
on the Weather Underground, select "?" from the main menu.
BYPASSING SUBMENUS
------------------
One can save keystrokes in the U.S. city forecast submenu and current weather
observation submenu by entering the desired code immediately upon entering
the submenu. For example, upon selecting "1" from the main menu to enter the
U.S. city submenu, one can then immediately enter "MIA" to get the forecast
for Miami, instead of typing a "1", carriage return, then "MIA". Similarly,
one can enter the 2-letter state or province code immediately upon entering
the current observations submenu.
```

Telnet to the NASA SPACELINK

THREE

1. Double-click on **Telnet** and the Telnet window will open.
2. Click on the **Connect** menu item and you will see the Connect To box.
3. In the Host Name: box, type `spacelink.msfc.nasa.gov`

4. Tab to the Port: box, and type `23`, and then click on **OK**

NOTE: You should see a screen similar to Figure 4-5. Notice that Connect on the menu bar has changed to Disconnect. If you get hung up or stalled while using Telnet, just click on Disconnect to break the remote host session.

```
Telnet - spacelink.msfc.nasa.gov
File  Edit  Disconnect  Settings  Script  Network  Help
UNIX(r) System V Release 4.0 (spacelink)

                              WELCOME TO
                            NASA SPACELINK

            NASA's Computer Information Service for Educators
                   Managed by the NASA Education Division
           In Cooperation with the Marshall Space Flight Center

    ********************  I M P O R T A N T !  ********************

                THE SPACELINK SYSTEM HAS BEEN CHANGED!!!!!

          TO LOG ON, ENTER guest (IN LOWER CASE) THEN PRESS RETURN

                           To use the system,
               YOUR SOFTWARE MUST EMULATE A VT-100 TERMINAL

     IF YOU ARE DIALING OUR MODEMS DIRECTLY, YOU MUST SET YOUR SYSTEM TO USE
                   8 DATA BITS, 1 STOP BIT AND NO PARITY

  For help with technical problems call the Spacelink Hot Line (205)961-1225.

login: █

Ready                                              VT100           24, 8
```

Figure 4-5
NASA SPACELINK

5. At the login prompt, type the word `guest` and press **<Return>** Press **<Return>** again.

You will be see a screen resembling Figure 4-6, the NASA Spacelink Electronic Library Main Menu.

```
Telnet - spacelink.msfc.nasa.gov
File  Edit  Disconnect  Settings  Script  Network  Help
                    NASA Spacelink Electronic Library

                    Main Menu from: spacelink.msfc.nasa.gov

-->  1.  About.Spacelink/
     2.  Educational.Services/
     3.  Instructional.Materials/
     4.  NASA.News/
     5.  NASA.Overview/
     6.  NASA.Projects/
     7.  Spacelink.Frequently.Asked.Questions/
     8.  Spacelink.Hot.Topics/

Press ? for Help, q to Quit                                   Page: 1/1

Ready                                           VT100          5, 5
```

Figure 4-6
NASA Spacelink Electronic Library Main Menu

As indicated, at any time you may press **?** for Help, **q** to Quit, and **u** to go up a menu.

You will notice that all of your choices can be made from this initial menu. Quite a bit of information about NASA Spacelink is provided. In addition, you will find that NASA Spacelink is an excellent repository of images taken from around the world, all of which are available using file transfer protocol (ftp). These gif files, as they are known, may be viewed using Mosaic.

Once you have finished exploring NASA SPACELINK, press **q** to Quit and then **y** to really quit, and you will be disconnected from NASA SPACELINK and returned to your main Telnet screen.

FOUR

Using Hytelnet

As you have seen in the preceding activities, Telnet is a powerful, easy-to-use Internet resource. However, one of the questions that is inevitably raised by those using Telnet is, "How do I find out about all of the Telnet sites that exist?" Fortunately, Peter Scott at the University of Saskatchewan has developed a resource known as *Hytelnet* which is intended to help us all. In an introductory screen to Hytelnet, Peter Scott states, "Hytelnet is designed to assist users in reaching all of the Internet- accessible libraries, Free-nets, CWISs, BBSs, and other information sites by Telnet, specifically those users who access Telnet via a modem, serial line, or direct network connection." Follow along as we begin to use Hytelnet.

1. Double-click on **Telnet** and the Telnet window will open.
2. Click on the **Connect** menu item and you will see the Connect To box.
3. In the Host Name: box, type `access.usask.ca`
4. Tab to the Port: box, type `23`, and then click on **OK**
5. When prompted, enter the login name: `hytelnet`

You should see a screen that resembles Figure 4-7.

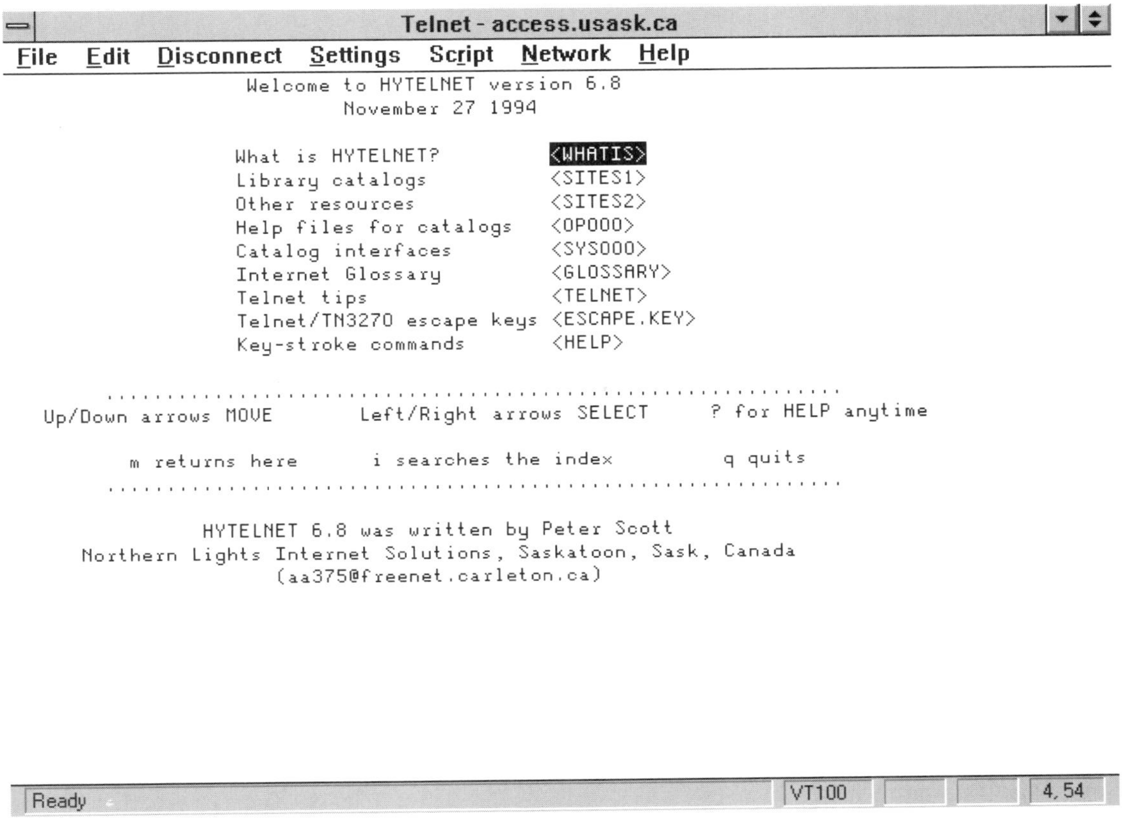

```
Telnet - access.usask.ca
File  Edit  Disconnect  Settings  Script  Network  Help
                    Welcome to HYTELNET version 6.8
                           November 27 1994

                   What is HYTELNET?          <WHATIS>
                   Library catalogs           <SITES1>
                   Other resources            <SITES2>
                   Help files for catalogs    <OP000>
                   Catalog interfaces         <SYS000>
                   Internet Glossary          <GLOSSARY>
                   Telnet tips                <TELNET>
                   Telnet/TN3270 escape keys  <ESCAPE.KEY>
                   Key-stroke commands        <HELP>

          ............................................................
  Up/Down arrows MOVE      Left/Right arrows SELECT     ? for HELP anytime

       m returns here      i searches the index        q quits
          ............................................................

              HYTELNET 6.8 was written by Peter Scott
      Northern Lights Internet Solutions, Saskatoon, Sask, Canada
                        (aa375@freenet.carleton.ca)

Ready                                              VT100            4, 54
```

Figure 4-7
Hytelnet Main Screen

For our first exploration of Hytelnet, we will see what library catalogs might be available via Telnet. Here is how to do so.

1. Use the **down-arrow key** to slide the cursor down to Library Catalogs <SITES1> and press **Enter**
2. Press **Enter** again to select <SITES1A> The Americas
3. Use your **down-arrow key** to slide down to <US000> United States and press **Enter**
4. Use your **down-arrow key** to slide down to <US000PUB> Public Libraries and press **Enter**
5. Your first screen of United States Public Libraries should resemble Figure 4-8.

```
Telnet - access.usask.ca
File  Edit  Disconnect  Settings  Script  Network  Help
                    United States Public Libraries

<US268> Abilene Public Library
<US514> Anoka County Library
<US455> Atlanta-Fulton Public Library
<US076> Bangor Public Library
<US402> Beaumont Public Library
<US011> Bemis Public Library
<US584> Berkeley Public Library
<US352> Boulder, Colorado, Public Library System
<US603> Canton Public Library
<US442> Carnegie Library of Pittsburgh
<US477> Carver County Public Library
<US395> Cedar Rapids Public Library
<US394> Central and Western Massachusetts Public Libraries (via CARL)
<US483> Chicago Public Library
<US010> Cleveland Public Library
<US478> Dakota County Public Library
<US011> Denver Public Library
<US038> Detroit Public Library
<US500> Douglas Public Library District
<US011> Estes Park Public Library
<US568> Farmington Community Library
-- press space for more --

Ready                                   VT100          3, 8
```

Figure 4-8
United States Public Libraries

6. We have selected <US352> Boulder, Colorado, Public Library System. The first screen we see is shown in Figure 4-9.

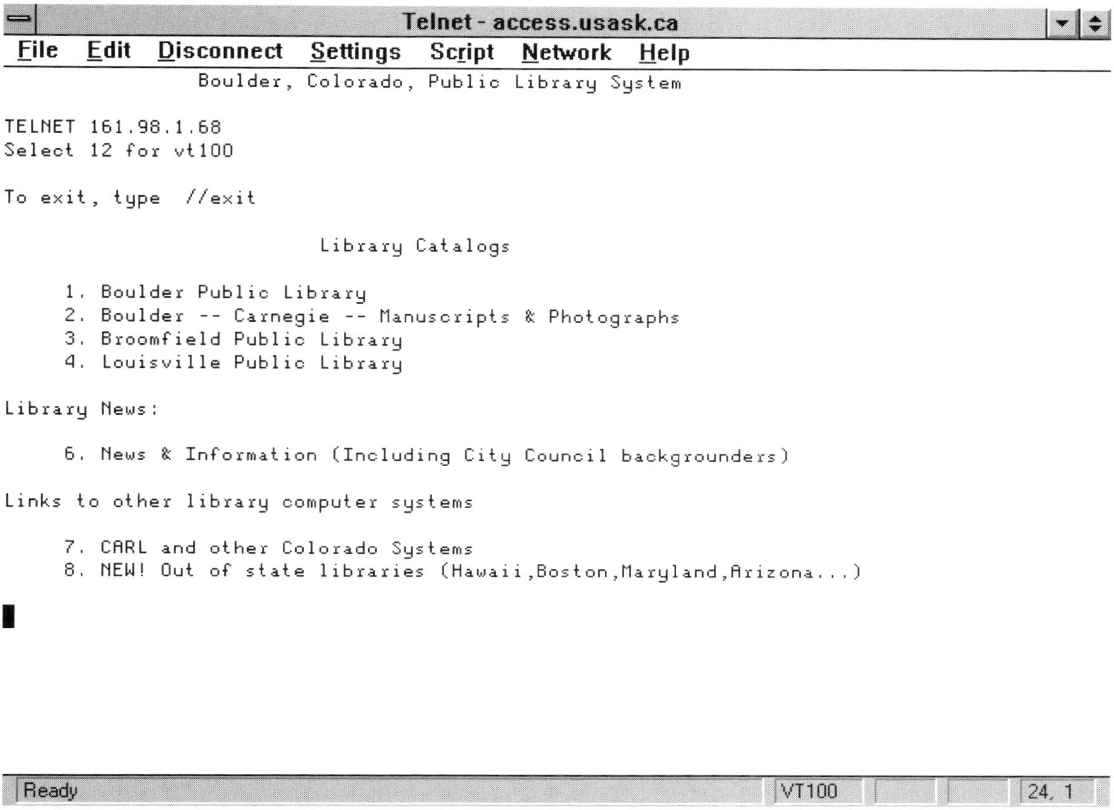

```
Telnet - access.usask.ca
File  Edit  Disconnect  Settings  Script  Network  Help
                Boulder, Colorado, Public Library System

TELNET 161.98.1.68
Select 12 for vt100

To exit, type  //exit

                          Library Catalogs

     1. Boulder Public Library
     2. Boulder -- Carnegie -- Manuscripts & Photographs
     3. Broomfield Public Library
     4. Louisville Public Library

Library News:

     6. News & Information (Including City Council backgrounders)

Links to other library computer systems

     7. CARL and other Colorado Systems
     8. NEW! Out of state libraries (Hawaii,Boston,Maryland,Arizona...)

Ready                                         VT100            24, 1
```

Figure 4-9
Boulder, Colorado, Public Library System

It is important to realize that because we are using Hytelnet on a remote host we cannot directly access the Boulder, Colorado, Public Library System resources. However, through the use of Hytelnet, we now know where these resources are located and how to access them. We will just have to Telnet to host 161.98.1.68 to be able to actually use the Boulder, Colorado, Public Library System resources. It is easy to do that.

7. Press **q** to quit Hytelnet

8. Now, click once on **Connect**

9. In the Connect To box, enter the following:

Host Name: `161.98.1.68`

Port: `23`

Emulate: `VT100`

10. When the CARL system welcomes you, enter the number `12`, which will tell it that your computer is emulating a VT100 terminal.

11. Press **<Return>** several times until you come to a screen that should resemble the one shown in Figure 4-9. However, it is important to note that this time you are actually logged into the Boulder, Colorado library system and can make choices that will be implemented.

12. Press 1 to see the Boulder, Colorado Database. It should resemble Figure 4-10.

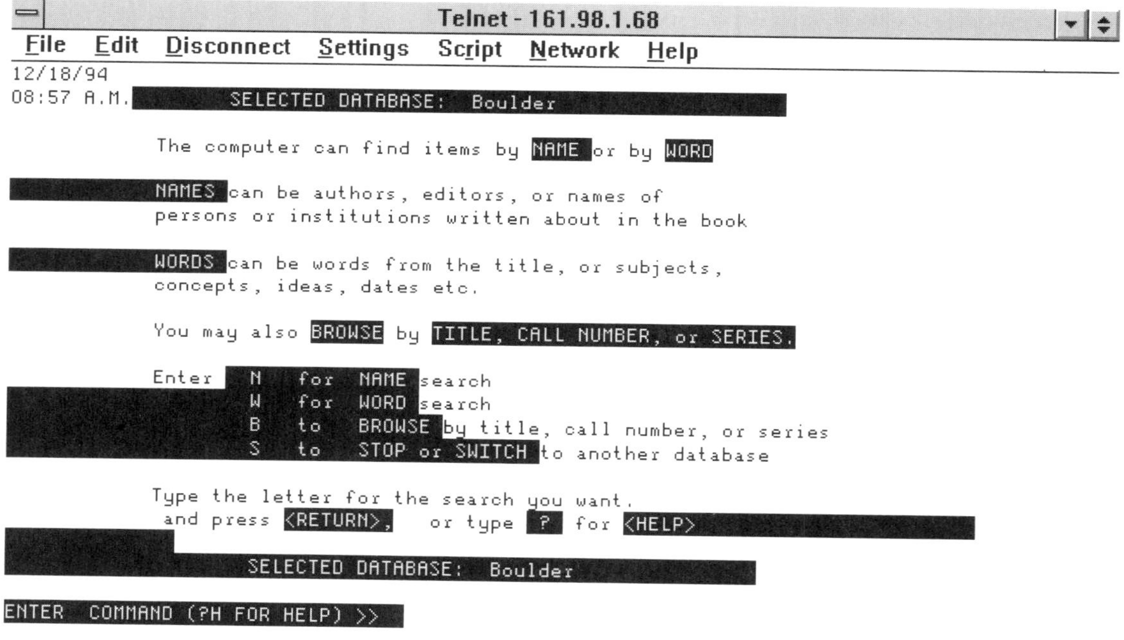

Figure 4-10
Boulder, Colorado Library Database

When you have finished exploring this marvelous resource, type //exit to leave the Boulder, Colorado Library Database and to disconnect from their system.

Session Summary

Telnet is an easy, powerful tool to use. As you have seen in this session's activities, for the most part you just need to know the name of the computer to which you wish to go, and Telnet will take care of the rest. Occasionally, as with the University of Michigan, you might have to change the port number. However, the default of 23 is usually the one that is required.

SESSION 5

Getting Internet Chameleon Mail Ready to Use

Creating and Sending Mail

Receiving Mail with Internet Chameleon

A Brief Introduction to E-Mail

Session Overview

This particular session is intended to provide you with a very brief introduction to the Internet Chameleon Mail program. Therefore, we will spend a short time helping you get the Internet Chameleon Mail program up and running. Should you wish to learn more about all of the many features that Mail contains, feel free to explore on your own or read the documentation provided with the full version of Internet Chameleon.

Overview of Internet Chameleon Mail

Internet Chameleon contains an extremely powerful program to facilitate your use of electronic mail. This program, which is called *Mail*, will permit you to do the usual E-mail activities such as sending and receiving E-mail. In addition, quite a few advanced choices and features permit you to customize the way your E-mail is received by others, as well as how your E-mail is handled by your computer.

When the Internet Chameleon Program Group initially appears on your screen, one of the seven icons you will see is the mailbox which is used to indicate Mail. Before you will be able to use Mail, you will have to set up a mail account for yourself and for any others who might be using your computer.

Getting Internet Chameleon Mail Ready to Use

There are really two parts to the process:

a. In the first part, you have to log in as *Postmaster*. This will enable you (as Postmaster) to define a user's name, password, real name, and mail directory.

b. In the second part, you have to log in as the *user* so you can define a mail gateway and mail server.

If some of this does not make sense to you right now, just keep on going; it will soon!

To Log in as Postmaster

1. Double-click on the **Mail Icon**. You should see the Mail - Login box that is pictured in Figure 5-1.

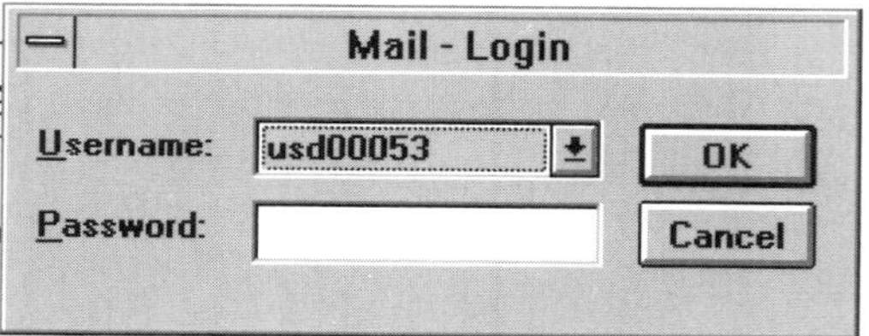

Figure 5-1
Mail - Login

2. Click on the **down arrow** in the Username: box and then click on the word **Postmaster** so it becomes active. Click on the **OK button**. Once you have done that, the Mail - Postmaster window will appear. It should resemble Figure 5-2.

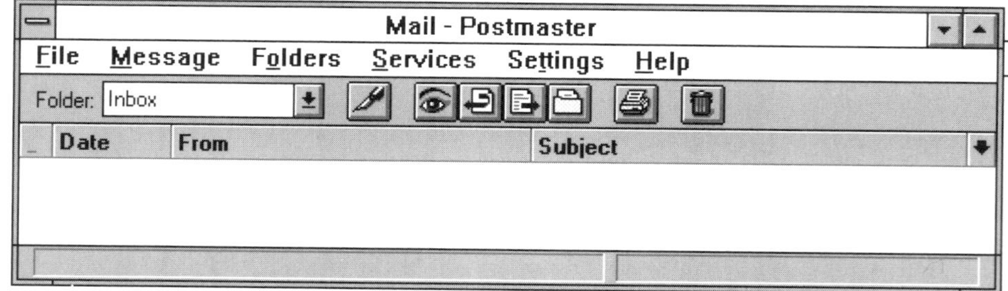

Figure 5-2
Mail - Postmaster

3. Click on **Services**. Then, click on **Mailboxes...** The Mailboxes window should resemble the one shown in Figure 5-3.

NOTE: The Mailboxes... option appears only when you are logged in as Postmaster. Should you wish to add additional users at a later time, you must remember to log in as Postmaster.

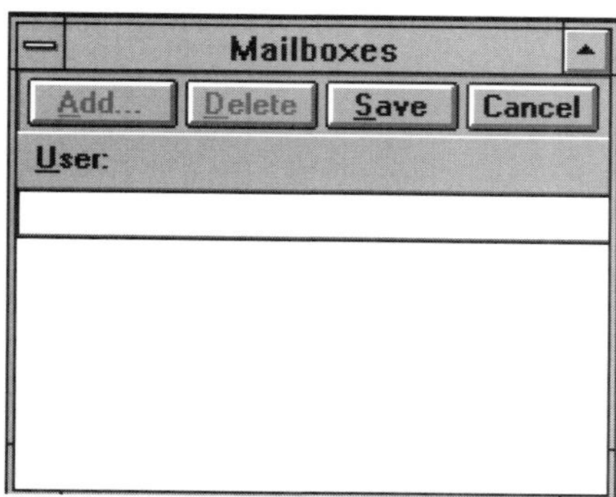

Figure 5-3
Mailboxes

4. Add your user name to the User: field. For example, I have always used dsachs as my user name, so that is what I will enter here.

NOTE: As soon as you do this, the Add... button becomes active.

---

5. Click on the **Add... button**. Once you have done so, a dialog box resembling Figure 5-4 should appear.

Figure 5-4
Mailboxes Dialog Box

6. You will need to add the following information:
   - **a.** the user's password
   - **b.** the user's name in real life
   - **c.** the mail directory where you would like to have your E-mail stored
7. Once you have done this, click on **OK**
8. You will be asked if you wish to have a Directory created for your mail. Click on **Yes** and Internet Chameleon will do this for you.

Once this has been done, you will be returned to the Mailboxes window shown in Figure 5-3. If you wish to do so, you can add other users and their information at this point.

IMPORTANT: When you have finished, be sure to click on **Save** in the Mailboxes window.

To Log in as User

1. Double-click on the **Mail Icon**. This should return you to the Mail - Login window.
2. Enter your user name and your password in the Username and Password: fields. Then, click on **OK**

When you have done that, the main Inbox Folder appears. Figure 5-5 is what mine looked like.

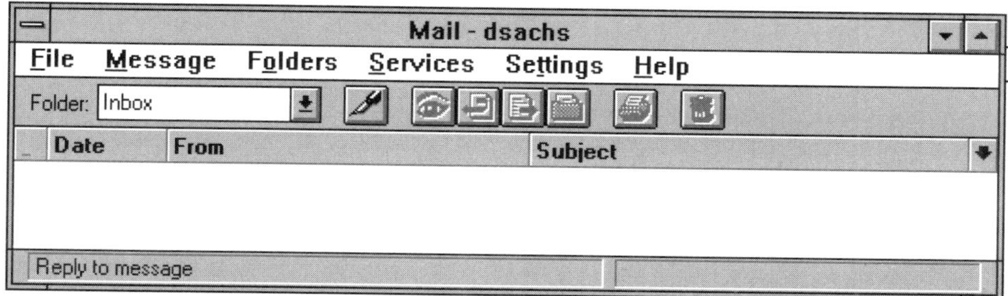

Figure 5-5
Mail Inbox

As you can see, there are quite a few choices here. We will return to some of them shortly. However, for the moment, we still have some information to enter before your E-mail address becomes fully functional with Internet Chameleon.

3. First, click on **Settings**

4. Next, click on **Network**

5. Finally, click on **Mail Gateway...**

The Mail Gateway dialog box should appear. It should resemble the one in Figure 5-6.

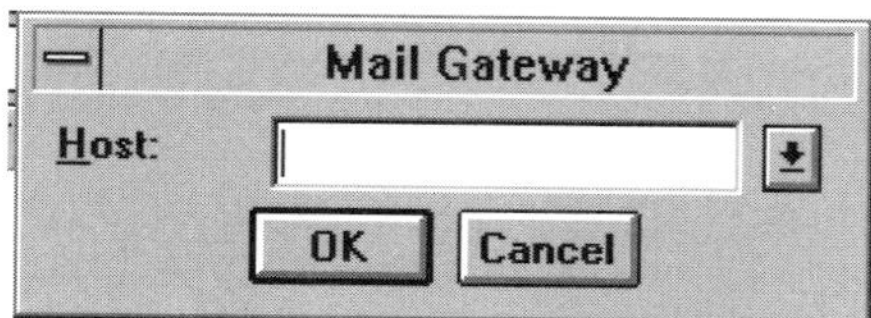

Figure 5-6
Mail Gateway

Your Internet service provider should have given you information about what is called the *mail (POP) server.* Sometimes, this information will be just a domain name (for example, panix.com). Other times, it may require that a host name be specified as well (for example, dialup.oar.net).

Carefully examine the information sent to you by your service provider. It is *very* important that you enter this information correctly into the Host: box. Once you have done that, click on **OK**

6. Three more steps!
   a. First, click on **Settings**
   b. Next, click on **Network**
   c. Finally, click on **Mail Server...**

The Mail Server window should appear. It should resemble the one shown in Figure 5-7.

Figure 5-7
Mail Server

7. You will have to enter the following required information:
   a. Enter the name of the mail (POP) server on the Host: line
   b. Enter your user name on the User: line
   c. Enter your password on the Password: line
   d. Leave an X next to Delete retrieved mail from server (or add one, if necessary)
   e. Finally, click on **OK**
8. One final step!
   a. Click on **Settings**
   b. Click on **Preferences...**
   c. Click on the **Advanced button**

d. In the From field be sure to enter your correct return E-mail address (for example, dsachs@panix.com)

e. Click on **OK** twice to return to your Mail Inbox.

Congratulations! If you have followed all of the directions in this first activity, you should have successfully configured Internet Chameleon Mail.

Creating and Sending Mail

TWO

1. From the main Internet Chameleon window, double-click on **Custom**. Then, click on **Connect** to connect to your Internet service provider.
2. Minimize the Custom application by clicking on the **down arrow** in the upper-right-hand corner.
3. From the main Internet Chameleon window, double-click on **Mail**
4. When the Mail - Login window appears, type in your password
5. Then click on **OK**

You should see the main Mail window, which is shown in Figure 5-8.

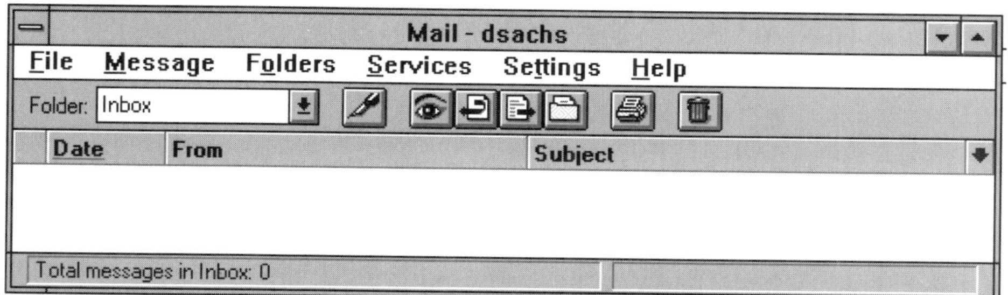

Figure 5-8
Main Mail Window

6. Click on **Message** and then click once on **Create**

A New Mail #1 window should appear. It should resemble the screen in Figure 5-9.

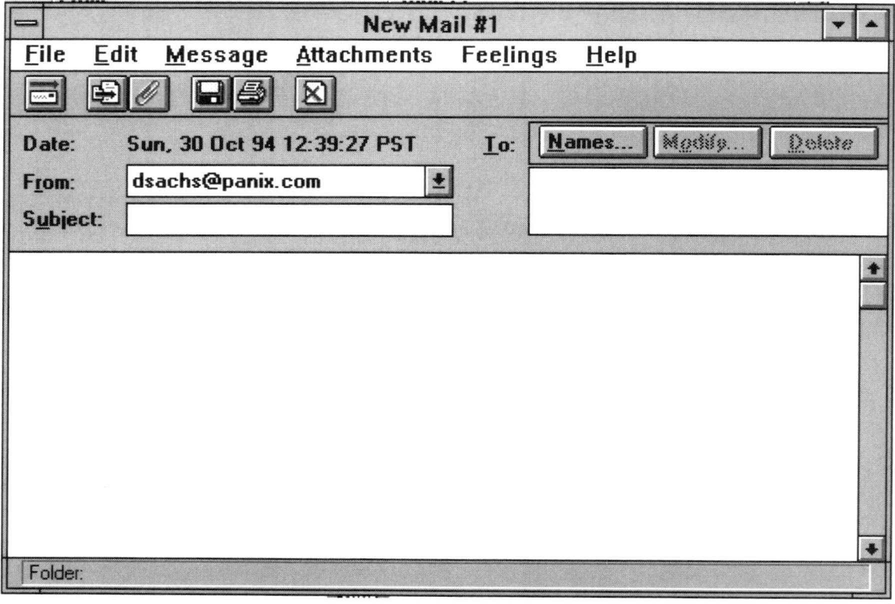

Figure 5-9
New Mail #1

As you can see, some information has been already added for you. Here are the steps to follow for the rest of the message:

1. Fill in the Subject: of your message. Since this is your first message, let's call it Just Practicing #1

2. Press **Tab** once to move your cursor to the Names… button. Click once.

   You will have to enter an address, if you wish to have your message sent. Since you are just practicing, enter your own Internet address. That way, you will not bother anyone else, and you can see if the message gets through all right.

3. Enter a practice message in the message area. If you would like to add some Feelings to your message, just click on **Feelings** and make your selection.

4. When you have finished adding your text, just click on **Message** and then on **Send** and your message will be sent.

So that you will be ready for the activities that follow, it might be a good idea to have three or four practice messages awaiting you in your Inbox. Follow the steps above and create a few more.

Receiving Mail with Internet Chameleon

THREE

1. Open your main Mail window. It should have a number of practice files in it by now and should resemble the one in Figure 5-10.

Mail - dsachs

File Message Folders Services Settings Help

Folder: Inbox

Date	From	Subject
10/30/94	<dsachs@panix.com>	Just Practicing #1
10/30/94	<dsachs@panix.com>	Practice Message # 2
10/30/94	<dsachs@panix.com>	Practice Message #3

Forward message

Figure 5-10
Receiving mail

2. To read one of your messages, do the following:
   a. Click on the message you wish to view
   b. Click on **Message** and then on **View**

Quite a few choices are available to you. Let's begin with the simplest.

3. Click on **Message** and then on **Reply to** and enter your response.

IMPORTANT: Most of the time, you will choose the default for this, which is Reply to and then Sender.

---

4. Once you have entered your text, click on **Message** and then on **Send** to send your message.

When you are viewing messages, two new buttons became active. The left arrow permits you to see the previous message; the right arrow permits you to see the following messages. Since these arrows are context sensitive, they will not be active if you are at the end of your messages (or if you have only one message), or if you are just beginning to look at your messages (or if there is only one message).

Session Summary

The Mail program included with Internet Chameleon is quite powerful. In this session, we have explored the concepts you will need to use once you begin using Internet Chameleon on a regular basis. Obviously, there are quite a few other features of Mail that we have left for you to explore. Should you be interested in reading more about them, feel free to use the Help that is included in the program, or purchase the complete Internet Chameleon program from NetManage, Inc.

SESSION 6

Activity 1 Using ftp to Get an ASCII File

Activity 2 Learning about Compression and Adding Host Computers to Your FTP File

Activity 3 Using ftp to Get a Copy of pkz204g.exe

Activity 4 Getting pkz204g.exe Ready to Use

Activity 5 Using ftp to Get Virus Protection Software

Activity 6 Using PKUNZIP to Get scn-212e.zip Ready to Use

File Transfer Protocol

Session Overview

This session is extremely important. You will use Internet Chameleon's file transfer protocol (ftp) to obtain copies of compression and virus protection software. In order to install much of the software you will encounter on the World-Wide Web, you will have to have compression software. If you are going to download binary files, you should have good virus protection software and use it regularly. By the end of this session, you will be completely ready to download and install many of the compressed files you will encounter later in this book.

Review of Anonymous File Transfer Protocol (ftp)

As you may be aware, one of the most exciting aspects of using the Internet is the process of transferring files from around the world to your own computer using the *file transfer protocol (ftp)*. File transfer protocol enables us to transfer ASCII and binary files from remote host computers to our own host computer.

We will use Internet Chameleon's ftp in the following activities as we continue to get set to use WebSurfer in the sessions to come. Using Internet Chameleon's ftp is a pleasurable and powerful way to experience anonymous ftp. It is a one-step process to move files from the remote host to your own computer using a very friendly point-and-click Windows interface.

Binary versus ASCII Files

As you are probably aware, *ASCII files* are the plain raw text that can be generated by many word processors (or spreadsheets). The files are stripped of all the code that might be particular to a given word processor, such as Word Perfect or Microsoft Word, and are, instead, just the text that forms those files. In addition, since you are retrieving "just text," you do not usually need to be concerned about introducing viruses to your computer or network.

Binary files, or *graphics files* as they are also known, are all of the other files that are out there. Typically, binary files are software programs, pictures, sounds, images, or video clips.

Downloading binary files enables you to have a new software program or a new set of graphics files. Potentially problematic, however, is the fact that you also run the risk of bringing an unintended virus to your own computer or computer network. We will return to this point later in this session.

ONE

Using ftp to Get an ASCII File

This first activity will provide you with an opportunity to become familiar with the file transfer protocol capabilities of Internet Chameleon as we download a text file. In addition, during this activity you will obtain a current copy of Scott Yanoff's *Internet Services List*. This wonderful Internet resource should be on your must have list; it is updated every two weeks (on the first and the fifteenth of each month) and is one of the best ways of keeping current about Internet resources. It is also a perfect illustration of how to use the Internet Chameleon to enable us to get, save, and print a text file using anonymous ftp.

The ftp application provided by Internet Chameleon is used to provide file transfer services across a wide variety of systems through the use of file transfer protocol (ftp). You will be pleased to see that the directory structure of the remote host (the one to which you are going for files) will be displayed just as local files and directories are displayed in Windows. You can use your usual point-and-click techniques to browse through directories as well as to transfer files. Let's get started!

Before we actually use ftp, let's take a few moments to configure it to our liking, as well as to become more familiar with its various options.

1. Open the Internet Chameleon window
2. Double-click on **FTP**

You will see the Internet Chameleon FTP window shown in Figure 6-1.

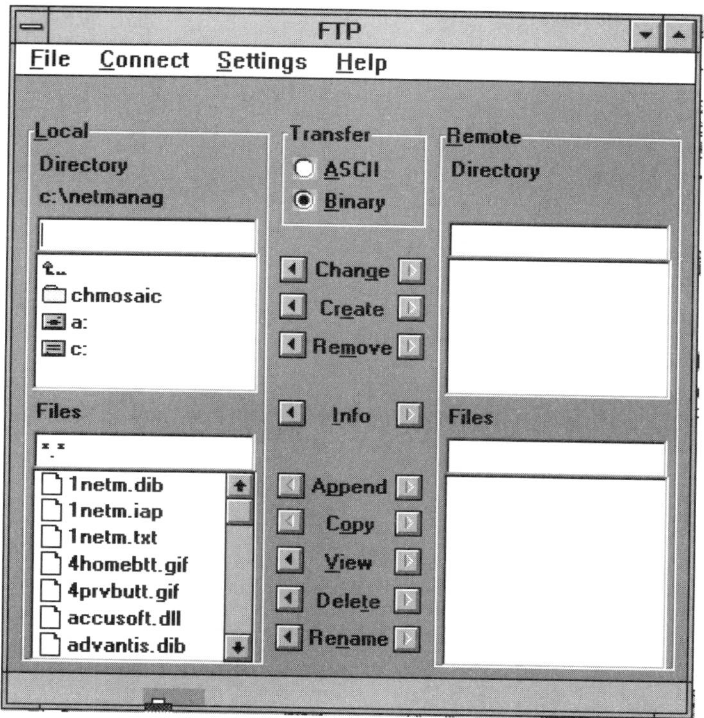

Figure 6-1
Internet Chameleon FTP Window

You will be transferring quite a few files from other computers to your own. It is probably wise to have a special directory into which these files will be transferred. We would advise that you create one now called INCOMING. If you do this, you will always know where to look for the files you download, and you will protect other files from being overwritten. Here is how to do so:

a. Move your cursor to the Local Directory box. Notice that the default directory is c:netmanag
   Just below that, type `c:\incoming`
b. Click once on the **left arrow** next to Create
c. Click once on the **left arrow** next to Change
d. Your local directory should be c:\incoming
e. Click on **File** and then **Save**

3. Click on **Settings** and then choose **Connection Profile...**

Your screen should look like the one in Figure 6-2.

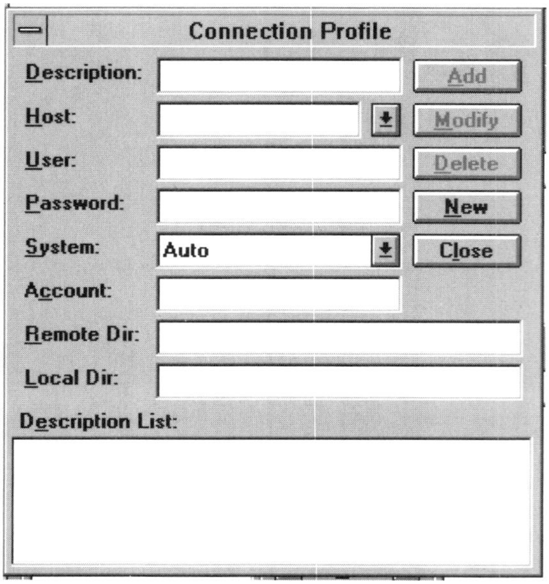

Figure 6-2
Connection Profile

4. We will enter some information that will enable us to retrieve Scott Yanoff's Internet Services file—and preserve our ability to do so easily and quickly whenever we again wish to have a current copy. To do so:

a. In the Description box, enter something that will remind you about this ftp archive and this particular set of files, for example, `Yanoff/U. of Wisconsin`

b. Tab to the Host box and enter the correct, fully qualified domain name for the remote host computer. For the Yanoff List, we will need to enter `ftp.csd.uwm.edu`

c. Tab to the User box and enter the name that is to be entered when the remote host prompts for a user name. Since we are using anonymous ftp as the protocol, we must enter the word `anonymous`

d. Tab to the Password box and enter the correct password. Assuming that you do not have a password on the University of Wisconsin host, you should follow Internet protocol and *enter your fully qualified E-mail address*. For example, I would enter `dsachs@cloud9.net`

When you do this, your password will *not* appear in the Password box, so be sure to type it correctly.

e. Tab to the System box and select **Auto**

f. Move your cursor to the Local Dir: box and type in the drive and pathname for where you would like to have your ftp files saved, for example, `c:\incoming`

g. Finally, click on the **Add button**, which will cause the Description to be added to the Description List and the configuration information to be added to your Internet Chameleon program.

If you have other favorite ftp locations, you should feel free to add them at this time. Otherwise, you can return to this set of operations at any time to add additional ftp locations.

5. When you have finished adding information about ftp hosts, click on **Close**

6. Click on **File** and then **Save**

Now, using the information that was just added, we can use the Internet Chameleon to download the Yanoff Internet Services file.

IMPORTANT: If you are not already online with your service provider, double-click on the **Custom Icon** and then click on **Connect**

---

7. Minimize the Custom Window into an icon by clicking on the **down arrow** in the upper-right-hand corner of your screen. Then, double-click on the **Ftp Icon**

8. Click on **Connect**

The FTP Connect window should appear and should resemble the one in Figure 6-3.

Figure 6-3
FTP Connect

9. Slide your cursor down to the Description: box and click on **Yanoff/U of Wisconsin**. Instantly, all the necessary information appears in the upper boxes on your screen.

   Since that is the remote host to which we wish to connect, click on **OK**

   Notice how quickly and efficiently you are connected to the host computer at University of Wisconsin.

10. The first thing you will see in the Remote Directory box is a slash (/) that indicates you are at the root directory. Since we wish to change to the pub subdirectory, double-click on **pub**

11. Move your cursor down to the Remote Files box in the lower-right-hand corner of your screen. By clicking on the **down arrow** in the scroll bar, you will be able to see a listing of the files in the pub directory.

    Stop when you come to one called inet.services.txt and click once on it. Your screen should resemble the one in Figure 6-4.

FTP - ftp.csd.uwm.edu
File Disconnect Settings Help
alpha2.csd.uwm.edu FTP server (Version wu-2.4(3) Wed Jun 22 17:23:50 CDT 1994) ready.
Local
Directory
a:\
a:
c:
Files
.
!inet.htm
!inet.txt
!inet00.txt
hoi06.asc
hom03.910
iim04.030
iim04.106
iim06.106
pfs.dir
Transfer
ASCII
Binary
Change
Create
Remove
Info
Append
Copy
View
Delete
Rename
Remote
Directory
/pub
..
ags
anamika
beatpunk
bhayes
Files
inet.services.txt
Custard_Flavors
fingerinfo
inet.services.html
inet.services.txt
inet2.html
internetwork-mail-guide
maple.ind
maple.lib
woo.html
zipcode.gz

Figure 6-4 Downloading inet.services.txt

We would, in effect, like to copy this file from the *remote* host computer (with the file in the right-hand Files box) to our own local host computer (with the list of files in the left-hand Files box).

12. Double-click on the **left-hand copy button** and watch the magic!

Internet Chameleon automatically converts the name into one that is more usable by your computer. In our case, the file was automatically named !inet00.txt

---

If you would like to give this file another name, do the following:

a. Highlight the name of the file
b. Click on the **left-hand Rename button**
c. Type in the new name on the To: line in the Rename box, and then click on **Yes** when you have finished.

If you wish to download any other files from the University of Wisconsin, you may do so now. Otherwise, click on **Disconnect** to end this ftp session.

NOTE: To read this file, just use your favorite word processor. It is a text file and should be accessible immediately. You may have to change the margins to one-half inch on each side.

Compressed Files

Binary files tend to be large. For example, it is not uncommon to find binary files that are 600,000 bytes or larger. It does not take very long to transfer files of this size from one host computer to another. However, as you might imagine, there are costs affiliated with files of this size.

All of the resources being used in this process cost time and money. There is a cost affiliated with your use of the remote host computer, as well as the cost affiliated with using your local host computer. Finally, there is a cost affiliated with using your own time. Consequently, people have developed methods that are intended to minimize these costs. This work has focused on compressing files, so they will be much smaller than they were originally.

The advantages are many. First of all, the file may be stored in a much smaller space on its resident host computer. Second, the file may be transferred from one host computer to another in much less time. Finally, the file may be saved in much less space than would otherwise be required. When added together, all of these represent sizable savings of time and money for all concerned.

Where Does Compression Take Place?

One location where compression may take place is on a remote computer. The person who has developed the program may wish to reduce its size before uploading it to a host computer, or before putting it on disks for distribution, and uses a file compression program to do so. Once you have retrieved such a file, you will need to have in your possession the compression program that can be used to uncompress the file. For example, if the program was *zipped* after it was created, it will need to be *unzipped* once it has been retrieved.

It is also possible that you may wish to compress files on your own computer in an attempt to conserve storage space. Once you begin to download large graphics and audio files using WebSurfer, you will quickly discover the value of being able to do this!

Learning about Compression and Adding Host Computers to Your FTP File

If the topic of compression is new to you, it is possible to become somewhat overwhelmed by it all. So, before learning about many of the possible methods of compression that can be used, let's just focus on a few of them. There are two parts to the compression discussion:

a. The first part has to do with the file extensions that are commonly used by those who have compressed files.

b. The second part has to do with the programs that are used to compress and uncompress software programs.

Typical File Extensions

In the DOS environment, you have probably seen file extensions such as the ones in Table 6-1.

Table 6-1: Typical file extensions

File Extension	ASCII or Binary	File Type
com	binary	executable file
doc	ASCII	text file
exe	binary	executable file
ps	ASCII	to be printed on a PostScript printer
txt	ASCII	text file
wp	binary	WordPerfect file

In this context, we are going to focus on files with some new file extensions. Some (of the many) are presented in Table 6-2.

Table 6-2: Typical file extensions

File Extension	ASCII or Binary	Compression Program Required
gif	binary	graphics file
tif	binary	graphics file
zip	binary	PKZIP/PKUNZIP

Notice, first of all, that these new files are all binary files. This means that when we are using ftp, we must be sure to indicate that we are getting and transferring binary, not ASCII files. In particular, you should notice that files ending in zip require compression programs to be used before you will be able to have a fully functional program on your personal computer.

In this second activity, we will prepare your Internet Chameleon FTP program for some of the activities that follow. To do so:

1. Open your Internet Chameleon Icon. Double-click on **Custom** and click on **Connect** so that you are connected to your service provider.
2. Minimize the Custom window to an icon by clicking on the **down arrow** in the upper-right-hand corner.
3. Double-click on **FTP**
4. First click on **Settings** and then click on **Connection Profile...**
5. Click on **New** and type the following:

    Description: `Washington University`

    Host: `wuarchive.wustl.edu`

    User: `anonymous`

    Password: This should be your actual fully qualified domain name, such as mine, `dsachs@cloud9.net`

    System: `Auto`

    Local Dir: `c:\incoming`

6. When you have finished typing this information, review it, and, if it is correct, click on **Add** If it is not correct, just retype it.
7. Now, let's add another host. First, click on **New** Then type the following:

    Description: `University of Illinois`

    Host: `ftp.cso.uiuc.edu`

    User: `anonymous`

    Password: This should be your actual fully qualified domain name, such as mine, `dsachs@cloud9.net`

System: `Auto`

Local Dir: `c:\incoming`

8. When you have finished typing, review the information. If it is correct, click on **Add** If it is not correct, just retype it.

9. Finally, let's add one more host. First, click on **New** Then type the following:

   Description: `Oakland`

   Host: `oak.oakland.edu`

   User: `anonymous`

   Password: This should be your actual fully qualified domain name, such as mine, `dsachs@cloud9.net`

   System: `Auto`

   Local Dir: `c:\incoming`

10. Review the information you have entered. If it is correct, click on **Add**

There is quite a bit of software available on the Internet. Some of it is known as *freeware*. This means that the people who developed it are purposely providing you with the software for free.

There is other software that is more properly thought of as *shareware*. In this latter instance, people develop software that they distribute in the hope that you will try their software, like their software, and then decide to upgrade your program to the full version, for which there will be a fee paid to them. Several of the programs that we are about to acquire fall into this latter category.

In each case, we will make you aware of where it is possible to purchase the full version of the software with the complete documentation and files that may be missing from the shareware version. We would urge you to purchase the full version should the software have value to you.

A much used file compression technique is known as PKZIP, and the files that are compressed this way typically have an extension of .ZIP . This program was developed by a company called PKWARE, Inc. To purchase the latest complete version of the software with all of the documentation, you may contact:

PKWARE, INC.
The Data Compression Experts
9025 N. Deerwood Drive
Brown Deer, WI 53223

For us to use the shareware version of PKZIP, we will have to first have a copy of pkz204g.exe. This file can be found most easily at Oakland or at the University of Illinois.

THREE

Using ftp to Get a Copy of pkz204g.exe

Many files on the Internet have been compressed using PKZIP, and you would be unable to use them if you were not able to unzip them once you had retrieved them. We will learn how to unzip files shortly. In this activity we will download a copy of pkunzip.exe. Here is how to do that.

1. With Internet Chameleon active, use the **Custom Icon** to log in to your service provider. Then, minimize the Custom window to an icon by clicking on the **down arrow** in the upper-right-hand part of the window.

2. Double-click on the **FTP Icon**

IMPORTANT: Since we are about to transfer a software program (a binary file), it is imperative that you change the Transfer mode from ASCII to binary. Click once on the **Binary button** to do this.

3. Click on **Connect** and highlight the name Oakland which is found in the Description box. Your screen should resemble the one in Figure 6-5.

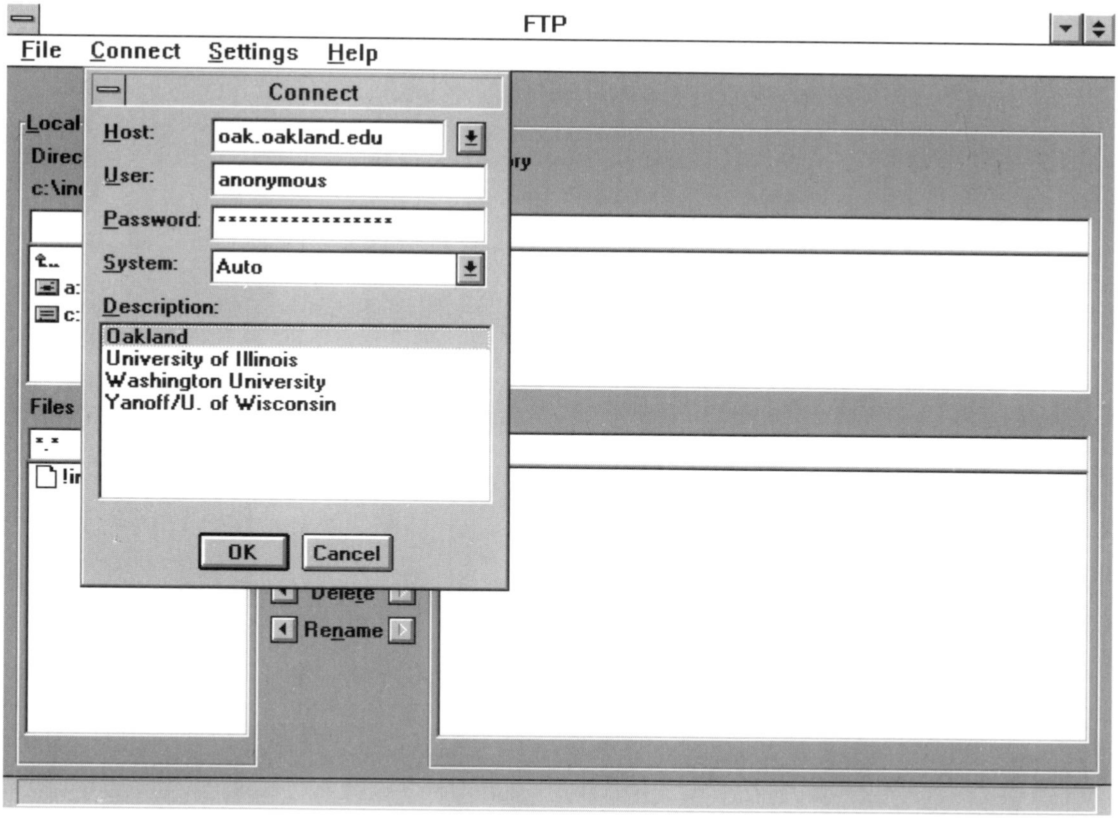

FTP
File Connect Settings Help
Connect
Host: oak.oakland.edu
User: anonymous
Password: *****************
System: Auto
Description:
Oakland
University of Illinois
Washington University
Yanoff/U. of Wisconsin
OK Cancel
Rename

Figure 6-5
Connection Profile—Oakland

4. Click on **OK** to connect to oak.oakland.edu

5. Click on the **down arrow** in the Remote Directory box to move the names of the files until you come to the one called SimTel

6. Double-click on **SimTel** so that you can see the subdirectories it contains. Since we are looking for a file that can be used in an MSDOS environment it seems logical to change to that subdirectory. Double-click on **msdos**

7. Click on the **down arrow** in the Remote Directory box, until you come to the sub-subdirectory called zip

8. Double-click on **zip** so that you can change to that sub-subdirectory.

   Once you have done so, click on the **down arrow** in the Remote Files box until the file called pkz204g.exe is visible. Your screen should resemble the one in Figure 6-6.

FTP - oak.oakland.edu

File Disconnect Settings Help

oak.oakland.edu FTP server (Version wu-2.4(2) Sun Aug 14 14:49:48 EDT 1994) ready.

Local
Directory
c:\incoming
..
a:
c:
Files
.
!index-b
!inet.txt
index
pkunzip.exe
scn-212e.zip

Transfer
ASCII
Binary
Change
Create
Remove
Info
Append
Copy
View
Delete
Rename

Remote
Directory
/SimTel/msdos/zip
..
Files
pkz204g.exe
pk2bugs.zip
pkbanner.zip
pkcnvt11.zip
pkinsv64.zip
pkv100.zip
pkz-ced.zip
pkz204g.exe
pkzdate.zip
pkzf11.zip
pkzm104.exe

Figure 6-6
Locating pkz204g.exe

IMPORTANT: Be sure that you are prepared to transfer a binary file.

---

9. Once you are ready to download the pkz204g.exe file, just click on the **left-hand arrow** for **Copy**.

If you have done this correctly, you should see a screen that resembles the one in Figure 6-7.

Figure 6-7
Downloading pkz204g.exe

Once the file has been successfully transferred to your computer, be sure to disconnect from oak.oakland.edu, as well as from your Internet service provider.

Getting pkz204g.exe Ready to Use

FOUR

First, you should be aware that pkz204g.exe is what is known as an *executable* file. That is, it may be executed (run) by just typing the name of the file. For example, if you wish to run pkz204g.exe, you just have to type `pkz204g`. **WARNING: Do not do that now!**

It is probably useful to have the pkunzip.exe file and the files which accompany it in their own subdirectory on your hard disk. We would

suggest that you copy the pkz204g.exe file to a new subdirectory called c:\pkware To do this:

- **a.** Make a new subdirectory on your hard drive. At the c: prompt, type `md pkware`
- **b.** Copy the file from incoming to the new subdirectory. Type `copy c:\incoming\pkz204g.exe c:\pkware`
- **c.** Now, let's explode the files that are contained within pkz204g.exe. First change to the pkware directory by typing `cd pkware`
- **d.** Next, type `pkz204g`

If all goes according to plan, you should wind up with 17 files in this subdirectory; you should have your original copy of pkz204g.exe as well as 16 files that have been exploded.

The important file for our purposes is the one called pkunzip.exe. We will not do any more with this file at this time. However, we will return to it momentarily.

FIVE

Using ftp to Get Virus Protection Software

If you have been using anonymous ftp for the transfer of ASCII files, then you should not have had to worry too much about the transfer of viruses to your personal computer or to your network. However, as soon as you begin to transfer new binary programs to your computer, you should begin to think carefully about protecting your computer and its software from viruses that might harm some or all of your programs. You would be well advised to have a virus protection program installed on your computer and to use it regularly.

There are quite a few commercial programs available. In addition, there is a well-known shareware program called *SCAN*, developed by McAfee Associates, that is available to us on the Internet. If you wish to order the latest commercial version of the software, you can order it from

McAfee Associates
2710 Walsh Avenue
Santa Clara, CA 95051
(408) 988-3832

Here is how to get the shareware version of SCAN and how to use it.

1. Double-click on the **Custom Icon** and then click on **Connect** so that you are connected to your service provider.

2. Minimize the Custom window into an icon by clicking on the **down arrow** in the top-right-hand side of your Custom window.
3. Double-click on the **FTP Icon**
4. Review the FTP screen and be sure that Transfer is set to Binary
5. Click on **Connect** and select **oak.oakland.edu** as the host
6. Click on the **down-arrow button** in the Remote Directory box until you find the subdirectory SimTel

   Next, double-click on **SimTel** so that you can see which directories it contains.
7. Double-click on the sub-subdirectory **msdos** to make it active.
8. Click on the **down-arrow button** in the Remote Directory box until you find the sub-sub-subdirectory named virus

   Double-click on **virus** to make it active.
9. Click on the **down-arrow button** in the Remote Files box to see the files that are contained in the virus sub-sub-subdirectory.
10. You will notice that one of the files is named scn-xxx.zip (when we did this, it was called scn-212e.zip). This is the SCAN file you would like to retrieve.

NOTE: This file is a binary file that has (most likely) been compressed using the PKZIP/PKUNZIP compression program we referred to and retrieved earlier. First, we will retrieve scn-212e.zip; then we will use PKUNZIP to convert it into a usable program.

---

11. You will need to copy this program from the remote host (oak.oakland.edu) to your computer. We will copy this file into the subdirectory on drive c: called incoming.

    Click once on **scn-212e.zip** to make it active. Once you have done so, just click on the **left-hand Copy button** and the file will be copied.
12. Once the file has been transferred, be sure to leave the oak.oakland.edu host by clicking on **Disconnect**. Then click on **Disconnect** again when it appears in the Disconnect window.
13. Finally, you should close the FTP window.

    Once the file has been successfully transferred to your personal computer, you may disconnect from your service provider and exit from the Internet Chameleon. Now we just need to get the SCAN program ready for use!

SIX

Using PKUNZIP to Get scn-212e.zip Ready to Use

We will assume that you have followed all of the directions in Activity 4 and that your PKUNZIP.EXE file is on your hard drive in a subdirectory called pkware.

1. First, you should put the SCAN program into its own directory. At the c: prompt, type `md scan`
2. Assuming that the scn-212e.zip file is on drive c: in the subdirectory incoming, type
   `copy c:\incoming\scn-212e.zip c:\scan`
   and press **ENTER**
3. In addition to the scn-212e.zip file, we would like to also have a copy of PKUNZIP.EXE in that same directory. To copy PKUNZIP.EXE from the pkware subdirectory to the SCAN subdirectory, type
   `copy c:\pkware\pkunzip.exe c:\scan`
   Once you press **ENTER**, the file will be copied.
4. Change to the SCAN directory by typing `cd scan`
5. Once you are in the SCAN directory, just type
   `pkunzip scn-212e.zip` and press **ENTER**

All of the files that have been compressed will be uncompressed, and you should wind up with approximately 19 files in your SCAN directory (the exact number will depend on the version of the program that you are unzipping).

To use the SCAN program to check your computer for viruses is remarkably simple.

1. At the c: prompt, change to the SCAN directory. Type `cd scan` and then type the word `scan` followed by the name of the drive you wish to check.

For example, type `scan c:` and the program will do the rest.

Session Summary

In this session, we have advanced our knowledge of anonymous ftp techniques and have added some new software to our Internet Toolbox in the process. If you have been following along, you have:

a. Used anonymous ftp to retrieve a text file known as Yanoff's Internet Services List.

b. Learned about three well-known sites for ftp files:
wuarchive.wustl.edu
ftp.cso.uiuc.edu
oak.oakland.edu

c. Used anonymous ftp to retrieve two binary files:
pkz204g.exe and scn-212e.zip

d. Inflated both software programs so that we now have fully functioning copies of both PKUNZIP and SCAN.

e. Used PKUNZIP to unzip scn-212e.zip into its actual program files.

f. Used SCAN to check your hard disk for viruses.

We are now extremely close to using WebSurfer. As will become obvious later in this book, the skills you have just learned in this session (and the software you have just acquired) are important if you are to implement many of the multimedia aspects of WebSurfer. We will put your new-found software and talents to work in Session Twelve.

SESSION 7

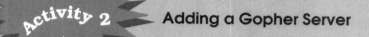

Activity 1 Getting Familiar with Your Gopher Client

Activity 2 Adding a Gopher Server

Activity 3 Continuing to Explore the Gopher Client

Activity 4 Exploring the NetManage Gopher

Activity 5 Exploring the University of Minnesota Gopher

Activity 6 Exploring Other Gopher and Information Servers

Activity 7 Learning about Symbols

Exploring GopherSpace

Session Overview

Gopher is the first of two major tools that have taken the Internet by storm. Browsers for the World-Wide Web are the other and they will be covered beginning in the next session. Gopher originated at the University of Minnesota whose mascot is a gopher. The Internet Gopher is a go-fer that goes 'fer information like a theater gofer goes 'fer coffee.

The Internet Gopher really comes in two types: Gopher Clients and Gopher Servers. You now have a Gopher Client as part of Internet Chameleon which can go to all the Gopher Servers in the world for information. Together the Gopher Servers in the world (with your Gopher Client) are considered to be GopherSpace. GopherSpace may seem to be a strange concept, but once you begin to move about in GopherSpace, it will seem wonderfully real.

Getting Familiar with Your Gopher Client

To begin, let's look at your Gopher Client. Find and double-click on the **Gopher Icon** in your Internet Chameleon Group. It is shown in Figure 7-1.

Figure 7-1
The Gopher Icon

This will open the Gopher window that is shown in Figure 7-2.

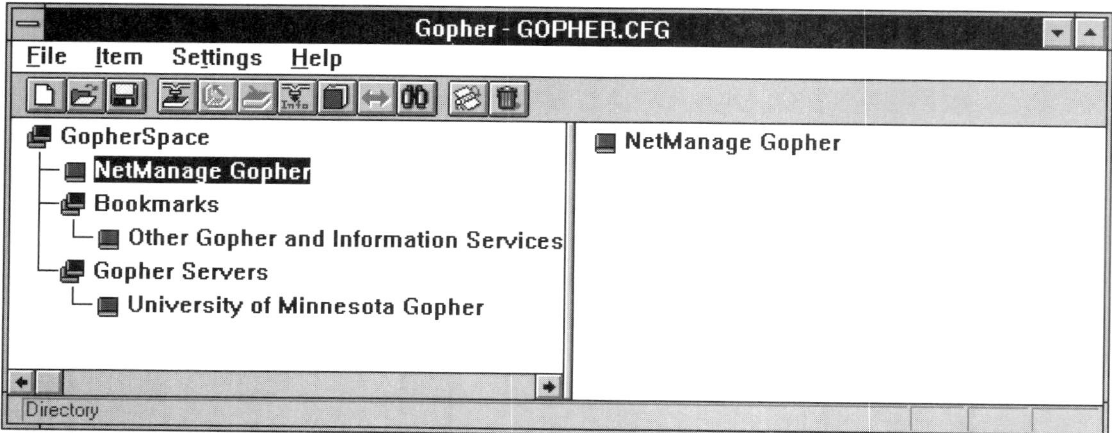

Figure 7-2
Gopher Window

The window is divided into left and right boxes. On the left-hand side is the directory tree for GopherSpace and on the right-hand side is the resource list. If you have used the File Manager in Windows, this will look familiar.

Note that one of the directories in the left-hand box is highlighted (in Figure 7-2 it is the NetManage Gopher). You will see the contents of this highlighted directory in the right-hand box. This allows you to see in an instant both *where* you are (left-hand box) in GopherSpace and *what* is there (right-hand box).

As you look at the left-hand box, you will see two kinds of book icons that are arranged in a hierarchy or directory tree. One icon is a closed blue book (with a red book behind it) and the other is a closed red book. In just a moment, we'll open one of the books.

Several Gopher Server locations are already in your directory tree. One is the NetManage Gopher and another is the University of Minnesota Gopher. We'll visit each of these in a moment to get you started. Later we'll add several more Gopher Servers to show how it's done.

Before we jump off into GopherSpace, let's look around your Gopher Client.

The top line of the Gopher Window is the Title Line. It tells you that you are in Gopher and are using a configuration file called

GOPHER.CFG. You can have several configuration files if you wish, but let's keep it simple for now.

The next line is the Menu Bar. Its headings include File, Item, Settings, and Help. Each of these has a drop-down menu allowing you to do different tasks. Following Window's convention, choices in each drop-down menu will be "shadowed" if they are not active.

In File, the choices are

New	Create a new Gopher Client Configuration File
Open	Open an existing Gopher Client Configuration File
Save	Save the currently open Configuration File
Save As	Save the currently open Configuration File under a new name
Exit	Close and leave the Gopher Client

You really won't have to use these too often unless you make changes while you are using Gopher. Then, you may either Save and Exit or just Exit. If you just Exit, Gopher will ask you if you want to save changes.

The Item heading on the Menu Bar will be used more often. It contains

Retrieve Item	Retrieve the selected item into local storage
Close Item	Close the selected item collapsing its substructure
Open Item	Open the selected item from local storage
Retrieve Info	Retrieve Gopher+ information on the selected item
Set Bookmark	Copy the current selection into the Bookmark section
Go Back	Select the previously selected item
Search	Search keyword index of the currently selected GopherSpace
Copy to File	Copy the currently selected information to a file
Move to File	Move the currently selected information to a file
Add Gopher Server	Add a new Gopher Server to your current configuration
Item Properties	Examine or change item properties
Remove Item	Remove the selected item from the hierarchy

You may use these drop-down menu boxes to perform these actions, or you may choose to click on the icon buttons on the Toolbar for many of them. We'll explain more about the Toolbar after the first activity.

When you find an item from a particular Gopher Server you wish to retain, you may use the Set Bookmark function to keep that item in your Bookmarks section. Then you will not need to go down through a long hierarchy to reach that selected item.

If you hear about a Gopher or find a Gopher server name in print and want to add it to your Gopher Client, you can use the Add Gopher Server function. You do this by clicking on **Item** and then **Add Gopher Server**. The Add Gopher Server dialog box should resemble Figure 7-3.

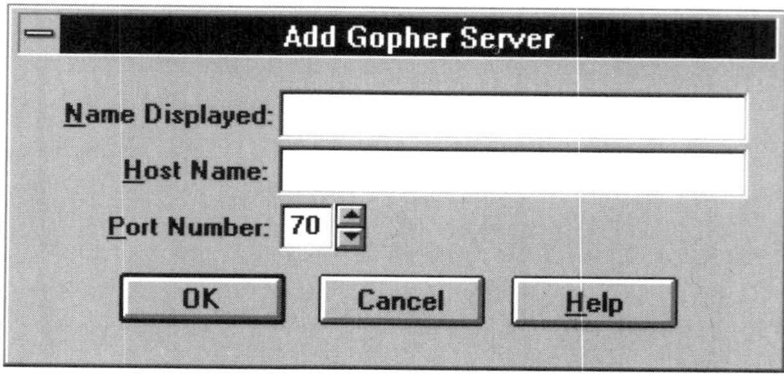

Figure 7-3
Add Gopher Server

In this box, you will type in the Name Displayed: (which is really the name you want to use for a particular Gopher Server) and the Host Name:. The hostname must be the exact name of the Gopher Server and must be typed with the correct lower- and upper-case letters. Almost all Gopher Servers in the world use port 70, so you will rarely need to change that.

TWO

Adding a Gopher Server

We're going to add a Gopher Server to your directory of Gophers. Here's how to do so.

1. Connect to your provider and open your Gopher Client if it's not already open.
2. Click on **Gopher Servers** in the left-hand box to make that directory active.
3. Click on **Item** and then on **Add Gopher Server...**

   You should see a dialog box resembling Figure 7-3.

4. In the Name Displayed: line, type `The InterNIC`

5. On the Host Name: line, type `gopher.internic.net`

6. Click on **OK** and the new server will appear in your directory tree in the left-hand box.

7. Now double-click on this new item.

You will see a pop-up box telling you that your Gopher Client is trying to connect to the Gopher Server at the Internet's Network Information Center, the InterNIC. Initially, it will say "Nothing Received". Then it should start telling you that information is being received. Finally, you will see the contents of the current Gopher Server at the InterNIC. We show what this looks like in Figure 7-4. It may look different on your screen as the information changes frequently.

Figure 7-4
The InterNIC Gopher

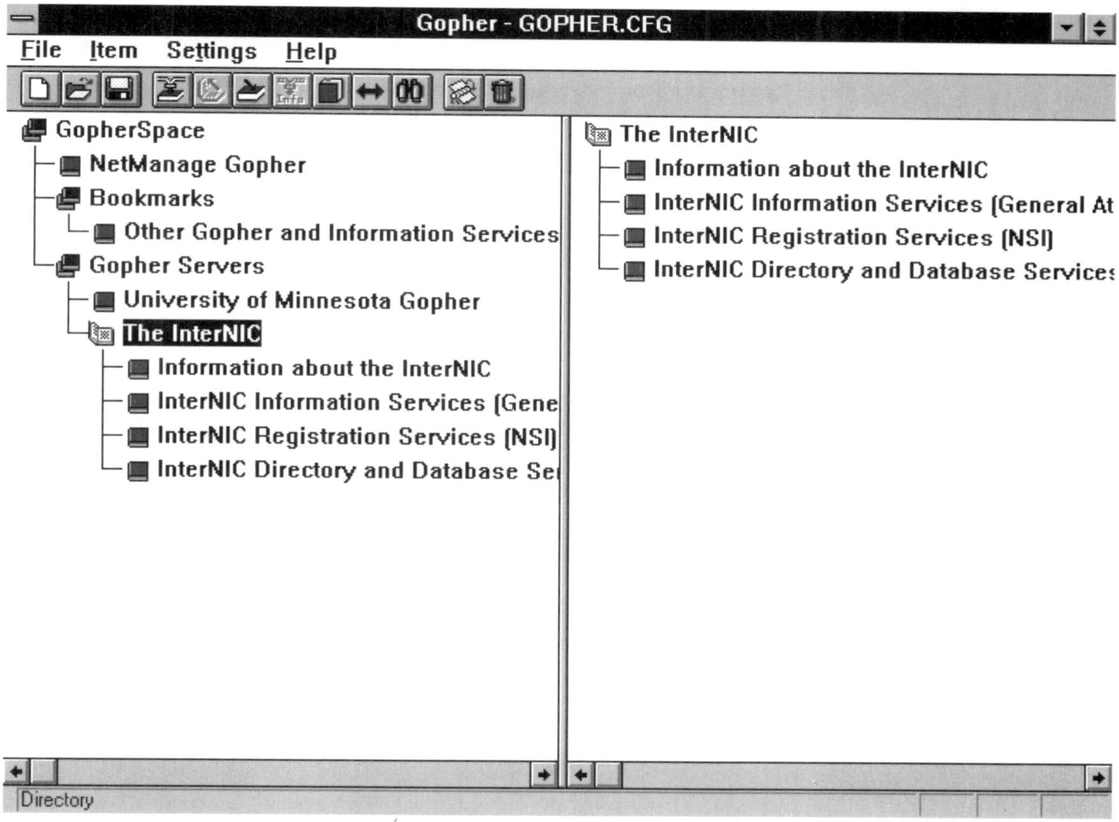

Notice that the book icon next to the words The InterNIC is now open. This tells us that the contents of The InterNIC "book" are displayed. The books below are still closed, which tells us that there is information in each one of them. We can access this information if we double-click on a particular book. This is illustrated in Figure 7-5.

The InterNIC
- Information about the InterNIC
- InterNIC Information Services (General Atomics)
- InterNIC Registration Services (NSI)
- InterNIC Directory and Database Services (AT&T)

Figure 7-5
The Open Book (The InterNIC)

Let's double-click on the closed book called **InterNIC Information Services** After a moment, you will see a screen similar to Figure 7-6.

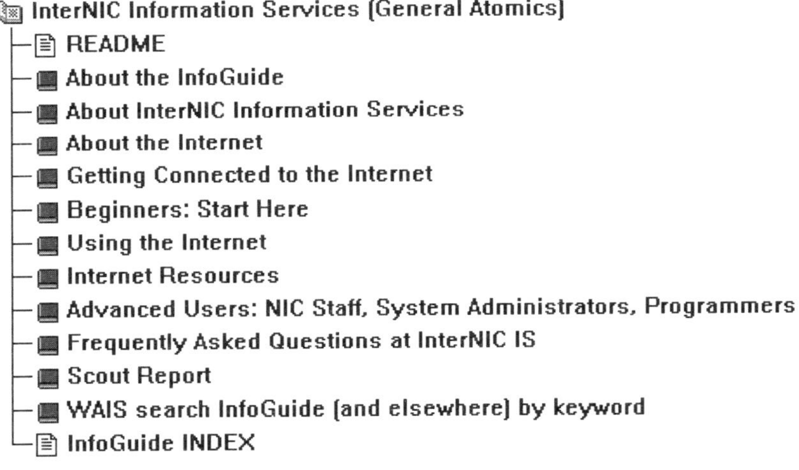

Figure 7-6
InterNIC Information Services (General Atomics)

Observe that we now see a new type of icon that looks like a page of a letter. This indicates that it is probably text information which we can read. If we double-click on the top page **README**, you will see some text that should resemble the text shown in Figure 7-7.

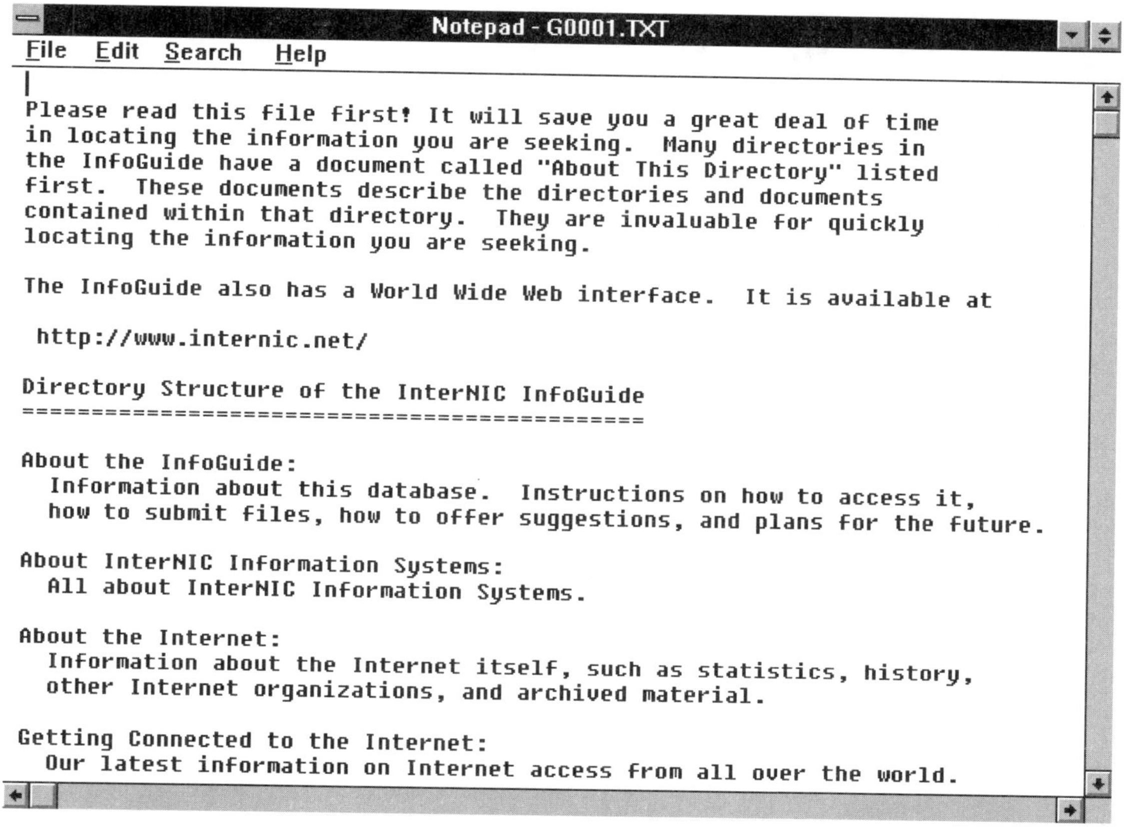

Notepad - G0001.TXT

File Edit Search Help

```
Please read this file first! It will save you a great deal of time
in locating the information you are seeking.  Many directories in
the InfoGuide have a document called "About This Directory" listed
first.  These documents describe the directories and documents
contained within that directory.  They are invaluable for quickly
locating the information you are seeking.

The InfoGuide also has a World Wide Web interface.  It is available at

 http://www.internic.net/

Directory Structure of the InterNIC InfoGuide
=============================================

About the InfoGuide:
  Information about this database.  Instructions on how to access it,
  how to submit files, how to offer suggestions, and plans for the future.

About InterNIC Information Systems:
  All about InterNIC Information Systems.

About the Internet:
  Information about the Internet itself, such as statistics, history,
  other Internet organizations, and archived material.

Getting Connected to the Internet:
  Our latest information on Internet access from all over the world.
```

Figure 7-7
The README Screen

You can now use your Gopher Client to begin exploring GopherSpace starting at the InterNIC. When you have finished exploring the wonderful resources of the InterNIC, we will look at some additional features of your Gopher Client.

THREE

Continuing to Explore the Gopher Client

The next Command on the Menu Bar is Settings. Settings contains

Preferences	Examine or change the operation of parts of your Gopher
Colors	Change or reset the colors used in your Gopher screen
Log	Open a Log window to follow information transfers
Toolbar	Display or hide the Toolbar and its buttons
Smart Buttons	Select small or large (with words) Toolbar buttons
Status Bar	Display or hide the Status Line at the bottom of the screen
Split Window	Move the line between the left and right boxes

You may choose to change Preferences and/or Colors to customize the look and operation of your Gopher Client. You may also choose to open the Log from time to time to see what is happening during an information transfer from a particular Gopher Server to your Gopher Client.

The Toolbar, Smart Buttons, and Status Bar may be used to cause those three sets of tools to appear or disappear from your screen. The original condition for your Gopher Client is to have the Toolbar checked ON, the Smart Buttons checked OFF, and the Status Bar checked ON. Whenever you click on **Settings** and then click on one of these three, it changes their status from ON to OFF or OFF to ON.

NOTE: The Toolbar must be checked ON for either the Toolbar with the small icons or for the Smart Buttons. Smart Buttons are really just the Toolbar with word reminders for each icon's function.

Whichever way you choose to display the icon buttons on the Toolbar, their actions remain the same. Notice that as you position your cursor over each button, a reminder of the button's action is shown in the Status Line at the bottom of your Client.

From left to right, the buttons are

New	Create a New Configuration File
Open	Open an existing Configuration File
Save	Save the current configuration in a Configuration File
Retrieve	Retrieve the selected item into local storage
Open Item	Open the selected item from local storage
Close Item	Close the selected item collapsing its substructure
Item Into	Retrieve Gopher+ information on the selected item
Bookmark	Copy the current selection into the Bookmark section
Go Back	Select the previously selected item
Search	Search keyword index of the currently selected GopherSpace
Properties	Examine or change item properties
Remove	Remove the selected item from the hierarchy

The last command on the Menu Bar is Help. A standard Windows-type help file exists for Gopher and all of its functions. Clicking on **Help** will take you to this information.

Exploring the NetManage Gopher

We are now ready to explore another Gopher Server, the NetManage Gopher. Move your mouse to the closed book just under the word GopherSpace in your left-hand screen. It should be labeled NetManage Gopher. Double-click on this book and you will shortly see a screen resembling Figure 7-8. (It may not be identical, as things do change quickly on the Internet.)

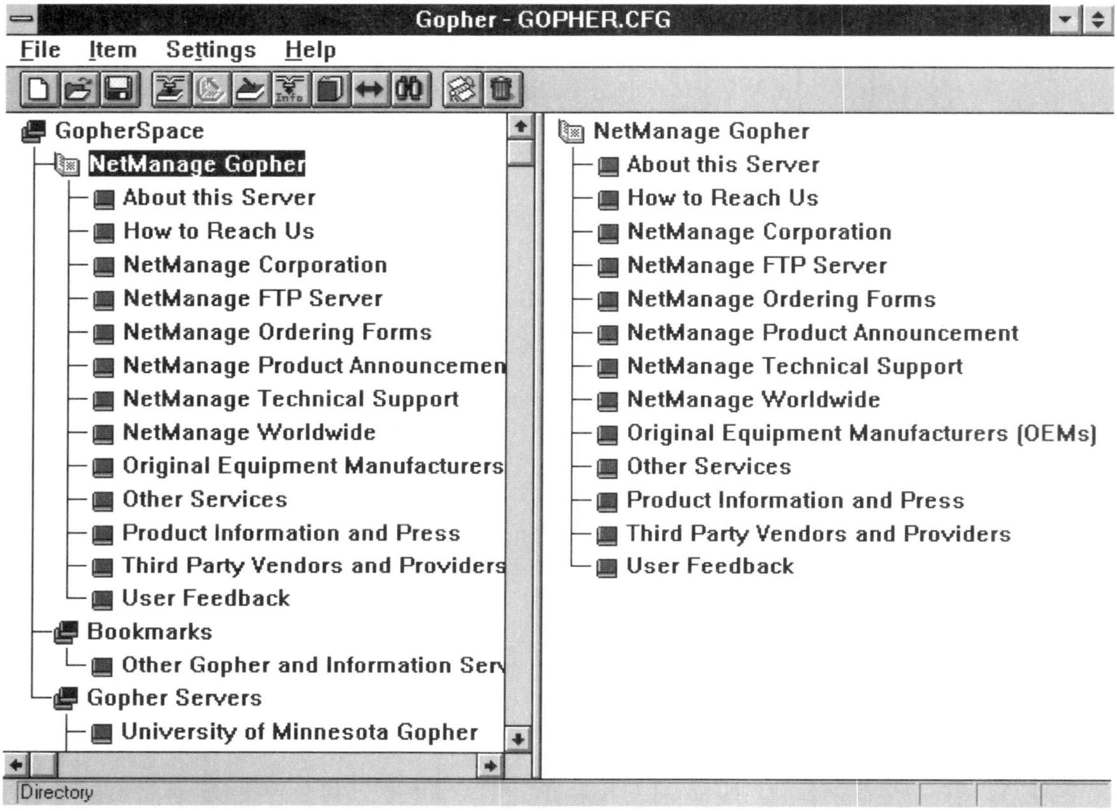

Gopher - GOPHER.CFG

File Item Settings Help

GopherSpace
NetManage Gopher
About this Server
How to Reach Us
NetManage Corporation
NetManage FTP Server
NetManage Ordering Forms
NetManage Product Announcemen
NetManage Technical Support
NetManage Worldwide
Original Equipment Manufacturers
Other Services
Product Information and Press
Third Party Vendors and Providers
User Feedback
Bookmarks
Other Gopher and Information Serv
Gopher Servers
University of Minnesota Gopher

NetManage Gopher
About this Server
How to Reach Us
NetManage Corporation
NetManage FTP Server
NetManage Ordering Forms
NetManage Product Announcement
NetManage Technical Support
NetManage Worldwide
Original Equipment Manufacturers (OEMs)
Other Services
Product Information and Press
Third Party Vendors and Providers
User Feedback

Directory

Figure 7-8
The NetManage Gopher

Here you will find more information about NetManage, their products, and your Internet Chameleon software. You may wish to browse here for a while or to come back later.

Exploring the University of Minnesota Gopher

Our next destination is to the "Mother of All Gophers" at the University of Minnesota.

If your Gopher screens are getting a bit cluttered, you may want to close some of the open books. Do this by double-clicking on the open books. They will close and their contents will vanish from your screen. If you want to see the contents again, you need only double-click on the closed book.

Double-click on the **University of Minnesota closed book** and you will receive a screen that should be similar to Figure 7-9. Notice yet another kind of icon, the file drawer for searching.

NOTE: The University of Minnesota Gopher is often very busy. You may need to try again later at a less busy time.

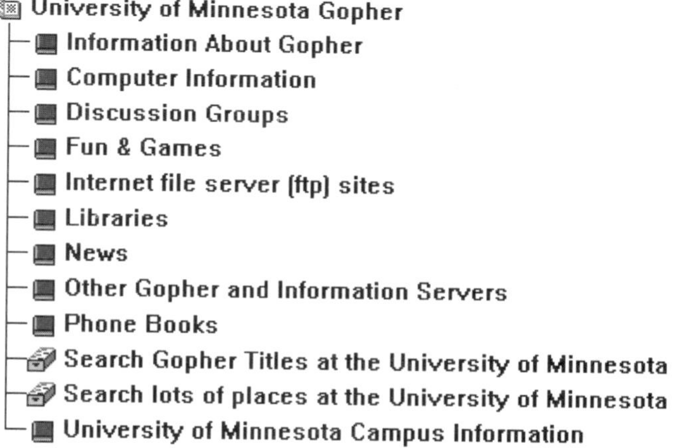

Figure 7-9
The University of Minnesota Gopher

SIX

Exploring Other Gopher and Information Servers

Finally, we will go to the line labeled Other Gopher and Information Servers. Click on it and you should see a screen resembling Figure 7-10.

Figure 7-10
Other Gopher and Information Servers

As you can tell, an amazing amount of information is presented to you on these screens. There are Gopher servers throughout the world just waiting to provide you with information.

SEVEN

Learning about Symbols

You have noticed several new icons in the previous pages. Internet Chameleon has a very full list of different icons for differing kinds of information. In Figure 7-11 you can see what some of these symbols are and what they mean. You can find them by clicking on **Help** on the Menu Bar and then by clicking on **Symbol Legend**

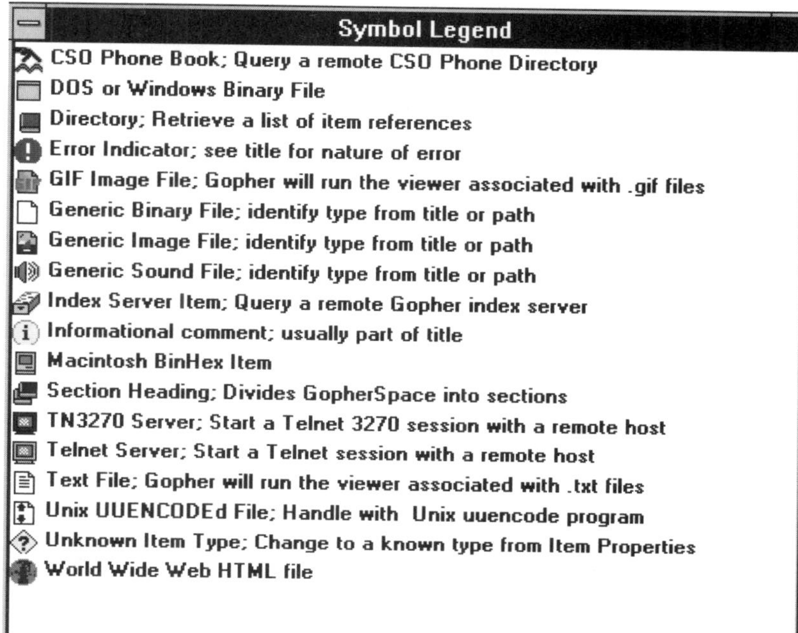

Figure 7-11
Symbol Legend

Session Summary

In this session, you have had a brief introduction to the Gopher Client that is part of Internet Chameleon. Gopher is an extremely useful Internet tool that should enable you to find a great deal of information, according to your interests and needs. In our next session, we will learn about the World-Wide Web and the Internet Chameleon browser known as the WebSurfer.

In *WebSurfer* you will learn a great deal about WebSurfer. You will learn most of the common WebSurfer terminology, as well as how to add audio and graphics capabilities to WebSurfer.

In **Session Eight**, you will learn about the World-Wide Web, HyperText Transport Protocol, Hypermedia, and Uniform Resource Locators. You will take a tour of the WebSurfer screen and we will highlight what you can do with each feature.

Session Nine introduces some of the many resources available on the World-Wide Web. You will have a chance to explore some of the well-known Home Pages.

Session Ten will teach you how to use WebSurfer to do Telnet, ftp, and gopher activities on the Internet. We will look at how WebSurfer might be used to enhance your use of these Internet tools.

In **Session Eleven**, you will learn how to use WebSurfer to search the World-Wide Web. You will learn about the World Wide Web Worm and the World Wide Web Wanderer, as well as some of the more recent searching tools and searching engines. In addition, you will learn about the expanding role of business on the Internet, and some of the markets that are beginning to appear on the World-Wide Web.

Session Twelve focuses on the multimedia capabilities of WebSurfer. You will download and install software that allows you to view PostScript files and other photos and to hear sounds. Then, you will use WebSurfer to download sound and photo files.

PART 3

WEB SURFER

INSTANT INTERNET

BASIC INTERNET TOOLS

SESSION 8

A Tour of the WebSurfer Screen

A WebSurfer Screen Tour

Session Overview

In this session we introduce the World-Wide Web of information that is available on the Internet through the use of WebSurfer, NetManage's browser for the World-Wide Web. Then, in the sessions that follow, we will begin to "Surf the Web." This brief WebSurfer tour will explain all parts of the WebSurfer screen and highlight what you can do with each feature. First a few words about the World-Wide Web.

The World-Wide Web

Until recently, the Internet was a difficult place to visit. The ease-of-use problem kept many people away from Internet information because of the complexity of access. Within the past few years, however, many people have put their energies into making the information and the access easier.

In Session Seven, we described gopher as a "friendlier" way to use the Internet. Now we introduce what many are calling the "killer application" on the Internet—The World-Wide Web or WWW. The Web, as it is also called, is a friendly and intuitive place to visit for three reasons.

a. Within the past two years, we have seen the emergence of a new series of very attractive graphic Web information browsers such as Mosaic and WebSurfer.

b. People providing information on the World-Wide Web have embraced the concept of presenting information using hypertext and hypermedia.

c. A consistent and uniform way of finding Internet resources known as *Uniform Resource Locators* or *URLs* has been accepted by those using the World-Wide Web. You will learn lots more about URLs in Sessions Nine and Ten.

Together, the Web, its browsers, and URLs have become the breakthrough to the Internet that users have been waiting for.

WebSurfer is the information browser we will introduce here. As you will see in the next several sessions, WebSurfer is not limited to the Web. The Web, however, is its starting point.

According to Kevin Hughes:

> The World-Wide Web has been officially described as a "wide area hypermedia information initiative aiming to give access to a large universe of documents." ... the Web project has changed the way people view and create information—it has created the first true global hypermedia network.
>
> The operation of the Web relies mainly on hypertext as its means of interacting with users. Hypertext is basically the same as regular text—it can be stored, read, searched, or edited—with an important exception: hypertext contains connections within the text to other documents.[1]

In other words, if you were reading a hypertext document about the Web and you came across the name Kevin Hughes, you might be able to point and click on the name **Kevin Hughes** and you would be connected instantly to a document that would tell you more about him. If you were interested in knowing more about Web browsers, if a hyperlink were in place, you would be able to click on the word **browsers** and be connected to additional hypertext that would tell you more.

In addition to hypertext, there is also hypermedia. Again, according to Kevin Hughes:

> Hypermedia is hypertext with a difference—hypermedia documents contain links not only to other pieces of text, but also to other forms of media—sounds, images, and movies. Images themselves can be selected to link to sounds or documents. Hypermedia simply combines hypertext and multimedia. Here are some simple examples of hypermedia:

---

1. *Entering the World-Wide Web: A Guide to Cyberspace Version 6.1*; `Kevin Hughes/eit/Webguide`, from `ftp.eit.com`; 1994

1. You are reading a book which contains some French passages. You select the French passage, and then are able to hear it spoken by a native French person.

2. You are planning a trip to Palo Alto. You browse through the information they have compiled, and then click on the hotels which are of interest to you. Instantly, you can see a picture of the hotel, and you are able to make a reservation.[2]

Credit for the creation in 1989 of the concept known as the World-Wide Web is given to Tim Berners-Lee, who was then at the European Particle Physics Laboratory known as CERN, a collective of European high-energy physics researchers. The project's original intent was to facilitate research and ideas throughout the organization. The Web's popularity has been enormous, and its use has been strong since its initial availability at the end of 1990.

What really caused the explosion of interest was the first availability in 1993 of graphic Web browsers. One of the best known is called Mosaic, which was developed at the National Center for Supercomputing Applications at the University of Illinois. These browsers allow users to follow hyperlinks with just a point and a click. Although many companies and research centers now offer Web browsers, we would like to introduce you to NetManage's WebSurfer.

A Tour of the WebSurfer Screen

ONE

WebSurfer Introduction

To begin our introduction, double-click on the **WebSurfer Icon** that is illustrated in Figure 8-1.

Figure 8-1
WebSurfer Icon

The WebSurfer screen then appears on your screen. We have selected a WebSurfer screen from NetManage to illustrate their Web browser. The WebSurfer screen is shown in Figure 8-2.

2. *Entering the World-Wide Web: A Guide to Cyberspace Version 6.1*

When you first bring up WebSurfer, you may receive a screen from your Internet service provider. Not to worry; all the features of the WebSurfer browser will be the same.

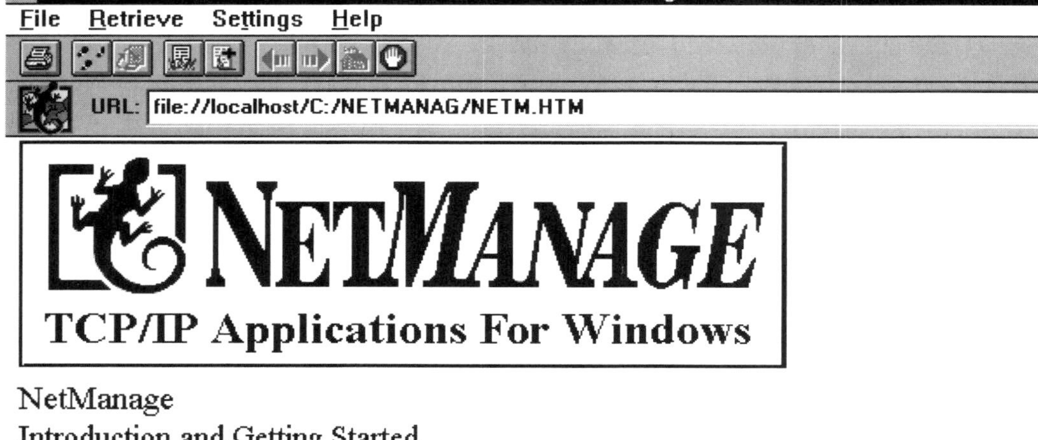

Figure 8-2
WebSurfer Screen

The WebSurfer Screen

Let's start with our overview of the WebSurfer screen at the top of the screen. Notice that WebSurfer has many of the features that are familiar to us from Microsoft Windows. The Title Bar of Figure 8-2 tells us that we are using the WebSurfer program and that we are looking at information provided to us by the NetManage World-Wide Web Server.

At the left end of the Title Bar is the usual Control Menu box, often called the File Drawer. A single click on this box will produce the Windows-type drop-down menu. A double-click on this box will close the window. At the right end of the Title Bar are the usual Windows minimize and maximize buttons.

The minimize button will shrink WebSurfer to a small icon at the bottom of your screen. It does not stop the program; it merely minimizes it. Double-clicking on the minimized **WebSurfer Icon** will bring it back as an open window. The maximize button will allow WebSurfer to occupy your entire screen. The maximize button will then change to a double-arrow button to allow you to return the program to a smaller window.

Continuing down the screen, we come to the Top Bars, the Document area, covering much of the screen, and at the bottom, the Status Line. The Top Bars help us manage and control what WebSurfer is doing. The Document area shows us the actual information from the World-Wide Web and the Status Line gives us status and descriptive information.

WebSurfer's Top Bars

Let's examine the Top Bars one at a time. Just below the Title Bar is a familiar Windows-type Menu Bar. This is illustrated on the top line of Figure 8-3.

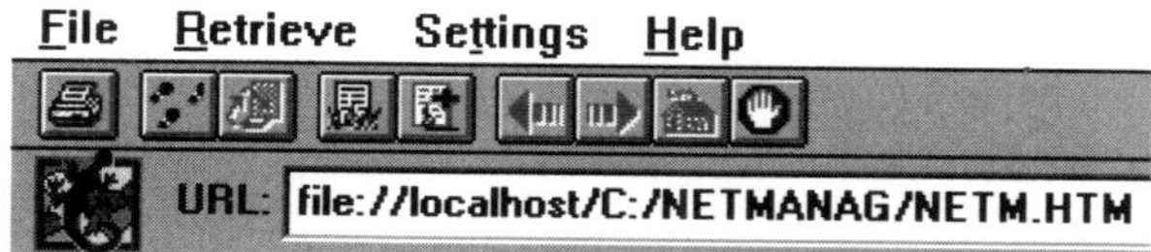

Figure 8-3
Top Bars

Here we see individual words: File, Retrieve, Settings, and Help, each with a single letter underlined. We can either single-click on the word or hold the ALT key and press the underlined letter to activate a drop-down menu. You may be aware that these underlined letters are sometimes referred to as accelerators. Later in this session, we will look at each drop-down box to see what it contains.

Continuing down the screen, we come to the Toolbar that is shown in the middle line in Figure 8-3. The Toolbar contains icons as a fast path to many WebSurfer commands. Not all of them are always active. That is, some may be dimmed to indicate that their function is not available at the present time.

Although each tool on the Toolbar is drawn to indicate its function, a reminder of that function is also shown on the Status Line. Glance down the WebSurfer screen and find the Status Line at the very bot-

tom. Now move your mouse slowly along the Toolbar. Stop on each tool and look at the Status Line. The function of that tool is shown on the Status Line.

For example, if we stop the mouse on the first tool (Print) that looks like a printer, the Status Line displays Print the active document. If you click on that tool, you will get a pop-up Windows menu allowing you to print the document that you see on the screen.

In the Settings Menu, you may also expand the tool icons with the Smart Buttons selection. This adds reminder words to each tool button.

Clicking on the next tool, the footsteps labeled Go to URL, takes us directly to the WebSurfer - Go To Document pop-up box. Here you can directly type in a URL or Uniform Resource Locator for Internet resources. In the next several sessions, we will show you how to find, interpret, and go to URLs. For now, remember that the Toolbar offers a quick tool to point to a new URL or address on the Internet.

The next tool with the circling arrows and the page (Get URL) allows you to "refresh" or get a fresh copy of the document from its source on the Internet.

Next come two tools to manage your Hotlist. The Hotlist is a list of your favorite places on the World-Wide Web. The first tool, with the fire under the page (Hotlist), pops up your Hotlist Favorite Places box. From this box, you can select locations quickly and go to them without any typing.

The second tool (Make Hot), with a plus and a minus on the page, allows you to add (or delete) the current document to (or from) your Hotlist.

The next three tools allow us to navigate through our current WebSurfer session. The left arrow moves us to previous documents, the right arrow moves us forward again, and the house (or home) returns us to the first document of the session.

The third line of the Top Bars, beginning with a Chameleon, is the Dialog Bar. Two key things to notice here are the Chameleon with its colorful background and the URL: box. The URL: box always displays the URL of the current document shown in the document area. The Chameleon's background will change colors when new information is being transferred to your computer from the Internet.

WebSurfer's Document Area

Next down the screen is our area of real interest—the Document area as shown in Figure 8-4.

Figure 8-4
Document Area

The entire center of your screen is the working document area that displays documents and images from Internet sources. Here you will find the blue underlines and blue boxes that indicate hyperlinks to other information.

At the right side of the screen, you will often find a Windows-type scroll bar. This will tell you that there is more information above or below the screen you are viewing. You may click on the up or down arrows to move slowly up or down or you may choose to put your cursor on the button and hold down the left mouse button to drag the button. You can also click on the scroll bar above or below the button to move in bigger jumps.

In Figure 8-4, you can see a scroll bar. If we scroll down we will see the bottom of the NetManage screen as displayed in Figure 8-5.

Your NetManage software is a Windows software package that connects you to the Internet. The suite of easy-to-use applications will help connect you to the world's largest network and guide you through its online information.

WebSurfer

The application that you are currently using is called WebSurfer. WebSurfer is NetManage's World Wide Web (WWW) client which lets you browse the fast growing portion of the Internet known as WWW. News, product information and entertainment are all available with WebSurfer.

Getting Started

This online document provides you with information concerning the Internet, your new NetManage software and how to use the two together successfully. To begin, double click on one of the three questions listed below in blue text or on one of the icons. If you are *already* connected to the Internet, click here to register to receive NetManage's newsletter and product update information. NetManage also provides great jump points to business, news, weather, sports, stock quotes, online shopping and more on its Home Page. To see the NetManage Home Page, click here.

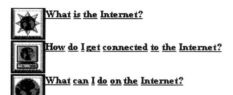

What is the Internet?

How do I get connected to the Internet?

What can I do on the Internet?

NetManage, 10725 N. De Anza Blvd., Cupertino, California 95014, (408) 973-7171, sales@netmanage.com

Figure 8-5
Document Continued

If a wide screen of data arrives, you may also get a scroll bar at the bottom of your screen. It works the same way but moves right or left.

WebSurfer's Cursors and Hyperlinks

Most of the time the cursor on your screen will look like a typical Windows arrow-type pointer cursor. However, when the cursor is placed over a hyperlink, it changes to a pointing hand. We have illustrated the pointing hand cursor in Figure 8-6.

Figure 8-6
Hand Cursor

When the normal arrow cursor changes to a pointing hand, the cursor has landed on a hyperlink and the Status Line at the bottom of the screen will show the command and address (URL) of that link. The Status Line is worth a glance whenever you are requesting a new hyperlink, as it will show you what you *didn't* have to type.

Remember that you can use the tools on the Toolbar if you wish to print a document, add the current URL to your Hotlist, to navigate back and forth or to stop a transfer of information. Another way to do these and several other activities is with the Menu Bar.

WebSurfer's Menus

Now we will go back to the Menu Bar and expand on each of the menus there. Although many functions can be done with both the Toolbar and the Menu Bar, the menus offer additional options. We will look at the first three Menu Bar options. The Help choice functions as a hypertext reference manual for Chameleon and may be used at any time to look up needed help references.

The File Menu

Figure 8-7 illustrates the choices you will have when you click on the word **File** on the Menu Bar.

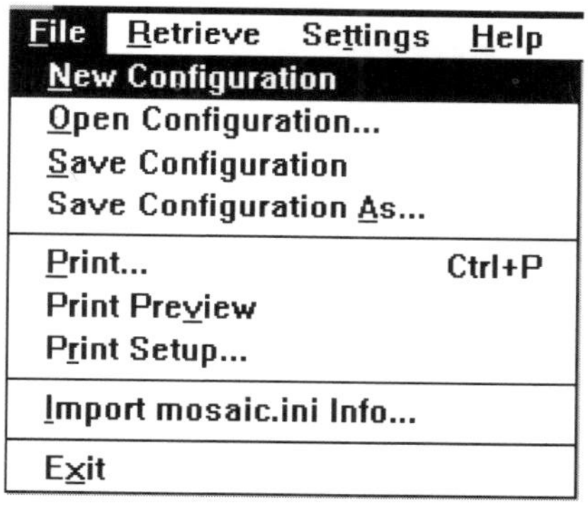

Figure 8-7
File Menu

The four Configuration choices (New, Open, Save, Save As...) allow you to set up one or more different WebSurfer configurations. Usually, you will regularly use just one configuration. However, if you have multiple users on the same Windows PC, each one may want to keep differing configurations under different names. The usual configuration file is called CHMOSAIC.CFG.

The Print choices invoke the usual Windows Print functions and Windows remains in charge of all printing. As with many other Windows applications, you may wish to preview what you will get with Print Preview. Notice that you can print more on one printed page than what you see on the screen.

Other than Exit, which can be used to leave WebSurfer, another choice is available to those who may already have used NCSA Mosaic. NCSA Mosaic is available from the National Center for Supercomputer Applications at the University of Illinois. If you have used this Web browser, you may have saved many favorite URLs (locations) with Mosaic.

WebSurfer offers you a way to visit these URLs and to save them on your WebSurfer Hotlist. This is the Import mosaic.ini Info... choice. Click on this choice if you have used NCSA Mosaic and the equivalent of your Hotlist will appear on the screen. (You will need to agree with WebSurfer's choice on the mosaic.ini file.) Much of this information will be in hyperlink format and you can add your favorites to your Hotlist with the Toolbar button. (You will need to be connected to your Internet service provider to do this.)

The Retrieve Menu

In Figure 8-8 we show the drop-down menu appearing from a click on **Retrieve** on the Menu Bar.

Figure 8-8
Retrieve Menu

The choices are grouped by type. The first two involve getting documents and perform the same functions as the Toolbar buttons. Go To URL... produces the pop-up box requesting that the name of a URL be entered. Refresh From Network reconnects with the current URL to bring in a new copy of the document.

This is possible because WebSurfer keeps documents in what is called a cache. Many documents are kept in this cache after you first receive them. This saves significant time and network resources but may not give you the latest copy. Select this choice (or use the Toolbar button) to get a refreshed copy.

The two Hotlist menu items perform the same functions as do the Toolbar buttons.

The next section of the menu permits navigation around your session. Although the Toolbar gives you Back, Forward, and Home, this menu choice also offers History... The History list differs from your Hotlist in that it records all of the places you have been (up to a limit). You may have been to a document but have forgotten what it was. A quick check of the History list may refresh your memory.

The last section of the Retrieve menu contains four useful functions not available from the Toolbar. Properties... gives you a very complete description of facts about the current document, including its type and when it was retrieved. Several options are available here for using cached documents.

Edit HTML... allows you to see the source text of a document. Most of the documents on the World-Wide Web are written in a markup language called HTML. HTML stands for HyperText Markup Language. Edit HTML... allows you to see, alter, and file this original HTML. You cannot, of course, alter the original HTML at the source. Only the originator can do that.

Connection Status... records the history of your connections to the current URL. As each document may involve many different files, Connection Status... shows what is coming in now and allows you to stop the transfer of this file (Cancel) or of all files related to this document (Cancel All). If you are interested in the inner workings of how the Web transfers documents, you may want to watch Connection Status... in action.

The last function, Cancel All, works just like the toolbar Stop tool to cancel all active transfers.

The Settings Menu

The last (other than Help) Menu Bar choice is Settings. As we show in Figure 8-9, you can customize your copy of WebSurfer with this menu item.

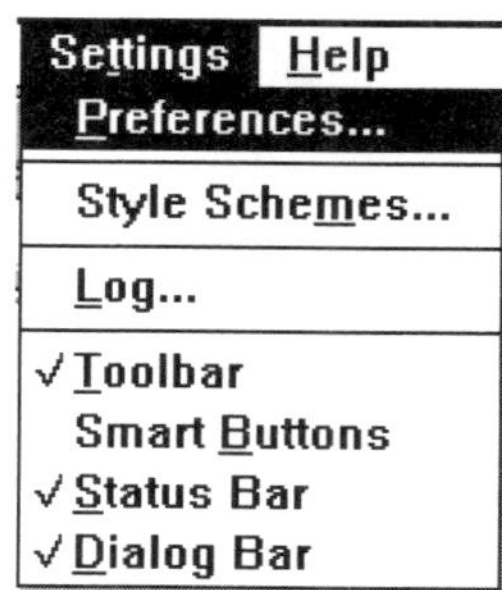

Figure 8-9
Settings

Preferences... and Style Schemes... allow you to personalize many of the attributes of WebSurfer. Perhaps the most important aspect of these has to do with what is known as caching documents. We will take a moment to explain this concept to you and review the options that are available. We will focus on the options that are presented in Figure 8-10.

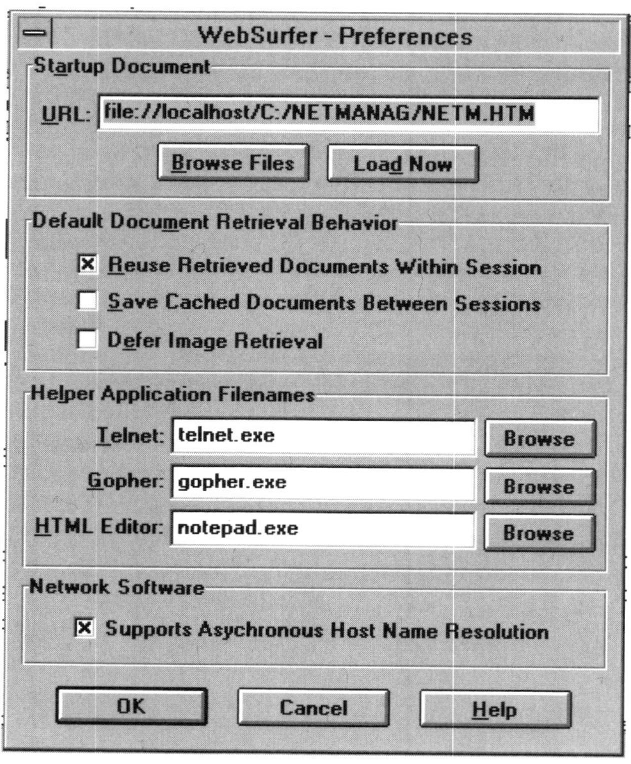

Figure 8-10
WebSurfer - Preferences

It is important to understand that WebSurfer provides the ability to cache documents or files. Documents or files may be stored on your local disk during a particular session when you are using WebSurfer. In addition, documents or files may be stored on your hard disk between sessions when you are using WebSurfer. If you look carefully at the box with the heading Default Document Retrieval Behavior in Figure 8-10, you will notice that three options are available:

Reuse Retrieved Documents Within Session

Save Cached Documents Between Sessions

Defer Image Retrieval

Choosing to Reuse Retrieved Documents Within Session means that once you have located a particular document or file using WebSurfer, the file or document is stored on your hard disk so you do not have to go back out onto the World-Wide Web network to retrieve it again during that particular session. This means the response time is quicker and also that you are using fewer of the World-Wide Web resources.

Choosing to Save Cached Documents Between Sessions means that the files or documents will be saved to your hard disk when you leave a particular WebSurfer session. This may or may not be a good thing. It will certainly provide you with faster access to the files or documents you have chosen to cache on your hard drive. However, it will also mean that you may miss the opportunity to learn about new resources available at a given location.

Defer Image Retrieval means that you will download only the text affiliated with a particular document or file. Placeholders for images will be inserted into the document; you can download these images later, should you so choose. The primary advantage of making this selection is that documents will be downloaded much more rapidly to your computer.

To select or deselect any of these three options in the Default Document Retrieval Behavior, just place your cursor in the appropriate box and click once. If you are new to the World-Wide Web, you may wish to accept WebSurfer's defaults until you have gained more experience. Remember that Preferences... and Style Schemes... are here and that they will allow you to change many of the appearance and support options of WebSurfer.

Now that we have examined the options in the Default Document Retrieval Behavior, let's return for a moment to the other available options on the Settings menu.

The Log... option allows you to turn on a transaction Log function to follow the actions of WebSurfer and the Web as they happen. This is also a good educational tool for those interested in the inner workings of the Web.

The last four options allow you to turn off (or on) the Toolbar, the Status Bar, and the Dialog Bar. Within the Toolbar, you may expand the buttons to be Smart Buttons, that is, buttons with reminder words for their functions.

Screen and Document Behavior

The last stop on our WebSurfer screen tour will reveal how the text and images will arrive in WebSurfer. You may already have noticed that the

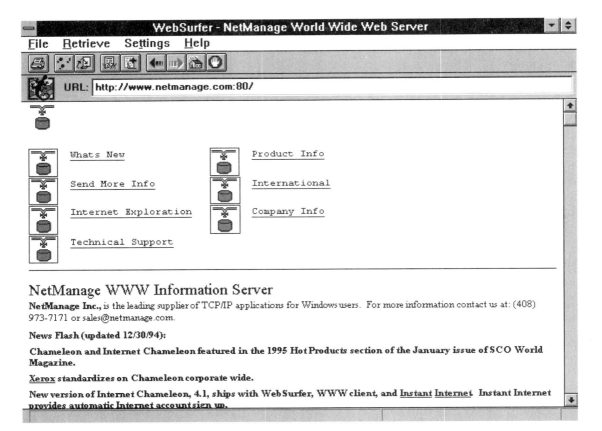

text of a document will arrive first and that the images and graphics will then pop up one at a time. This is a feature designed into WebSurfer to enable you to see the text quickly. Over modem lines text usually comes in faster than the larger graphics and image files.

WebSurfer brings in the text and puts little graphic placeholders where the images will go. We have illustrated this process in Figures 8-11, 8-12, and 8-13. The screen is the same original NetManage screen we showed earlier in this session. Here we have captured the NetManage Home Page as it actually appeared on our computer screen as it came in from the Internet.

The first capture, Figure 8-11, shows WebSurfer bringing in just the text and leaving the placeholders for the graphic images.

WebSurfer - NetManage World Wide Web Server
File Retrieve Settings Help
URL: http://www.netmanage.com:80/
Whats New
Product Info
Send More Info
International
Internet Exploration
Company Info
Technical Support
NetManage WWW Information Server
NetManage Inc., is the leading supplier of TCP/IP applications for Windows users. For more information contact us at: (408) 973-7171 or sales@netmanage.com.
News Flash (updated 12/30/94):
Chameleon and Internet Chameleon featured in the 1995 Hot Products section of the January issue of SCO World Magazine.
Xerox standardizes on Chameleon corporate wide.
New version of Internet Chameleon, 4.1, ships with WebSurfer, WWW client, and Instant Internet. Instant Internet provides automatic Internet account sign up.

Figure 8-11
Text Only

The second capture shows a partial fill of full text and one graphic image in place. One by one, the remaining graphic images will arrive and replace the placeholders until the screen is complete. Figure 8-12 shows this in progress.

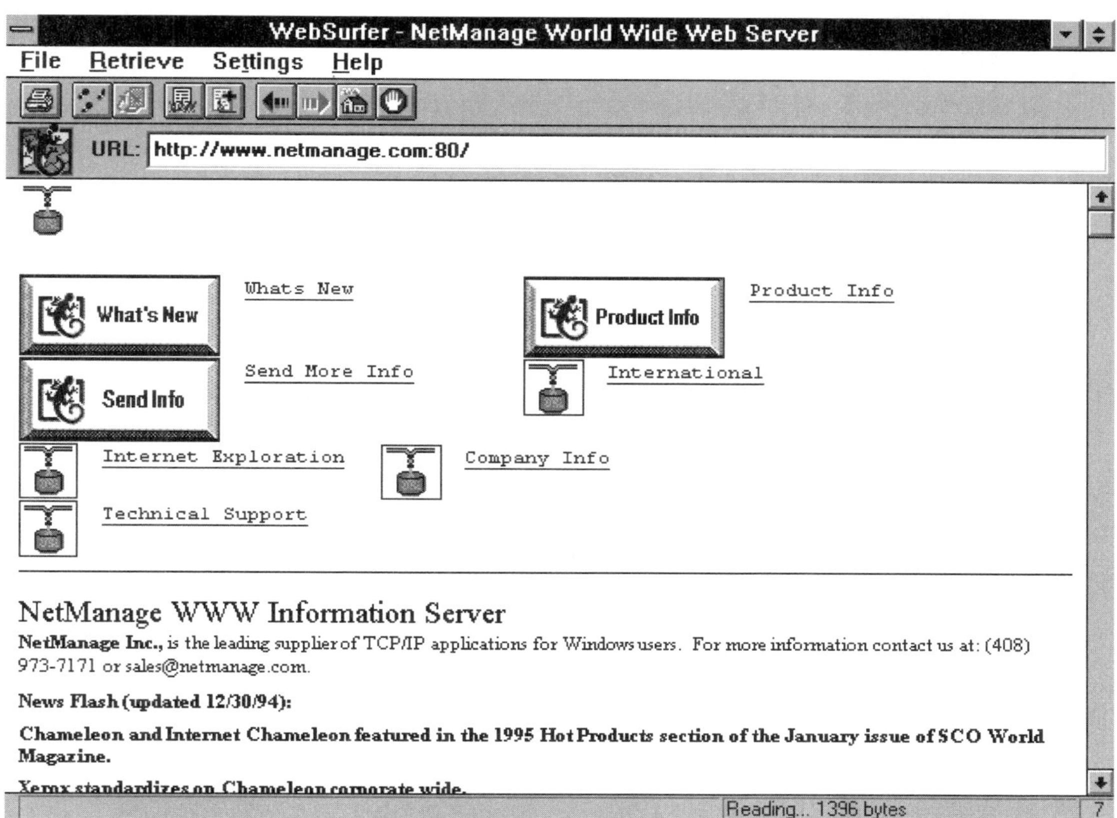

Figure 8-12
Partial Graphics

The completely filled screen is shown in Figure 8-13.

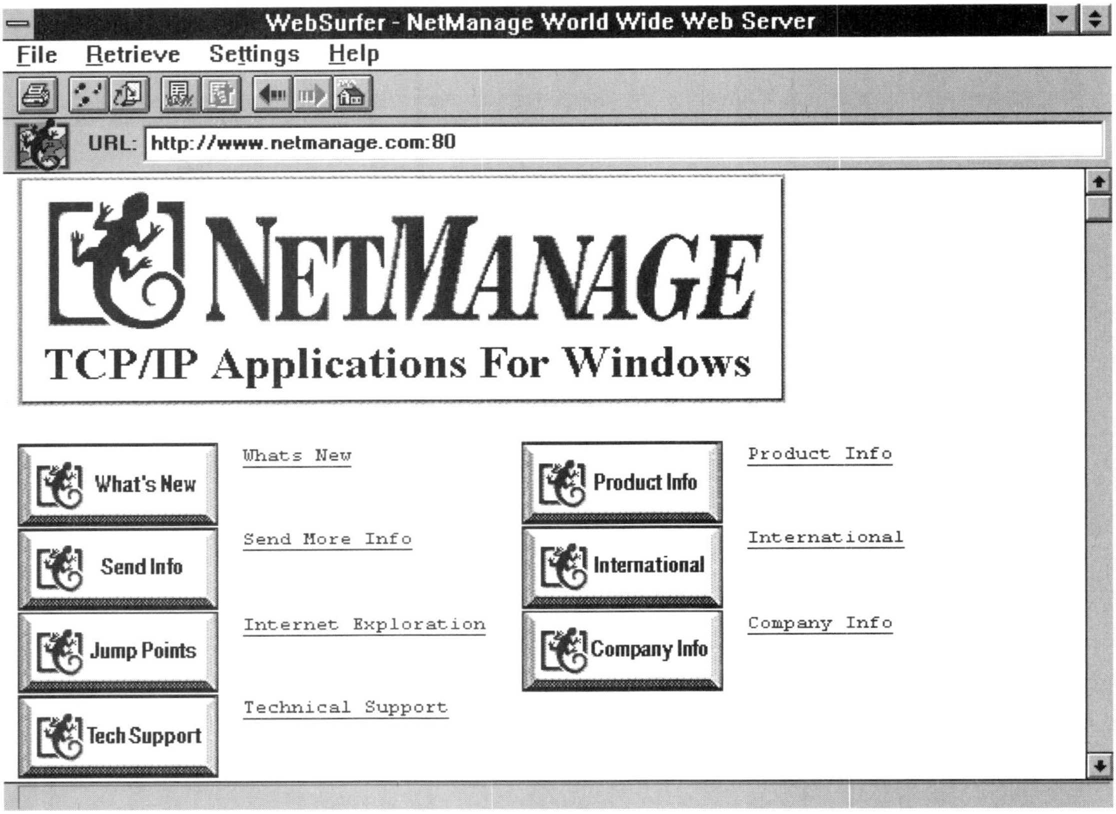

Figure 8-13
Full Graphics

Session Summary

This session has been intended to provide you with an overview of the WebSurfer browser provided by NetManage. Hopefully, you should have a good idea of the features included in WebSurfer and ways to modify it to suit your needs. Having done this, we're ready to begin our real explorations of the Internet using WebSurfer. In Session Nine, we will begin discovering home pages and learning how to find and visit them.

Session 9

What's Out There on the World-Wide Web?

Home Pages—Getting Started

Home Pages—Continued

Getting Started with WebSurfer

Session Overview

In this session you will have an opportunity to broaden your understanding of the World-Wide Web and WebSurfer. We will look at some of the many resources that are available. Then we will download a wide array of home pages. Let's get started!

What's Out There on the World-Wide Web?

The short answer is *everything!* The longer, and probably more useful, answer would provide you with some sense of the wide array of resources that can be found on the World-Wide Web. They include:

- General Information about the World-Wide Web
  - Information about WWW
  - A List of World-Wide Web Clients
- Mailing Lists
  - Hypertext Discussion Lists
  - Hypertext Archives
- Courseware
  - World-Wide Web Courseware
  - World-Wide Web Literature

- Lists of Tools and Convertors
- Commercial Sites
  - *Wired* Magazine
  - MTV
  - CommerceNet
  - Global Network Navigator
  - Silicon Graphics
- Country Sites
  - Guide to Australia
  - Spain Web Sites
  - Austria
  - Chile
  - Costa Rica
  - Czechoslovakia
  - Germany
- Educational Sites
  - Honolulu Community College
  - The University of Notre Dame
  - The Chinese University of Hong Kong
- Interactive Sites
  - Michigan State University Weather Movies
  - Interactive World Map Interface
- Legal Information and Government Sites
  - Legal Information at Cornell
  - U.S. Bureau of the Census
  - U.S. Department of Commerce
  - NASA
  - The City of Palo Alto, California
- Literature
  - English Server at Carnegie-Mellon
  - Internet Book Information Center
- Museums and Art
  - San Francisco's Exploratorium
  - University of California Museum of Paleontology

Music and Audio

Internet Music Resources

Internet Talk Radio

Organizations

Electronic Frontier Foundation

Association for Computing Machinery

World Health Organization

This short list is intended to provide you with an awareness of some of the many resources that can be found on the World-Wide Web. As we will show you shortly, you can use WebSurfer to help you find all of these resources from among the many that exist.

How Do We Address These Places?

As you learned earlier, it is the Transmission Control Protocol and the Internet Protocol (TCP/IP) that permit us to have so many host computers effectively communicating with each other. As you might imagine, there are other similar protocols and conventions in place that make it possible for WebSurfer to exist and to function.

The first protocol that we encounter goes by the acronym *URL* which means *Uniform Resource Locators*. According to Kevin Hughes:

> The World-Wide Web uses what are called Uniform Resource Locators (URLs) to represent hypermedia links and links to network services within HTML documents. (More about HTML in a moment.) It is possible to represent nearly any file or service on the Internet with a URL.
>
> The first part of the URL (before the two slashes) specifies the method of access.
>
> The second part is typically the address of the computer on which the data or service is located.
>
> Further parts may specify the names of files, the port to connect to, or the text to search for in a database. [1]

IMPORTANT: A URL is always a single unbroken line with no spaces.

---

1. *Entering the World-Wide Web: A Guide to Cyberspace Version 6.1*; `Kevin Hughes/eit/Webguide`, from `ftp.eit.com`; 1994

Here are some examples of URLs:

- `http://www.hcc.hawaii.edu`
  Connects to Honolulu Community College WWW Service
- `http://www.eff.org`
  Connects to the Electronic Frontier Foundation
- `http://www.xerox.com`
  Opens a connection to Xerox, the document company
- `gopher://gopher.netmanage.com`
  Connects to NetManage's gopher server

As you can see, all of these URLs have the same general format, and, in fact, look remarkably similar to the fully qualified Internet addresses you may have seen before. In all likelihood, it is the first part of the URL (http: or gopher:) that might be new for you.

Hypertext Transfer Protocol: http

You will notice that several of these URLs begin with the initials *http*.

You will see this term frequently being used at the beginning of URLs. http is an abbreviation for *Hypertext Transfer Protocol*, which refers to the language that is used by all of the World-Wide Web clients and servers to communicate with each other. All Web clients and servers must be able to use http if they are going to "speak" to each other.

Hypertext Markup Language: html

Many URLs contain the extension *html*. You will see this extension used frequently; html is the abbreviation for what is known as *Hypertext Markup Language*. This is the programming language that is used by the World-Wide Web for creating and recognizing hypermedia documents. html permits those who are interested in doing so to take standard ASCII files and mark them up with all of the formatting codes that are necessary to describe their layout and any hyperlinks they might have.

Now, let's look at several URL addresses again.

Main CERN World-Wide Web Home Page

http://info.cern.ch/hypertext/WWW/TheProject.html

http:	on the far left, tells us that this document adheres to the Hypertext Transfer Protocol

//info.cern.ch	is the host address that was used in an earlier telnet session to take us to Switzerland so that we could try out the World-Wide Web in text mode
hypertext/WWW/TheProject.html	The Project.html the final part of this URL provides us with the names of the directories and the file name of this home page and indicates that it was created using html, the hypertext markup language

CommerceNet

http://www.commerce.net

http:	on the far left, tells us that this document adheres to the Hypertext Transfer Protocol
//www.commerce.net	tells us that this is a World-Wide Web server, provided by commerce.net—in all likelihood, this will be their home page (More about home pages in a minute.)

U.S. Bureau of the Census

http://www.census.gov

http:	on the far left, tells us that this document adheres to the Hypertext Transfer Protocol
//www.census.gov	tells us that this is a World-Wide Web server provided by the governmental organization known as the Bureau of the Census

What's Out There on the World-Wide Web?

ONE

This activity will actually be comprised of many short exercises. We will take a few minutes to sample some of the many World-Wide Web servers that exist. As noted above, all of them communicate with each other using the Hypertext Transfer Protocol (http)—which is why you will notice that many of the places we will visit during this session (although not all) begin with http.

Before seeing what our first exercise looks like, let's take a minute to dissect the address we are given. This is for the WebSurfer - NetMan-

age Internet Jump Points page. We will find it by going first to the NetManage Home Page.

The address is http://www.netmanage.com/netmanage

Reading from left to right:

http:	refers to the Hypertext Transfer Protocol used to address this server
www.netmanage.com	tells us that this is a World-Wide Web server (WWW) provided by NetManage which is a commercial organization (com)
netmanage	name of the directory

It is important to realize that the World Wide Web is made up of many thousands of computers, each of which is under the control of its particular webmaster. Consequently, resources on the World Wide Web come and go with amazing frequency. New resources are appearing at an exponential rate, while old resources sometimes are moved to another location, incorporated into another address, or deleted entirely. So the resources that are referred to in books such as this one may be different by the time that you try to find them. Do not be discouraged! If you encounter difficulty reaching a particular location, you should certainly try it a second time, just to be sure. However, if you are convinced that it is really not where it should be, then feel free to move on to the next example. With luck, you might find the missing resource at a later time.

Exercise A: NetManage's Internet Jump Points

http://www.netmanage.com:80/netmanage/nm11.html

1. Double-click on **Custom** and connect to your Internet service provider
2. After connecting, click once on the **upper-right-hand down arrow** to minimize the Custom window into an icon
3. Double-click on **WebSurfer**
4. Once the WebSurfer - Chameleon Getting Started main window is open, be sure to maximize it by clicking on the **up arrow** in the upper-right-hand corner

You should see Figure 9-1, the NetManage Home Page.

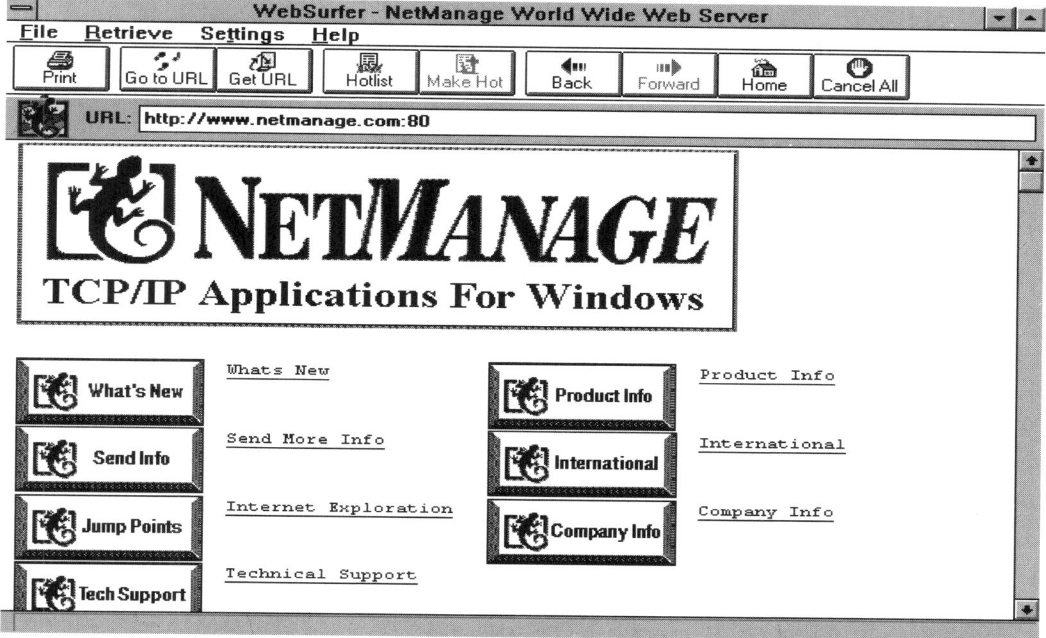

Figure 9-1
NetManage Home Page

NOTE: For the rest of the examples, we will *not* repeat steps 1 through 4; we will just assume that the Open URL window is open.

We are particularly interested in proceeding to the page of useful start-up points that NetManage refers to as the Jump Points page. Move your cursor to the hyperlink Jump Points and click once. You should see a page resembling Figure 9-2.

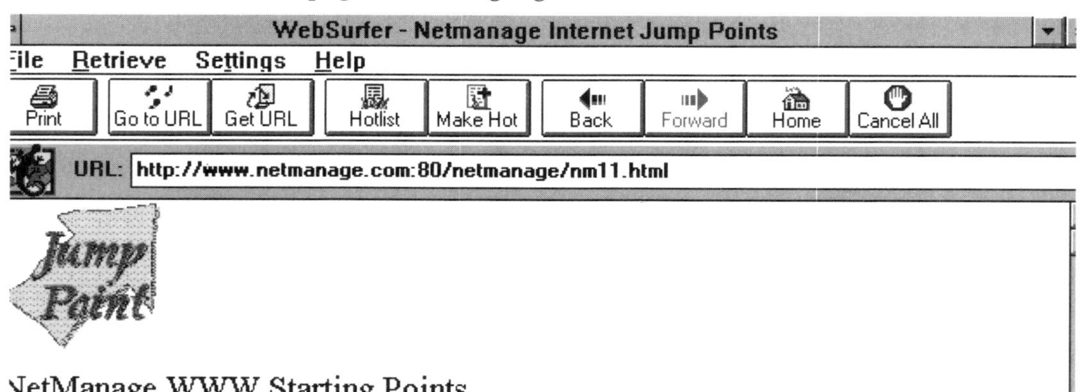

Figure 9-2
NetManage WWW Starting Points

Take a minute to wander through the Jump Points page. Click on the **down arrow** on the right-hand scroll bar to move down through the many screens of information. You can also use your Page Down key to move more quickly through the screens.

As you might imagine, you can click on your **up arrow** (or your **Page Up key**) to move back up through the Jump Points page.

Navigation Hints:

- **a.** When you move your cursor across one of the items that is in blue, your cursor becomes a hand with the forefinger pointing. Clicking once will take you to the item printed in blue.
- **b.** If you have chosen one of the words or boxes or names that is printed in blue and then decide that you would like to return to the home page where you began, just click on the left-pointing arrow (Back) on WebSurfer's Toolbar at the top.
- **c.** If you decide you would like to save this URL in what is known as your Hotlist (more about that shortly), just click once on **Make Hot** on WebSurfer's Toolbar.

Exercise B: *Wired* Magazine

http://www.wired.com

1. Click once on **Go to URL**
2. In the URL box, type `http://www.wired.com`
3. Click on **OK**

NOTE: You could also move your cursor down the Jump Points page until you arrived at the hyperlink for *Wired Magazine*. Then you could just click on it once.

You should see a page resembling Figure 9-3.

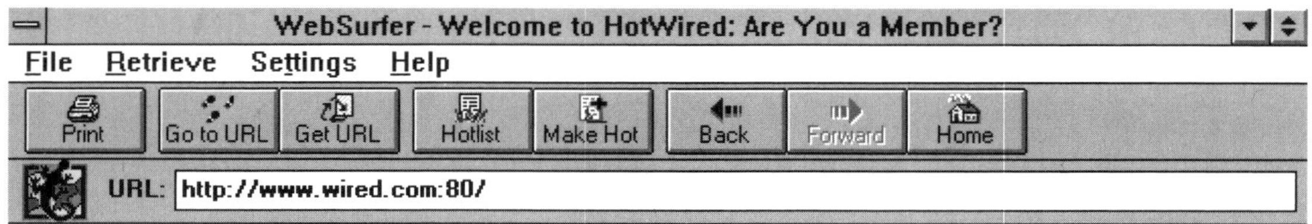

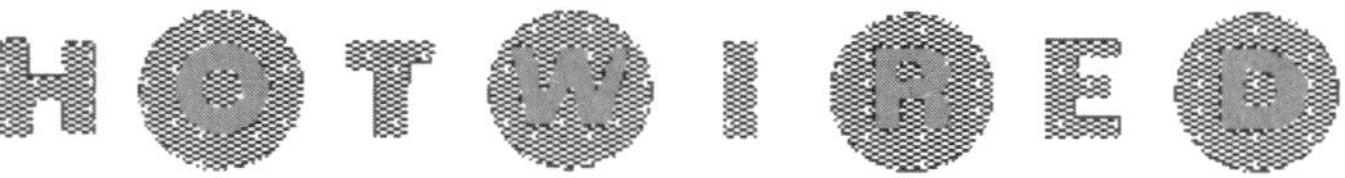

Figure 9-3
Welcome To HotWired: Are You a Member?

In all likelihood, you are not yet a member of Hotwired. In this case, click on **No** and you will be provided with a screen that resembles Figure 9-4.

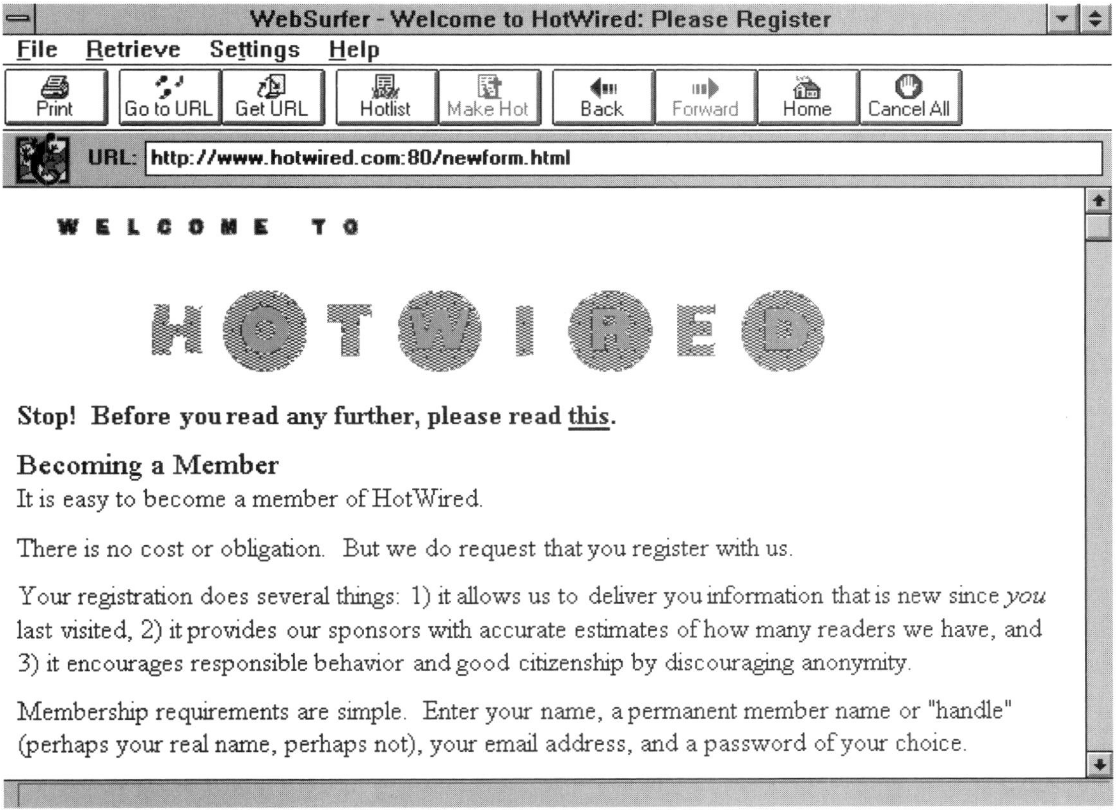

WebSurfer - Welcome to HotWired: Please Register

File Retrieve Settings Help

Print | Go to URL | Get URL | Hotlist | Make Hot | Back | Forward | Home | Cancel All

URL: http://www.hotwired.com:80/newform.html

WELCOME TO

HOTWIRED

Stop! Before you read any further, please read this.

Becoming a Member

It is easy to become a member of HotWired.

There is no cost or obligation. But we do request that you register with us.

Your registration does several things: 1) it allows us to deliver you information that is new since *you* last visited, 2) it provides our sponsors with accurate estimates of how many readers we have, and 3) it encourages responsible behavior and good citizenship by discouraging anonymity.

Membership requirements are simple. Enter your name, a permanent member name or "handle" (perhaps your real name, perhaps not), your email address, and a password of your choice.

Figure 9-4
Welcome to HotWired: Please Register

Navigation Hints

- **a.** Use your up- and down-arrow keys (on the right-hand scroll bar) to navigate through this screen.
- **b.** Use your left-arrow button (located at the top on the Toolbar) to jump back to the last document(s). Once you have done that, use your right-arrow button to jump forward to this one.

If you choose to register with HotWired, feel free to do so at this time. If not, then just continue along with us as we proceed to see what the Global Network Navigator is all about.

Exercise C: Global Network Navigator

http://gnn.com:80/gnn.html

1. Click once on **Go to URL**
2. In the URL box, type `http://gnn.com:80/gnn.html`
3. Click on **OK**

NOTE: You could also move down the Jump Points page until you come to the hyperlink for Global Network Navigator. Once you do, just click on it once.

Either way, you should arrive at the Global Network Navigator Home Page.

Navigation Hints

a. Use your up- and down-arrows (on the right-hand scroll bar) to navigate through the Global Network Navigator.

b. Use your left-arrow button (Back) to jump back through the last few documents. Use your right-arrow button (Forward) to jump forward to this one.

The Global Network Navigator Home Page contains an amazing array of information about the Internet. You would be well advised to take some time to get to know more about all that this page has to offer. In addition, you may wish to add it to your Hotlist. Just click on the **Make Hot button** on your Toolbar to do so.

Exercise D: Guide to Australia

http://www.csu.edu.au:80/education/australia.html

1. Click once on **Go to URL**
2. In the URL box, type
   `http://www.csu.edu.au:80/education/australia.html`
3. Click on **OK**

You should see a screen resembling Figure 9-5.

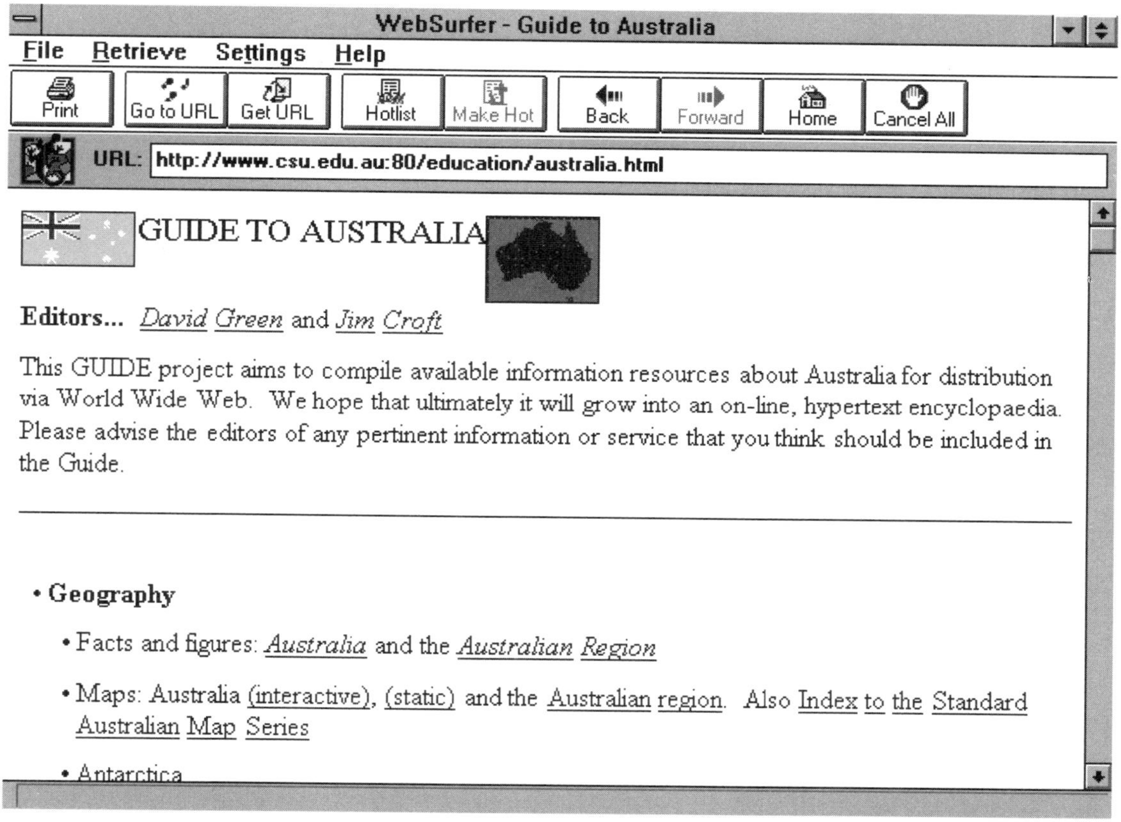

WebSurfer - Guide to Australia

File Retrieve Settings Help

Print | Go to URL | Get URL | Hotlist | Make Hot | Back | Forward | Home | Cancel All

URL: http://www.csu.edu.au:80/education/australia.html

GUIDE TO AUSTRALIA

Editors... *David Green* and *Jim Croft*

This GUIDE project aims to compile available information resources about Australia for distribution via World Wide Web. We hope that ultimately it will grow into an on-line, hypertext encyclopaedia. Please advise the editors of any pertinent information or service that you think should be included in the Guide.

- **Geography**
  - Facts and figures: *Australia* and the *Australian Region*
  - Maps: Australia (interactive), (static) and the Australian region. Also Index to the Standard Australian Map Series
  - Antarctica

Figure 9-5
Guide to Australia

Navigation Hints

a. Use your up- and down-arrow keys (on the right-hand scroll bar) to navigate through the Guide to Australia.

b. Use your left-arrow button (Back) to jump back through the last few documents. Use your right-arrow button (Forward) to jump forward to this one.

Take some time to explore the Guide to Australia. Notice how much information is available to you by clicking on hyperlinks on this one page. You can quickly learn about Australia's geography, environment, communications, travel and culture, and government and history. When you have finished exploring this wonderful resource, join us as we visit the city of Palo Alto.

Exercise D: The City of Palo Alto, California

http://www.city.palo-alto.ca.us/home.html

1. Click once on **Go to URL**
2. In the URL box, type `http://www.city.palo-alto.ca.us/home.html`
3. Click on **OK**

Figure 9-6 provides you with an introduction to the information that the City of Palo Alto, California, has chosen to present to the world.

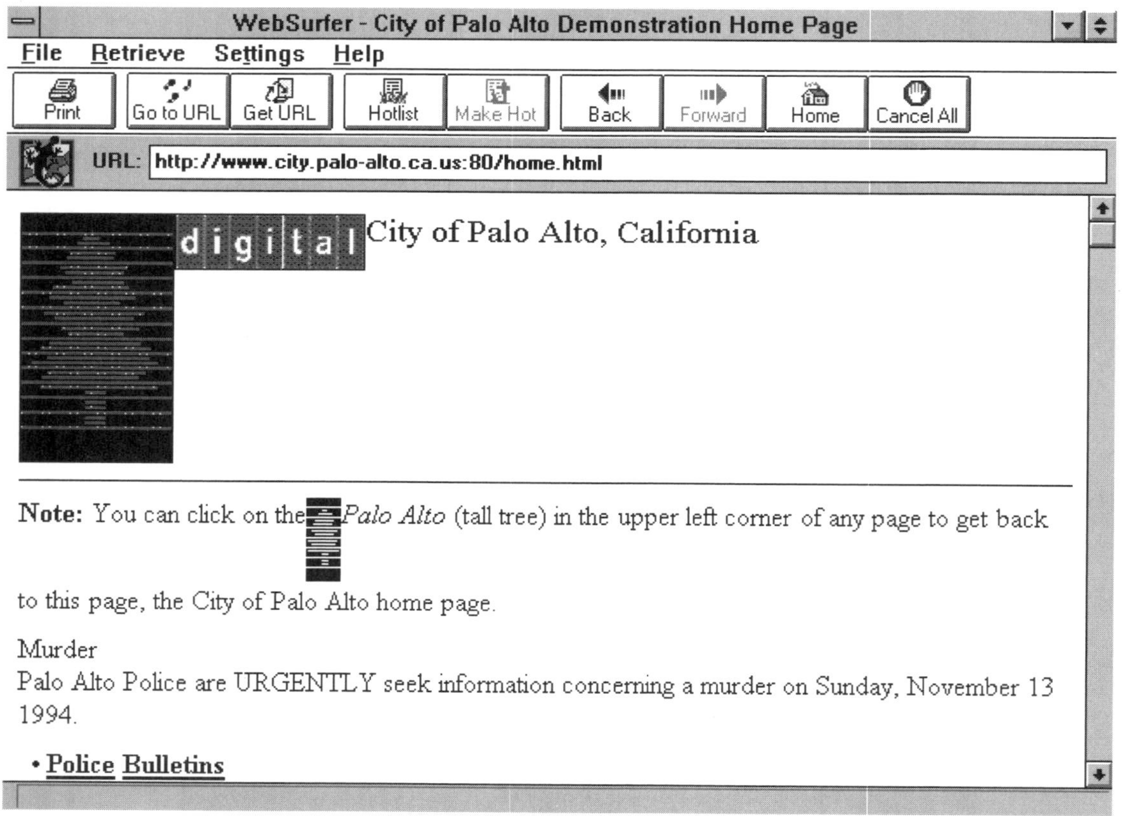

Figure 9-6
City of Palo Alto Demonstration Home Page

Again, notice how much information is potentially available to you by just clicking on a hyperlink. You can obtain police bulletins, a city profile, maps of the Bay Area, and information about parks, schools, and libraries. In addition, you can have access to information about their city government. Also, there is information about transportation, community services, and the Chamber of Commerce. When you have tired of exploring Palo Alto, join us as we learn about the Internet Book Information Center.

Exercise E: The Internet Book Information Center

http://sunsite.unc.edu:80/ibic/IBIC-homepage.html

1. Click once on **Go to URL**
2. In the URL box, type
   `http://sunsite.unc.edu/ibic/IBIC-homepage.html`
3. Click on **OK**

You should see the home page for the Internet Book Information Center (or the World Wide Web Virtual Library, as it is also known). It should resemble Figure 9-7.

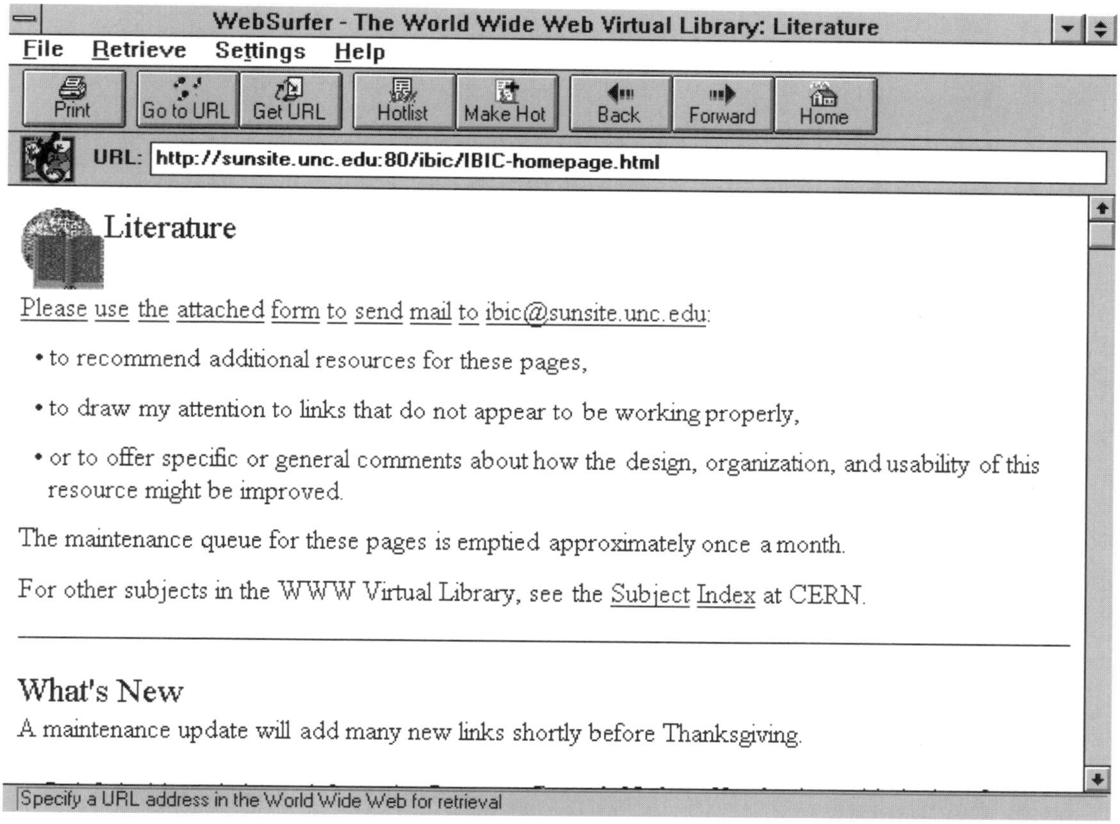

WebSurfer - The World Wide Web Virtual Library: Literature

File Retrieve Settings Help

Print | Go to URL | Get URL | Hotlist | Make Hot | Back | Forward | Home

URL: http://sunsite.unc.edu:80/ibic/IBIC-homepage.html

Literature

Please use the attached form to send mail to ibic@sunsite.unc.edu:

- to recommend additional resources for these pages,
- to draw my attention to links that do not appear to be working properly,
- or to offer specific or general comments about how the design, organization, and usability of this resource might be improved.

The maintenance queue for these pages is emptied approximately once a month.

For other subjects in the WWW Virtual Library, see the Subject Index at CERN.

What's New

A maintenance update will add many new links shortly before Thanksgiving.

Specify a URL address in the World Wide Web for retrieval

Figure 9-7
The World Wide Web Virtual Library: Literature

The Internet Book Information Center (IBIC) is intended to serve people who love books by providing them with useful and interesting information via the Internet. Feel free to take some time to browse through the resources that have been assembled on this home page.

The URL Hotlist

It quickly becomes apparent that URLs often are composed of extremely long lines of information. Certainly, it is possible to type the URL information each time you need it. However, for many of us, this becomes a real chore, especially if there are URLs you find yourself using repeatedly. Therefore, WebSurfer provides you with what is known as a *Hotlist*. Here is how to find it:

1. First connect to your Internet service provider. Then double-click on **WebSurfer**
2. Click once on the button labeled **Hotlist**
3. When the WebSurfer - Hotlist - Favorite Places screen appears, it should resemble Figure 9-8.

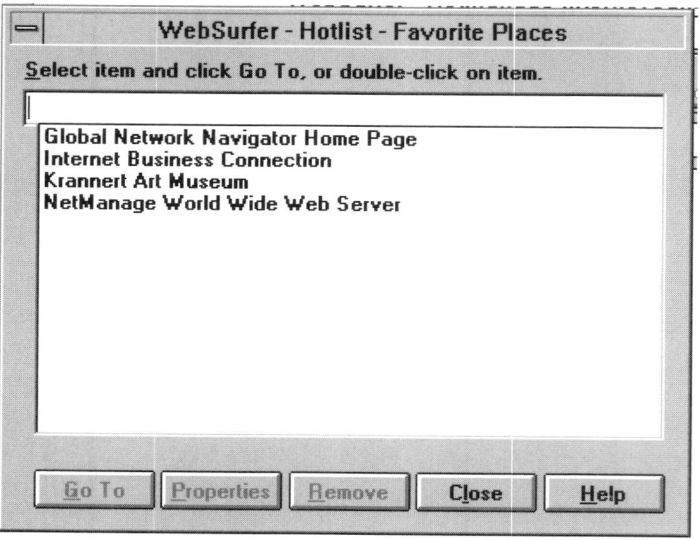

Figure 9-8
WebSurfer - Hotlist - Favorite Places

When you first begin, the Hotlist will not contain any items. However, as you explore the World-Wide Web and encounter home pages to which you wish to return, you can add them to your Hotlist by clicking on the **Make Hot button** on your Toolbar. Each time you do so, the URL of the particular page and its Document Title will be added to the Hotlist. The URLs that are listed make up what is known as your Hotlist.

Using the Hotlist

To invoke any of the URLs that are listed,

1. Click on your selection once to make it active
2. Click once on the **Go To button**

Try doing this several times now to see how this works.

Adding URLs to the Hotlist

Should you wish to add a URL to your Hotlist, it is remarkably simple to do so.

1. When you are connected to a Web server, just click once on **Make Hot**

   The Status Bar at the bottom of your screen will ask you if you want to Add or Drop the current document to or from the Hotlist.
2. Click once on **Make Hot**, and the current Web server will be added to your Hotlist.

Home Pages—Getting Started

TWO

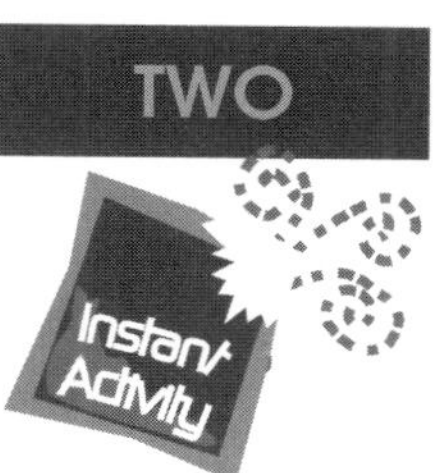

The key to the way in which many places (cities, states, companies, organizations) are presenting themselves on the World-Wide Web is through the use of what is known as a *home page*. This document is typically used to provide an overview of all the resources that a given entity wishes to provide to the world. The closest analogy might be the table of contents for a book. Using the table of contents, a reader should be able to

1. get a sense of what the whole book is all about
2. determine how the book has been organized
3. determine where in the book particular topics might be found

A well-designed home page should do all of the above, and more. For remember, we are working with hypertext and hypermedia. So, the reader of a home page can really choose to explore any or all of the topics listed on the home page in whatever order he or she might wish. Let's take the NCSA Home Page as an example. First, let's find it, and then we can take a look at it. Here is how to do that.

1. Begin by having the WebSurfer - NetManage Internet Jump Points on your screen. First, go to the NetManage Home Page. The URL for this is http://www.netmanage.com

2. Once there, click on the **Jump Points button**. Move down the Jump Points screen until you come to the phrase that says

   Click here for a WWW overview

3. Click once on the hyperlink here. You should see a screen resembling Figure 9-9.

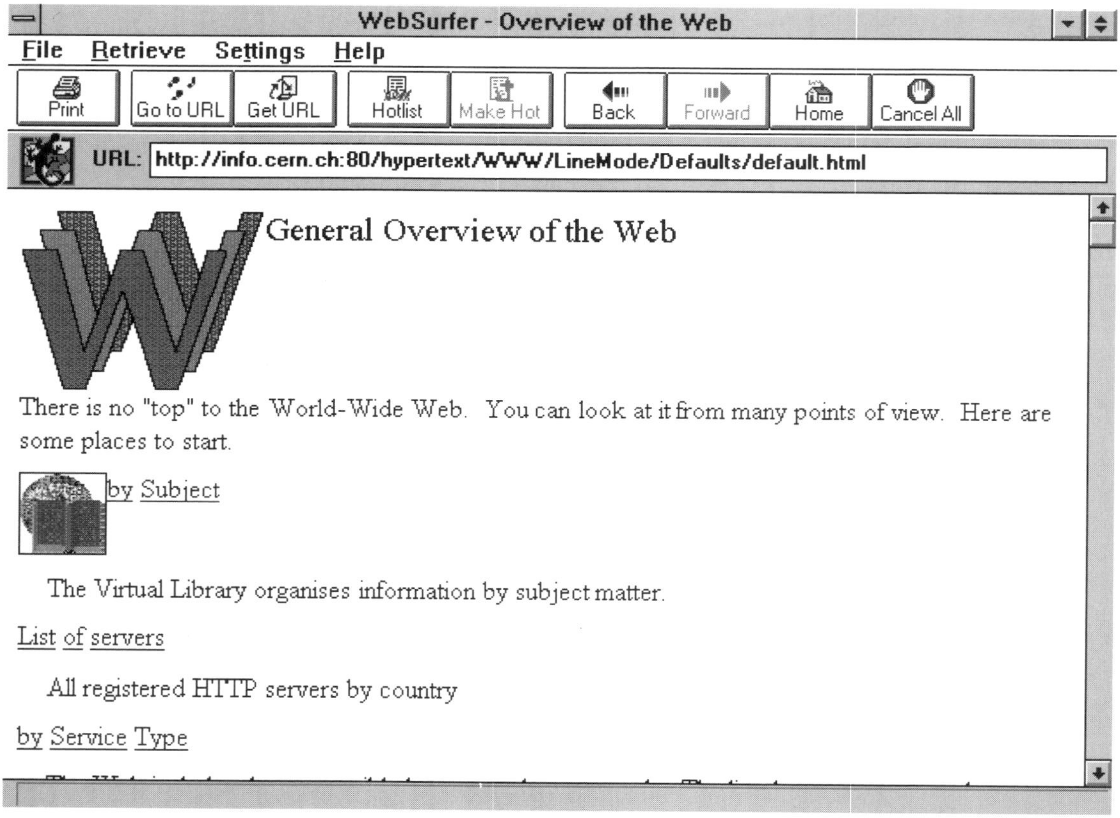

WebSurfer - Overview of the Web

File Retrieve Settings Help

Print | Go to URL | Get URL | Hotlist | Make Hot | Back | Forward | Home | Cancel All

URL: http://info.cern.ch:80/hypertext/WWW/LineMode/Defaults/default.html

General Overview of the Web

There is no "top" to the World-Wide Web. You can look at it from many points of view. Here are some places to start.

by Subject

The Virtual Library organises information by subject matter.

List of servers

All registered HTTP servers by country

by Service Type

Figure 9-9
Overview of the Web

Let's spend a minute or two reading the screen.

1. There is a Document Title at the top of the home page. In this case, it is called Overview of the Web
2. There is a Document URL similar to those we have seen before. It is

http://info.cern.ch:80/hypertext/WWW/LineMode/Defaults/default.html

As we learned earlier, this tells us the following:

   a. *http:* is a host computer that is using the Hypertext Transfer Protocol
   b. *info.cern.ch:80* is a World-Wide Web host computer maintained by CERN in Geneva, Switzerland
   c. *hypertext/WWW/LineMode/Defaults* is the directory being used for the storage of these files
   d. *default.html* is a document with the name default that was created using html

As we did earlier, if we wish to see more than just the first screen, we can click on the down or up arrows on the scroll bar on the right-hand side of the screen.

There are lots of words and phrases in blue on the screen. All of these phrases in blue type are hyperlinks, designed to take you to other documents, files, programs, and so forth.

3. Slide your cursor over to the phrase List of servers

   Notice that the cursor has become a hand with the forefinger extended.

4. Click once on the **hand** and a new document (Servers.html) will be transferred from the http Server to your computer. It should resemble Figure 9-10.

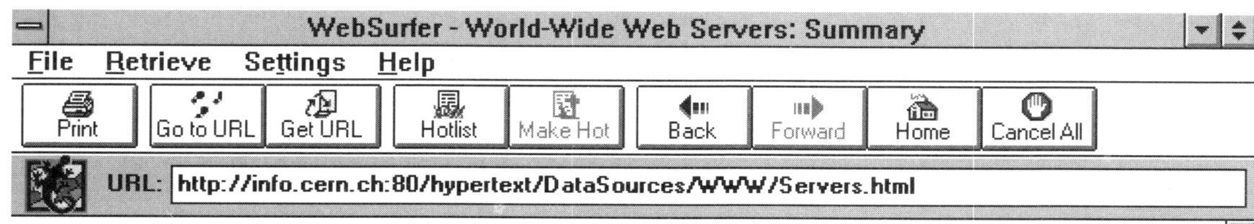

W3 servers

This is the summary of a list of registered WWW servers alphabetically by continent country and state. (About this list)

See also: data available by other protocols, data by subject, how to make a new server, test servers, automatically collected list of Home Pages, What's New, and the clickable world map. If servers are marked "experimental", you should not expect anything. Please see how to send announcements of new servers (or modify your server's description).

- **Africa**
  - South Africa (sensitive map, general info)

- **Asia** (see Southwest Asia, Northeast Asia, and Southeast Asia sensitive maps, and Southeast Asia sensitive maps, and Asian Studies)

Figure 9-10
World-Wide Web Servers: Summary

The Document Title is World-Wide Web Servers: Summary

The Document URL is

http://info.cern.ch:80/hypertext/DataSources/WWW/Servers.html

As before, you can use the up and down arrows on the right-hand scroll bar to see other parts of the document.

If you find an item on this screen of interest to you (and it has a word or phrase that appears in blue type), just slide your cursor to that word or phrase and click once.

Navigation Notes

a. Each time you click on a blue word or phrase, you will be taken to the html document to which that blue word or phrase refers. In effect, you will be going deeper and deeper into the original home page.

b. When you get to this new page, if you find additional information that is of interest to you and there is a word or phrase in blue, just click on it to get to the next html document.

c. Should you decide to go back toward your original beginning, just click on the left-arrow button on the Toolbar at the top of your screen. Clicking once on it will take you back to the preceding html document.

d. Using the left-arrow button on the Toolbar at the top of your screen, you can return to the WebSurfer Jump Points page where we began. Click on the **left arrow** as many times as necessary until you are back at the WebSurfer Jump Points page.

e. Once there, click on **File** and then **Exit** to return to the WebSurfer Icon.

Home Pages—Continued

In this activity, we will look at four of the best-known home pages. Here they are.

NASA's Jet Propulsion Lab

1. Double-click on the **WebSurfer Icon**
2. When WebSurfer appears, be sure to maximize it by clicking on the **up arrow** in the upper-right-hand corner.
3. Click once on **Go to URL**
4. In the URL box type `http://www.jpl.nasa.gov:80`
5. Then, click on **OK**.

You will be taken to the NASA Jet Propulsion Laboratory. The NASA Jet Propulsion Laboratory Home Page should resemble the one in Figure 9-11.

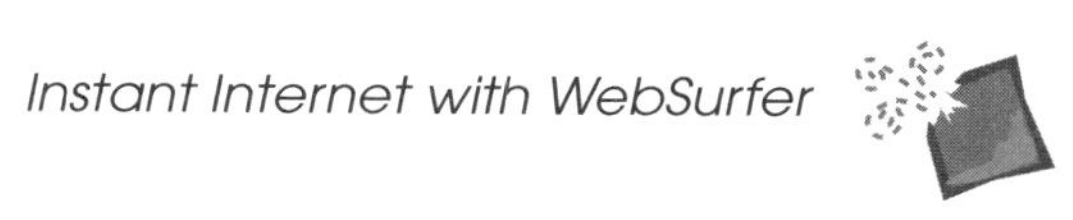

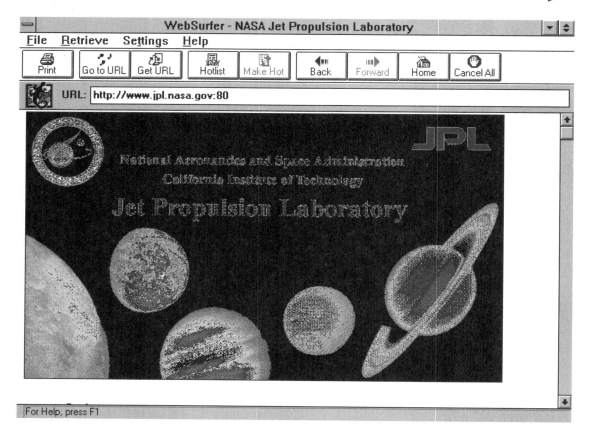

Figure 9-11
NASA Jet Propulsion Laboratory

To add this home page to your Hotlist, just click once on the **Make Hot button** on your Toolbar.

Spend some time exploring this home page. When you have finished, return to your WebSurfer Icon.

What's New With NCSA Mosaic

This is an extremely important home page to know about, since NCSA is the developer of NCSA Mosaic, a well-known World-Wide Web browser. As you will see momentarily, this home page will provide you with very valuable information about the Web and access to resources you may desire. Here is how to get there:

1. Double-click on **WebSurfer**
2. Be sure to maximize the WebSurfer for Windows window by clicking on the **up arrow** in the upper-right-hand corner of the scroll bar.

3. With the WebSurfer window open, click once on **Go to URL** and enter the URL for the NetManage Jump Points page: http://www.netmanage.com:80/netmanage/nm11.html
4. Then, click once on **OK**

If all goes according to plan, you should see a screen resembling the one in Figure 9-12.

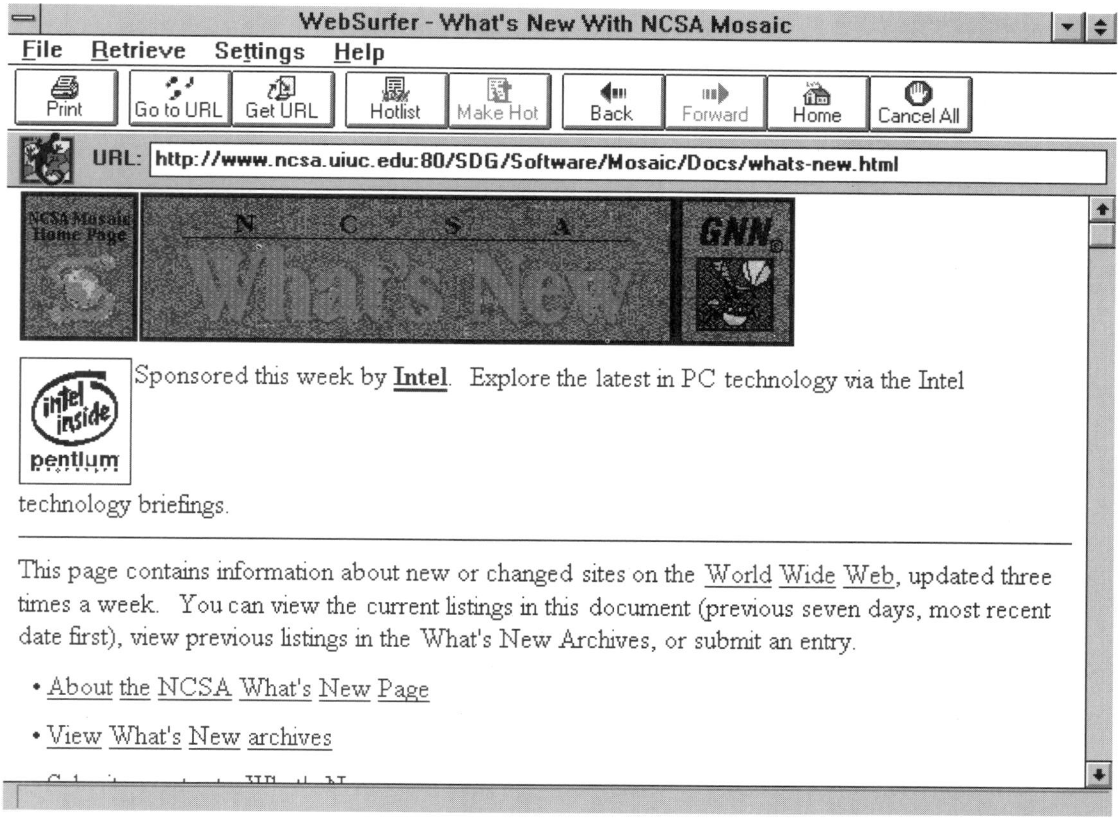

WebSurfer - What's New With NCSA Mosaic

File Retrieve Settings Help

Print | Go to URL | Get URL | Hotlist | Make Hot | Back | Forward | Home | Cancel All

URL: http://www.ncsa.uiuc.edu:80/SDG/Software/Mosaic/Docs/whats-new.html

NCSA Mosaic Home Page | N C S A What's New | GNN

intel inside pentium

Sponsored this week by Intel. Explore the latest in PC technology via the Intel technology briefings.

This page contains information about new or changed sites on the World Wide Web, updated three times a week. You can view the current listings in this document (previous seven days, most recent date first), view previous listings in the What's New Archives, or submit an entry.

- About the NCSA What's New Page
- View What's New archives

Figure 9-12
What's New With NCSA Mosaic

This initial screen provides you with a hint of the wonderful resources that are available. In particular, being able to learn quickly about the new or changed World-Wide Web sites is invaluable.

A Little Bit of History

1. You should be on the What's New With NCSA Mosaic Home Page
2. Click once on **Retrieve**
3. Click once on **History**

When you do this, you should see the WebSurfer - History window, which should resemble the one in Figure 9-13.

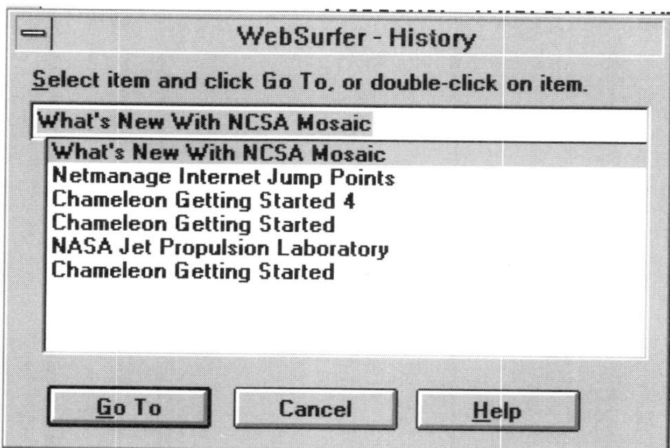

Figure 9-13
WebSurfer - History

WebSurfer - History provides you with a record of the pages you have looked at during this session, as well as an ability to go quickly to any one of them. To do so,

- **a.** Highlight the page that interests you by clicking on it once
- **b.** Then, click once on **Go To** and you will be taken to that page

The Power of Hyperlinks

A good example of the power of hyperlinks is provided by the following exercise.

1. Using the **left-arrow button** on the Toolbar at the top of your screen, return to the What's New With NCSA Mosaic Home Page.
2. Click once on **View What's New archives**
3. Click once on **Best of the Web '94**

Your screen should resemble Figure 9-14.

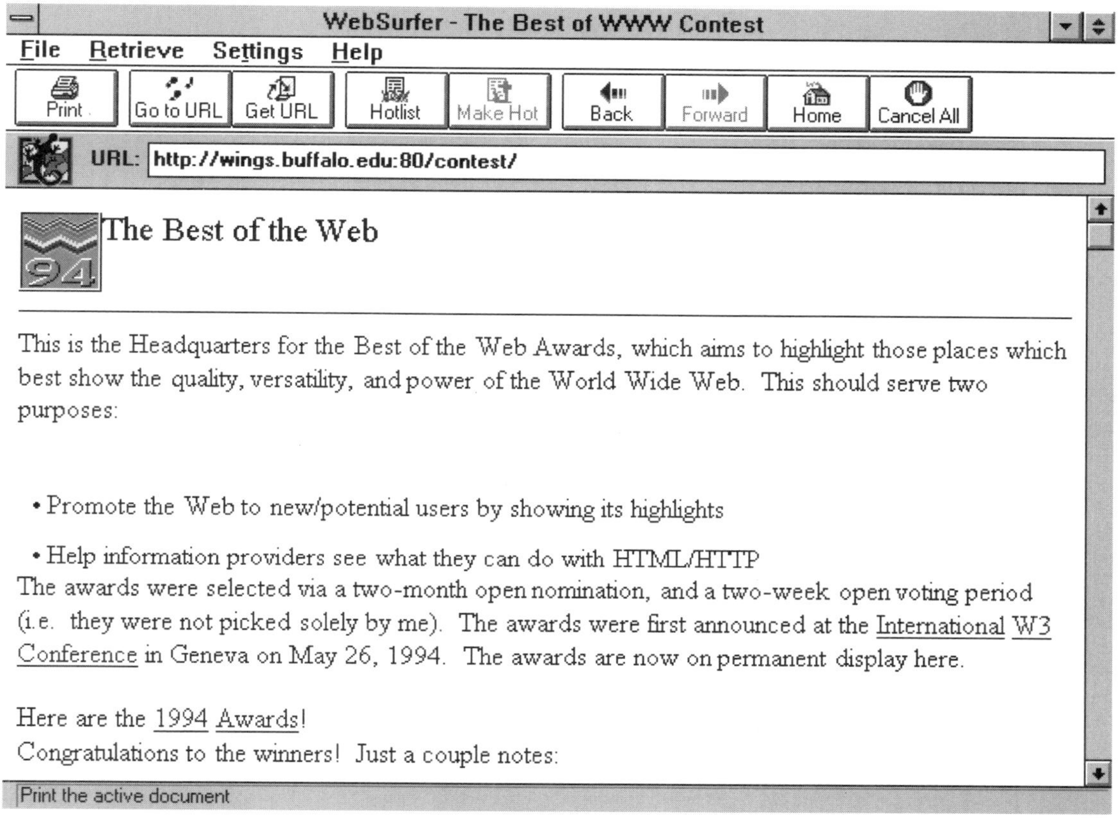

WebSurfer - The Best of WWW Contest

File Retrieve Settings Help

Print | Go to URL | Get URL | Hotlist | Make Hot | Back | Forward | Home | Cancel All

URL: http://wings.buffalo.edu:80/contest/

The Best of the Web

This is the Headquarters for the Best of the Web Awards, which aims to highlight those places which best show the quality, versatility, and power of the World Wide Web. This should serve two purposes:

- Promote the Web to new/potential users by showing its highlights
- Help information providers see what they can do with HTML/HTTP

The awards were selected via a two-month open nomination, and a two-week open voting period (i.e. they were not picked solely by me). The awards were first announced at the International W3 Conference in Geneva on May 26, 1994. The awards are now on permanent display here.

Here are the 1994 Awards!

Congratulations to the winners! Just a couple notes:

Print the active document

Figure 9-14
The Best of the Web

Notice how quickly you have traveled from the NetManage Jump Points screen (NetManage is located in California), to the What's New With NCSA Mosaic Home Page (NCSA is located in Illinois), to the Best of the Web Home Page (located at the University of Buffalo in New York) all at the click of a button!

Session Summary

As you have seen in this session, there is an amazing number of things that we can do with WebSurfer. You have complete access to all of the HyperText Transfer Protocol hosts out there on the World-Wide Web. It is also possible to use WebSurfer to access more traditional Internet tools such as ftp, telnet, and gopher. In our next session, you will learn how to do this.

Activity 1 Using WebSurfer for Telnet Sessions

Activity 2 Using WebSurfer for ftp Sessions

Activity 3 Using WebSurfer for Gopher Sessions

Using WebSurfer for Telnet, ftp, and Gopher

Session Overview

As you may have noticed earlier, WebSurfer seemingly has the ability to permit you to do all of the Internet activities that are commonly described, including telnet, ftp, and gopher. In this session, we will look at how WebSurfer might be used to facilitate the use of these Internet tools.

Using WebSurfer For Telnet Sessions

Telnet addresses can be entered as you would enter other URL information. The format for this is always going to be
`telnet://address/`

You will note that WebSurfer permits you to enter the URL information and then switches you to Telnet for the actual application. Here is one to try.

1. Connect to your Internet Service Provider and make WebSurfer active.
2. Click on **Retrieve** and then click on **Go To URL...**
3. In the WebSurfer - Go To Document box, type `telnet://www.njit.edu`
4. Click on **OK**

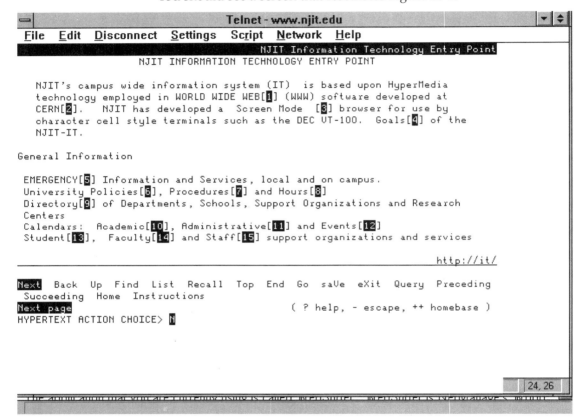

5. When you are prompted to log in, type www
6. Press **Enter**
7. When prompted for a password, press **Enter**

You should see a screen that resembles Figure 10-1.

```
Telnet - www.njit.edu
File  Edit  Disconnect  Settings  Script  Network  Help
                                    NJIT Information Technology Entry Point
                    NJIT INFORMATION TECHNOLOGY ENTRY POINT

   NJIT's campus wide information system (IT)  is based upon HyperMedia
   technology employed in WORLD WIDE WEB[1] (WWW) software developed at
   CERN[2].   NJIT has developed a  Screen Mode  [3] browser for use by
   character cell style terminals such as the DEC VT-100.  Goals[4] of the
   NJIT-IT.

General Information

 EMERGENCY[5] Information and Services, local and on campus.
 University Policies[6], Procedures[7] and Hours[8]
 Directory[9] of Departments, Schools, Support Organizations and Research
 Centers
 Calendars:  Academic[10], Administrative[11] and Events[12]
 Student[13],  Faculty[14] and Staff[15] support organizations and services

                                                                  http://it/

Next  Back  Up  Find  List  Recall  Top  End  Go  saVe  eXit  Query  Preceding
 Succeeding  Home  Instructions
Next page                                 ( ? help, - escape, ++ homebase )
HYPERTEXT ACTION CHOICE> N
                                                                      24, 26
```

Figure 10-1
New Jersey Institute of Technology

This is the New Jersey Institute of Technology's text-only version of hypertext. This screen permits you to make a HYPERTEXT ACTION CHOICE, as it is called. Each time you do so you will be taken to linked documents that will provide you with information.

Notice several things:

- **a.** You are actually using the Telnet client software that is part of the Internet Chameleon software suite.
- **b.** Documents are retrieved quite quickly, since there are no graphics.
- **c.** Many of the links (from this home page to other resources) are in the (by now) familiar URL form of http://info.cern.ch/hypertext/WWW/The Project.html

---

IMPORTANT: This means that by using these same hyperlinks you may have already seen many of these documents in the full multimedia WebSurfer format; here they are presented in text-only fashion.

---

1. Press **X** followed by **Enter** and you will return to a blank Telnet screen.
2. Click on **File** and then **Exit** to return to the WebSurfer screen where you began.

Let's use WebSurfer for Telnet once more. This time we will explore The Electronic Newsstand. Here is how to do so:

1. Click on **Retrieve** and then on **Go To URL...**
2. In the WebSurfer - Go To Document box, type `telnet://internet.com`
3. Click on **OK**
4. At the login prompt, type `enews`

You should see a screen resembling Figure 10-2.

```
Telnet - internet.com
File  Edit  Disconnect  Settings  Script  Network  Help
                    Internet Gopher Information Client v1.11

                         Root gopher server: localhost

-->  1.  Introduction to The Electronic Newsstand/
     2.  Notice of Copyright and General Disclaimer -- Please Read.
     3.  Magazines, Periodicals, and Journals (all titles)/
     4.  Business Publications and Resources/
     5.  Electronic Bookstore/
     6.  Music! (8 magazines and 80,000 CD titles)/
     7.  Travel, Trade Shows etc./ Lufthansa Takes Off/
     8.  The Electronic Car Showroom(tm)/
     9.  News Services/
     10. The Merchandise Mart/
     11. WIN A TRIP TO EUROPE SWEEPSTAKES/
     12. Search All Electronic Newsstand Articles by Keyword /



Press ? for Help, q to Quit, u to go up a menu                  Page: 1/1


Ready                                              VT100            5, 5
```

Figure 10-2
The Electronic Newsstand

In this case, The Electronic Newsstand has chosen to use a Gopher menu for their information. As you have done previously, feel free to browse among the information that is provided by just pointing and clicking on the information of interest to you.

When you have finished exploring The Electronic Newsstand, enter **q** and **ENTER** several times which should take you back to the main Telnet screen. Once there, just click on **File** and then **Exit** to be returned to WebSurfer.

TWO

Using WebSurfer for ftp Sessions

ftp addresses may be entered as you would enter other URL information. The format for this is always going to be `ftp://address/` You will note that WebSurfer permits you to enter the URL information but does not require you to add the other information that ftp traditionally requires, such as a user name of anonymous and your actual Internet address as a password.

An excellent illustration of the power of using WebSurfer as the *front end* for ftp activities is provided in the following exercise. We will use our WebSurfer front end to enable us to connect to an ftp server at the University of Illinois, Urbana-Champaign.

Here is how to do this:

1. Click on **Retrieve** and then on **Go To URL...**
2. In the WebSurfer - Go To Document box type `ftp://ftp.ncsa.uiuc.edu`
3. Then click on **OK**

If this works successfully, you should be connected to the ftp server at the University of Illinois, Urbana-Champaign and should see a screen resembling the one in Figure 10-3.

Figure 10-3
University of Illinois ftp Server

Contents of/

```
 2048 bytes   Nov 23 14:24   .
 2048 bytes   Nov 23 14:24   ..
  784 bytes   Aug 22 12:16   .index
  835 bytes   Aug 24 10:17   .message
 2048 bytes   Jul 27 11:56   BIMA
25819 bytes   Jun 20 09:10   Brochure
 2048 bytes   Aug 22 12:23   DTM
 2048 bytes   Aug 22 12:19   Documentation
 2048 bytes   Nov 21 11:09   Education
 2048 bytes   Aug 22 12:21   GlobalModels
 2048 bytes   Oct 12 20:22   HDF
 2048 bytes   Aug 22 12:26   Mac
   10 bytes   Aug  1 16:29   Mosaic -> Web/Mosaic
 2048 bytes   Aug 22 12:26   PC
16979 bytes   Aug 24 11:35   README
 2434 bytes   Aug  1 10:28   README.FIRST
 2048 bytes   Oct 31 10:43   SGI
 2048 bytes   Aug 22 12:24   Telnet
 2048 bytes   Aug 24 16:08   Unix
 2048 bytes   Oct 27 13:01   VR 2048 bytes Oct 27 15:54 Visualization 2048 bytes Aug 22
```

Notice several important facts:

- **a.** The ftp server contents are arrayed for you as a series of hyperlinks.
- **b.** Most significantly, you are provided with the number of bytes in various items before you download them!
- **c.** In each instance, should you make a selection, the ftp server will swing into action. You will move to the selected subdirectory, or you will be able to retrieve the particular file you have chosen.

The true power of WebSurfer's ability to work in collaboration with the ftp client software that is built into Internet Chameleon is made evident in the following exercise. Follow along as we use WebSurfer as both an ftp front end and in its usual capacity as a World-Wide Web browser.

1. Click on **Retrieve** and then on **Go To URL...**
2. In the WebSurfer - Go To Document box, type
   `ftp://ftp.csd.uwm.edu`
   Then click on **OK**

This will take you to the University of Wisconsin in Milwaukee, where we can find Scott Yanoff's Internet Services file in both text and html formats. The initial screen that you see should resemble Figure 10-4.

Contents of/

```
1024 bytes   Nov 23 01:57   incoming
1536 bytes   Nov 24 23:57   pub
 512 bytes   Mar 25 1994    sbin
 512 bytes   Mar 25 1994    usr
```

Figure 10-4
Contents of/

3. Click once on the hyperlink **pub** to change to that directory.
4. Once you are in the pub subdirectory, click on the **right arrow** on the bottom of your screen until you see two files. The first is called inet.services.html and the second is inet.services.txt
5. Click once on **inet.services.txt** and you will be greeted with a Save As box that should resemble Figure 10-5. Enter the drive and file name (i.e., `a:yanoff.txt`) and the file will be downloaded to your computer.

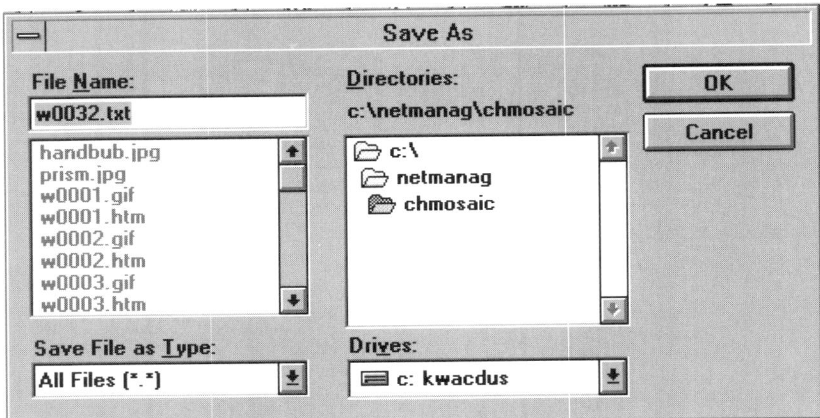

Figure 10-5
Save As Box

6. This time, click once on the file called **inet.services.html** Again, you will be prompted with a Save As box. As you have done before, determine the drive and file name for the incoming file and then click on **OK**.

However, the most interesting aspect of this exercise is about to happen. You should see, in a few moments, a screen that resembles Figure 10-6.

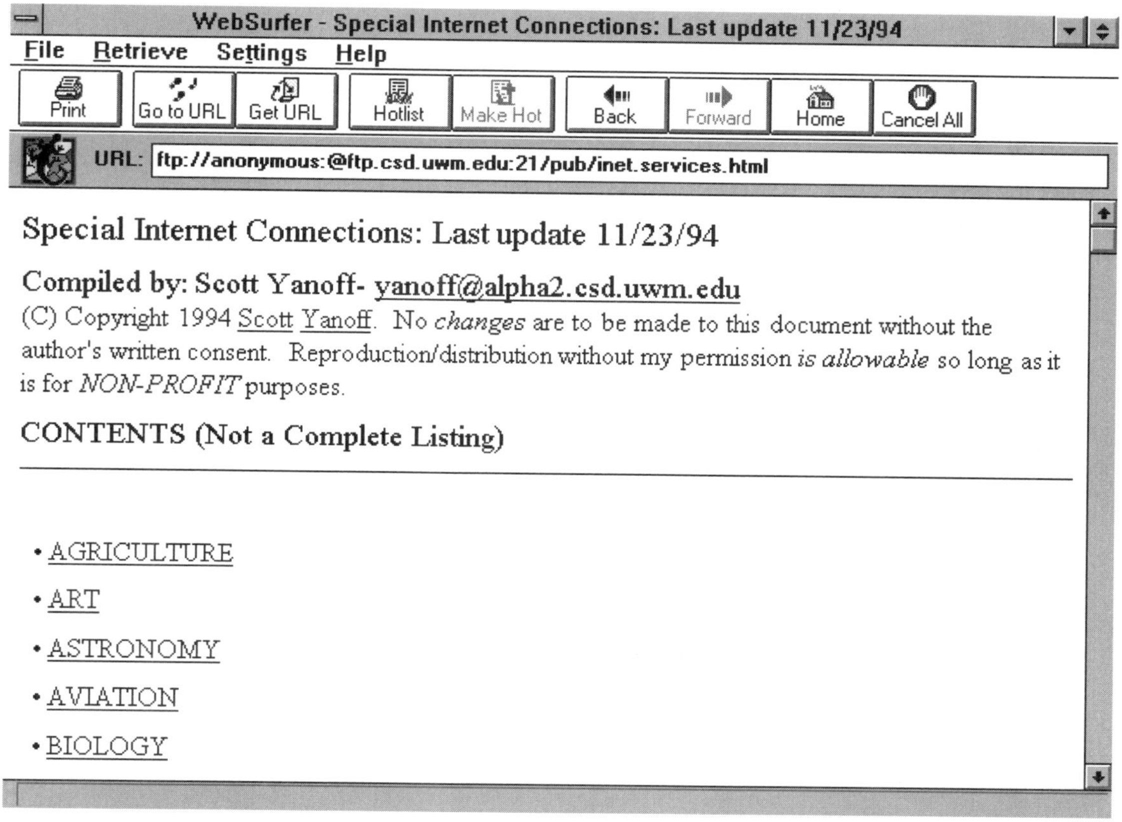

WebSurfer - Special Internet Connections: Last update 11/23/94

File Retrieve Settings Help

Print | Go to URL | Get URL | Hotlist | Make Hot | Back | Forward | Home | Cancel All

URL: ftp://anonymous:@ftp.csd.uwm.edu:21/pub/inet.services.html

Special Internet Connections: Last update 11/23/94

Compiled by: Scott Yanoff- yanoff@alpha2.csd.uwm.edu

(C) Copyright 1994 Scott Yanoff. No *changes* are to be made to this document without the author's written consent. Reproduction/distribution without my permission *is allowable* so long as it is for *NON-PROFIT* purposes.

CONTENTS (Not a Complete Listing)

- AGRICULTURE
- ART
- ASTRONOMY
- AVIATION
- BIOLOGY

Figure 10-6
Special Internet Connections

This document is so important that you should definitely add it to your Hotlist. The Special Internet Connections list (or the Yanoff List, as it is often called) is filled with a wonderful array of Internet resources.

Let's pause for a moment to reflect on what has just happened.

First, we began this activity by using WebSurfer to enable us to connect to ftp sites. As you have seen, this functions similarly to the ftp activities you did in Session Six, although when using WebSurfer, you did not have to be concerned about entering the name anonymous or your Internet address.

Second, we were able to download files as we typically do when using file transfer protocol.

Third, while using WebSurfer, we were immediately shifted back to WebSurfer itself when we encountered an html document that would be viewed better by the WebSurfer Client.

Finally, when we look at the Special Internet Connections document, it becomes obvious that WebSurfer is able to provide us with connectivity to servers that provide us with http, telnet, ftp, and gopher information.

Let's now use WebSurfer to enable us to view some Gopher resources.

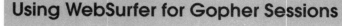

THREE

Using WebSurfer for Gopher Sessions

Gopher addresses can be entered as you would enter other URL information. The format for this is always going to be `gopher://address/` You will note that WebSurfer permits you to enter the URL information and then switches you to Gopher for the actual application. However, since you are now using WebSurfer as your front end to Gopher, you will find that your experience with Gopher is much more graphical than it has been before.

In this exercise, we will use WebSurfer as our front end to Gopher. Let's try the following:

1. With your WebSurfer window open, click once on **Retrieve** and then on **Go To URL...**
2. In the WebSurfer - Go To Document box, type `gopher://ds.internic.net`
3. Click on **OK**

You are quickly taken to a Gopher Server for the Internet Information Services that is provided by General Atomics. Your screen should resemble Figure 10-7.

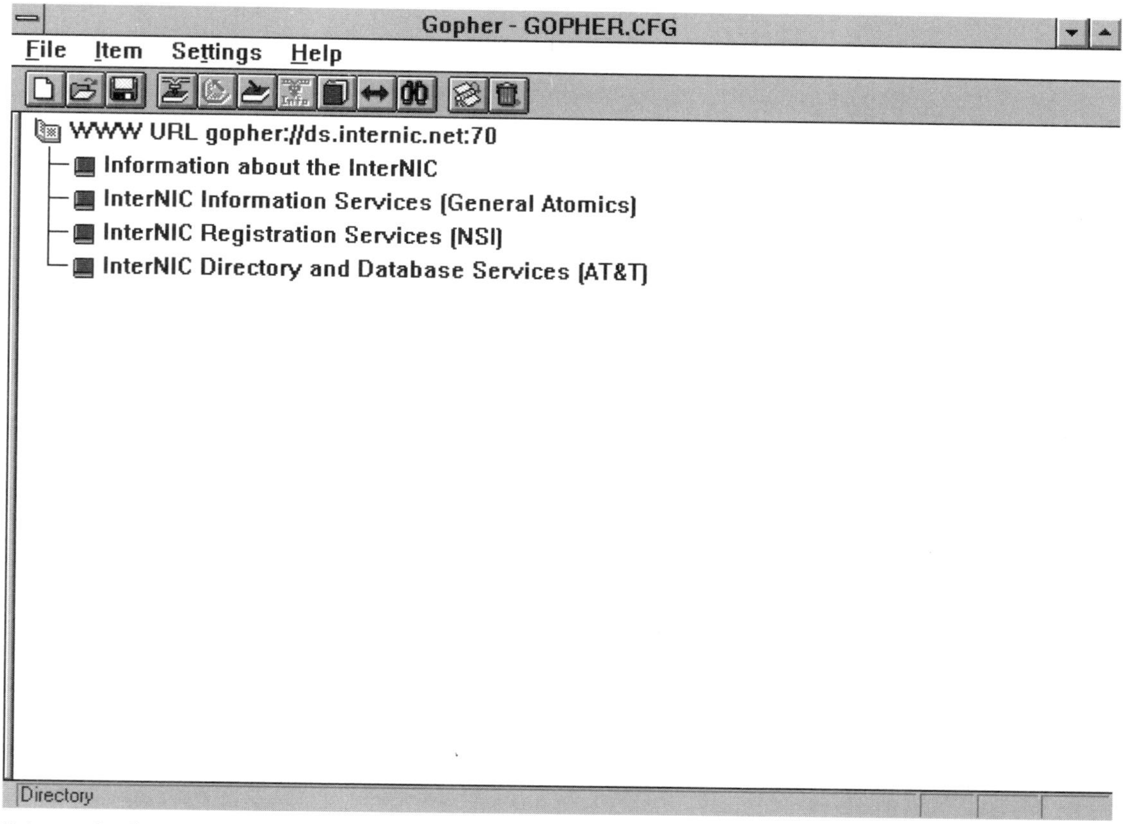

Gopher - GOPHER.CFG

File Item Settings Help

WWW URL gopher://ds.internic.net:70
- Information about the InterNIC
- InterNIC Information Services (General Atomics)
- InterNIC Registration Services (NSI)
- InterNIC Directory and Database Services (AT&T)

Directory

Figure 10-7
InterNIC Information Services

Select whichever items are of interest to you.

When you have finished, click on **File** and then **Exit** to return to the WebSurfer Icon.

As we noticed while looking at the Special Internet Connections provided by Scott Yanoff, there are many Gopher resources accessible to you via WebSurfer. Feel free to return to the Special Internet Connections file to explore the many Gopher resources that are listed.

Session Summary

As you have seen in Sessions Nine and Ten, you can do an amazing number of things with WebSurfer. You have complete access to all of the HyperText Transfer Protocol hosts out there (approximately 5,000 as of this writing). You can also use WebSurfer to access more traditional Internet tools such as ftp, telnet, and gopher. In our next session, you will learn how to use WebSurfer to quickly and effectively search for information located on the World-Wide Web.

SESSION 11

Activity 1 Searching with Menus—The Jump Points

Activity 2 Searching with Keywords—The W3 Search Engine

Activity 3 Yellow Pages

Activity 4 Markets on the World-Wide Web—Open Market

Activity 5 Markets on the World-Wide Web—Shopping2000

Searching for Information

Session Overview

In Session Nine we discovered home pages and learned how to type in URLs. While this allows you to find things you have heard about or that we have shown you, it doesn't help you to find things on your own. In this session, we will show you several ways to search for information on the World-Wide Web. We will begin with a menu approach, allowing you to follow a tree of menus to find information by category.

Then we will introduce you to search tools, search engines, and what are called meta-indexes. These will enable you to look for topics based on keywords and search terms. Finally, we will show you some of the newest markets on the Web.

Searching with Menus—The Jump Points

Earlier, you visited an excellent starting place to which we will return for our first explorations. This is the NetManage Home Page (http://www.netmanage.com). We will focus on the button labeled Jump Points - Internet Exploration as shown in Figure 11-1.

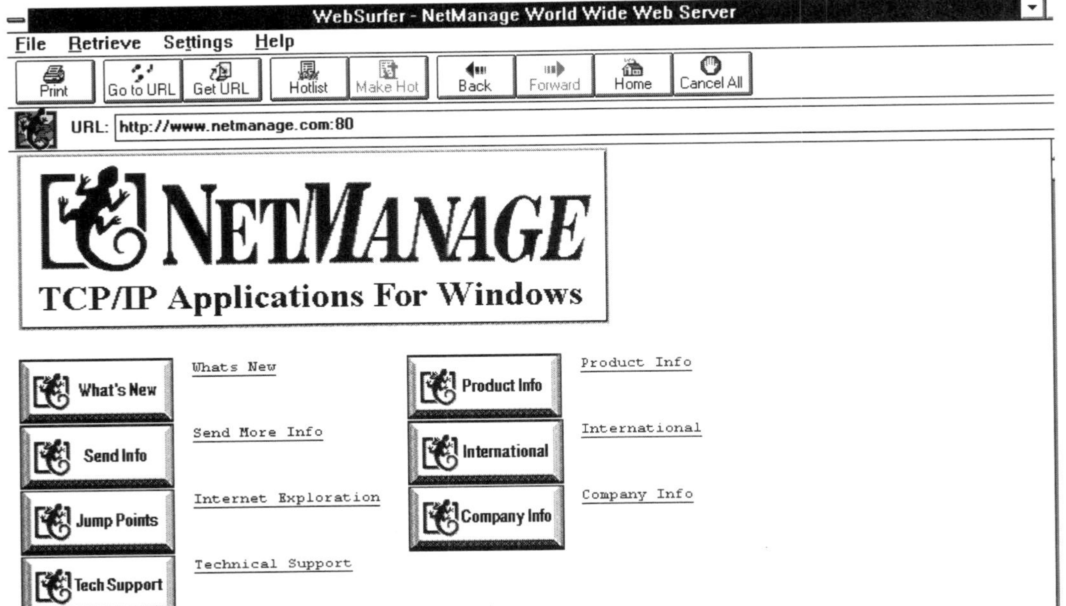

Figure 11-1
NetManage Home Page

1. Double-click on the **Jump Points button** and we will enter a series of starting points prepared for us by NetManage.

In the figures that follow, we have displayed the Jump Points page in many sections as it is quite long.

When you reach this page, you may find that quite a few things have changed. You must remember that the Internet is constantly growing and revising itself. The figures that follow will give you a close approximation of what you will find when you visit.

The Jump Points Page

Figure 11-2 shows the Index to broad categories. For each category in this Index, there are many listings as you scroll down the page.

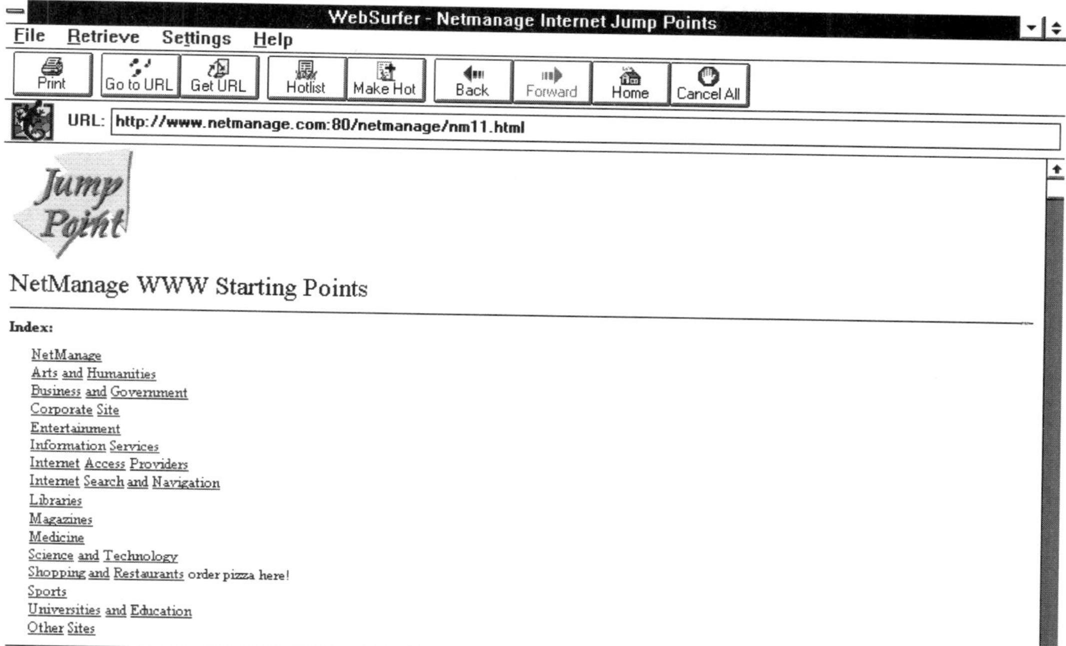

Figure 11-2
Jump Points

Now let's move down the Jump Points page. Under each of the broad categories, there are many one-line pointers. Many of the pointers contain the underlined hyperlink word here. As you move your cursor onto that hyperlink, you will see the URL displayed on WebSurfer's Status Line at the bottom of the screen. (We have not shown these in the figures.)

Figures 11-3 through 11-13 show us scrolling down the NetManage Jump Points page. Take a moment and scan down the lists.

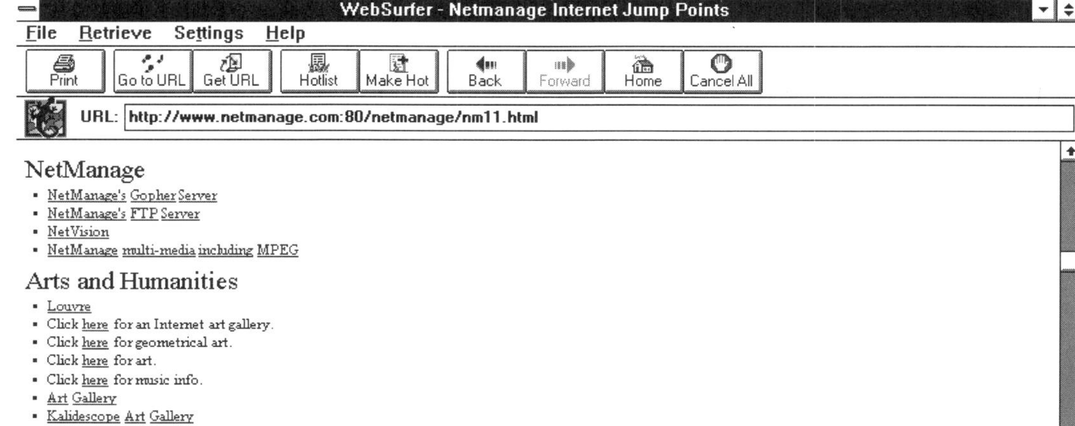

Figure 11-3
Jump Points Page—NetManage and Arts and Humanities

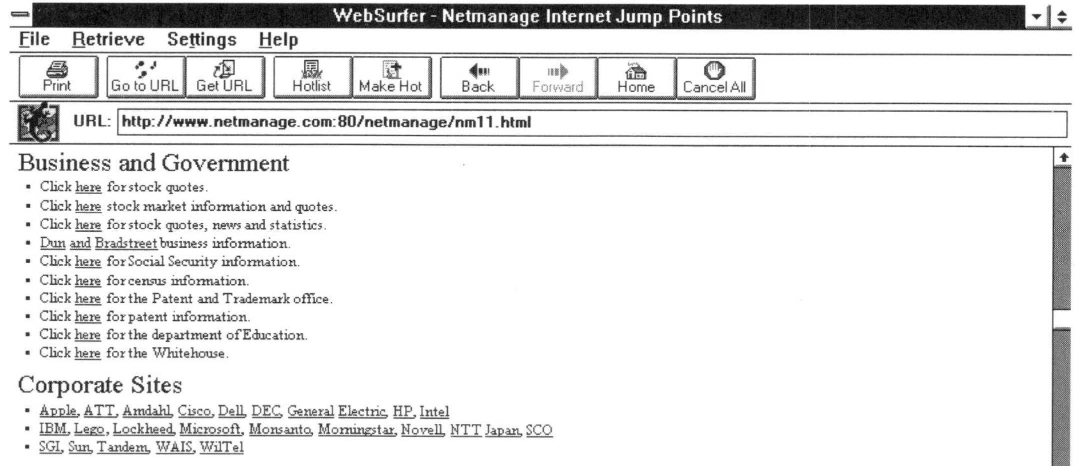

Figure 11-4
Jump Points Page—Business and Government and Corporate Sites

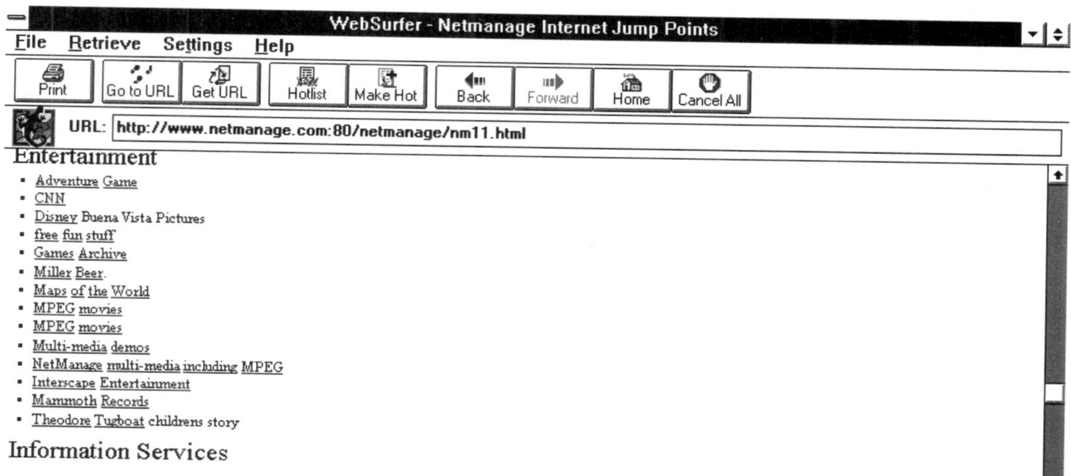

Figure 11-5
Jump Points Page—
Entertainment

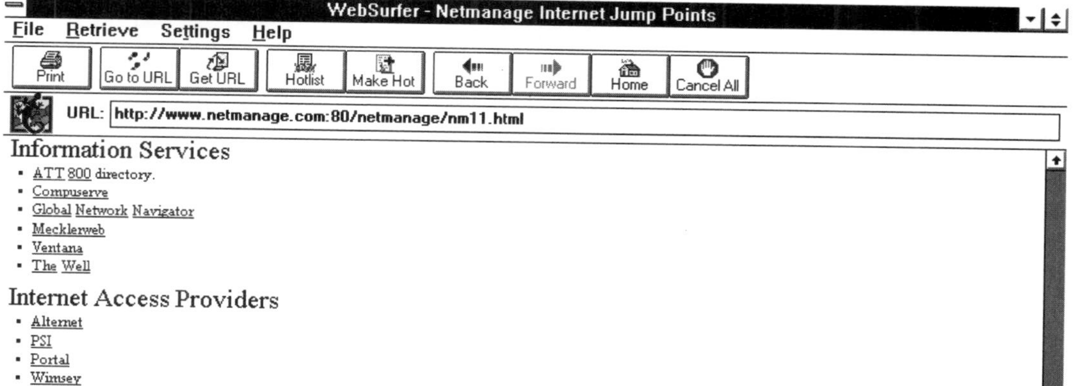

Figure 11-6
Jump Points Page—
Information Services

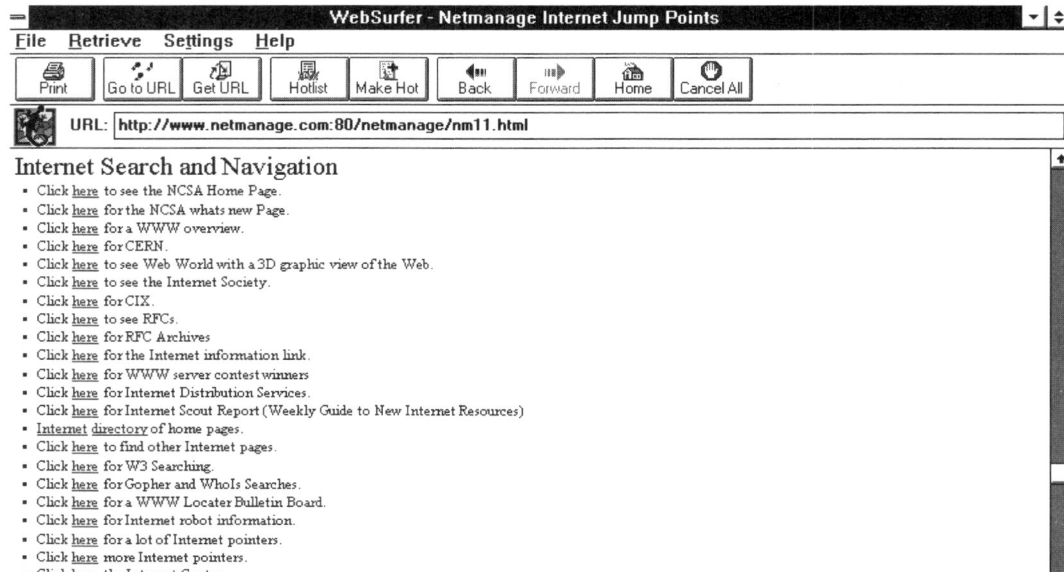

Figure 11-7
Jump Points Page—Internet

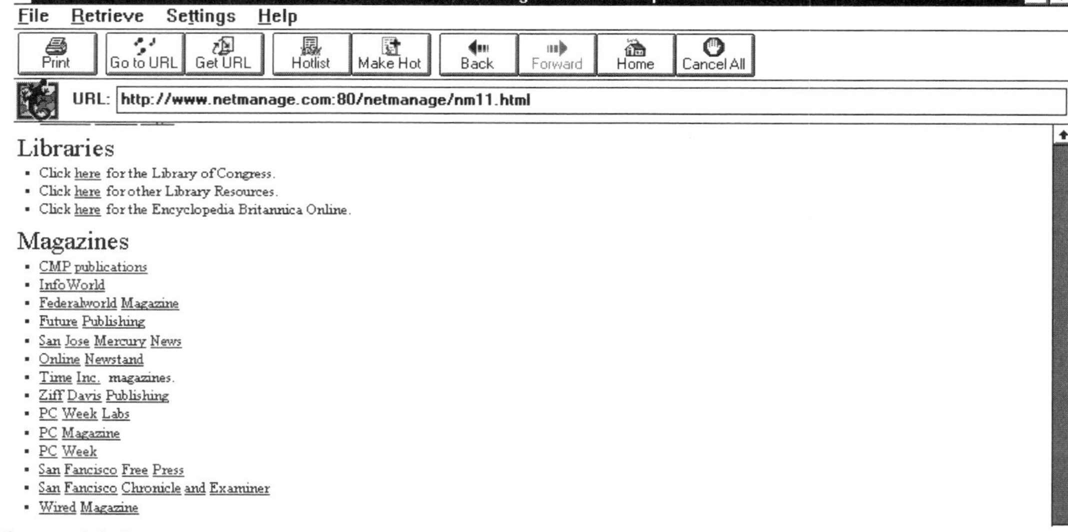

Figure 11-8
Jump Points Page—Libraries and Magazines

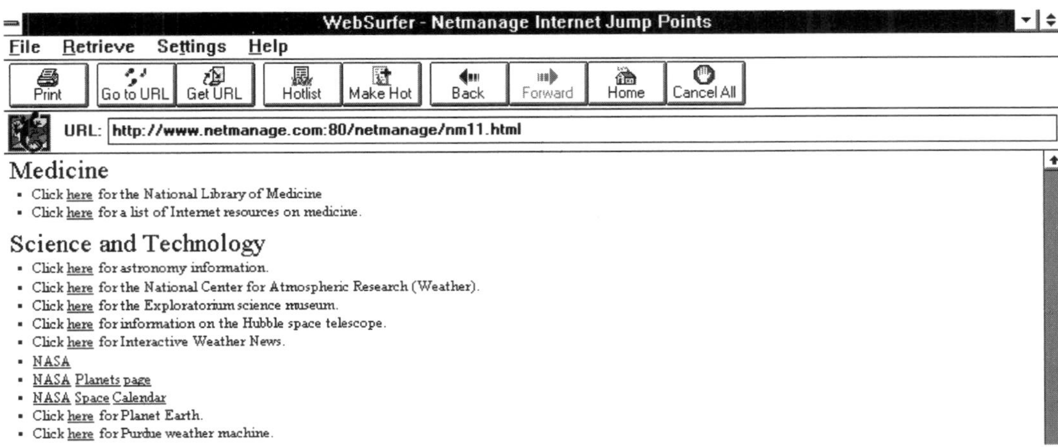

Figure 11-9
Jump Points Page—Medicine and Science and Technology

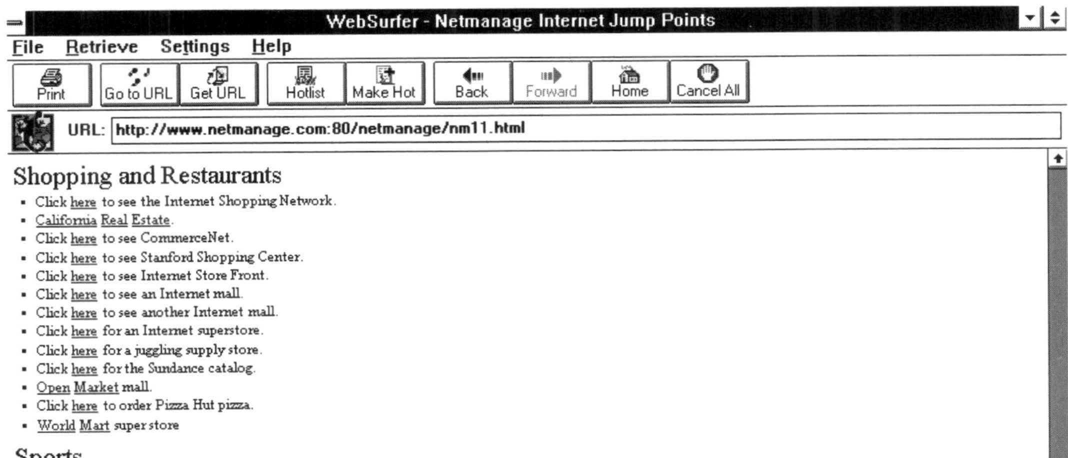

Figure 11-10
Jump Points Page—Shopping and Restaurants

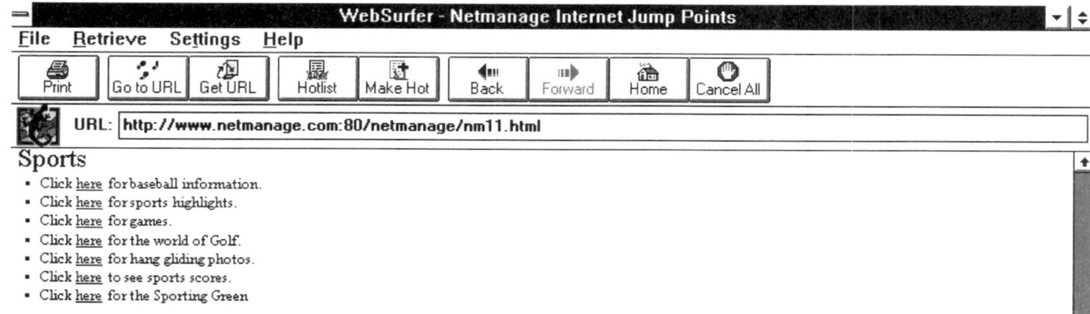

Figure 11-11
Jump Points Page—Sports

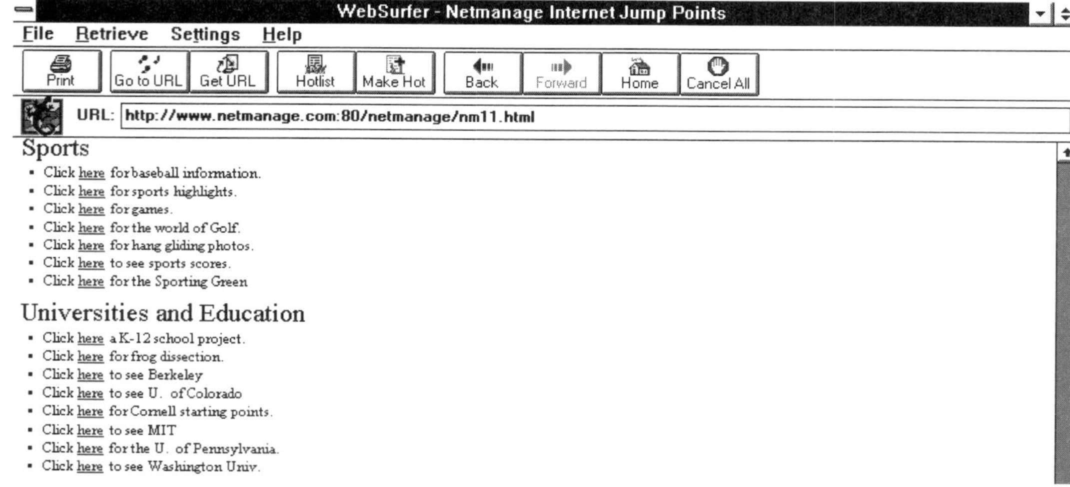

Figure 11-12
Jump Points Page—Universities and Education

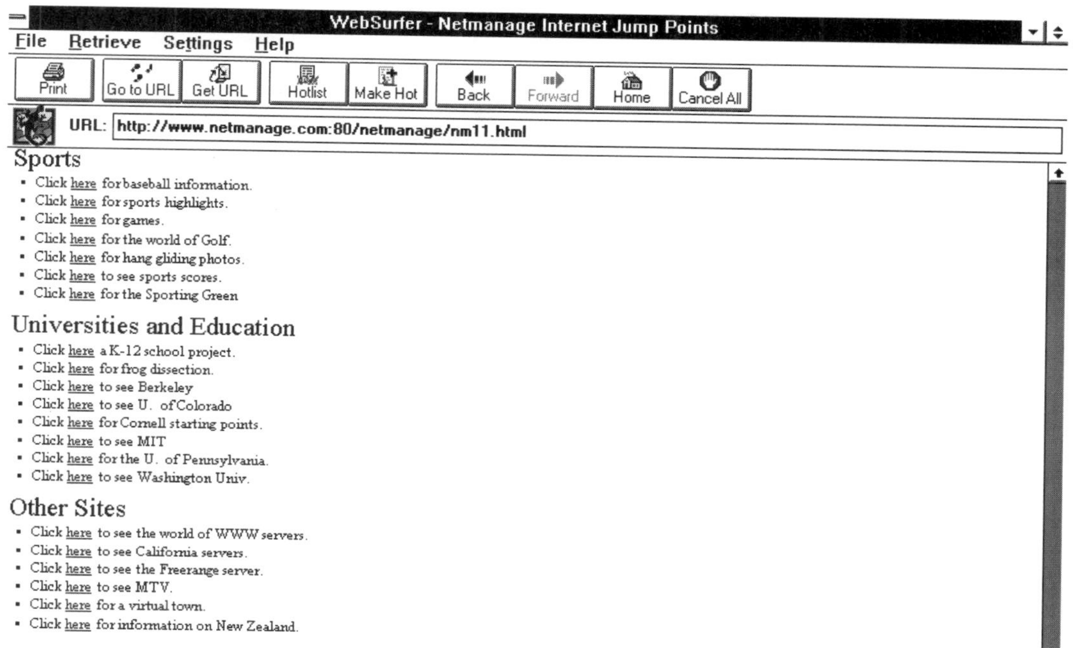

Figure 11-13
Jump Points Page—Other Sites

When you have finished browsing through this page and its associated hyperlinks, join us as we continue to find other ways to search and explore the World-Wide Web.

Searching with Keywords—The W3 Search Engine

As you have gathered by now, the World-Wide Web is an enormous place, filled with a tremendous and growing array of resources. Following indexes down to your areas of interest is a fast and well-organized way of locating information. What if, however, you go down the index trees and don't find what you are after? You would like to see what else is out there. Keyword searches may help you here. A number of searching tools now exist on the Web. We will illustrate one and then suggest a way to find others.

1. Go to the NetManage Jump Points page and click on **Internet** and **Click here for W3 Searching**.

This should take you to a page similar to Figure 11-14.

You are looking at one of the newer search tools on the Internet and the World-Wide Web known as a *meta-index*. Here, you will find a number of different search tools collected in one place. This allows you to use many different search engines to locate a particular item of interest. Each tool will search the "space" defined by its creator for your topic. Each tool, however, uses different methods and techniques to uncover your selection. This permits you to research a topic with a higher level of indexing (meta-indexing).

Although our example search uses only one of the engines (WebCrawler), you may wish to try either our sample topic or one of your own to follow many different paths and compare the results.

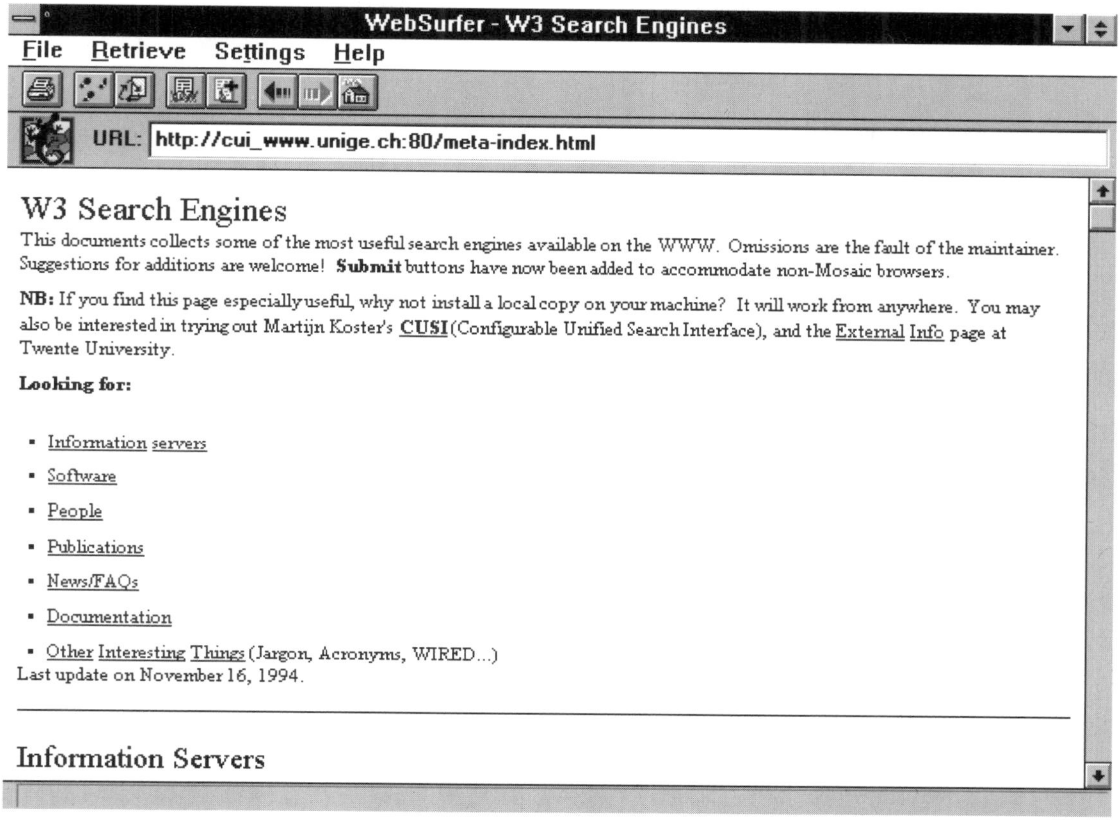

WebSurfer - W3 Search Engines

File Retrieve Settings Help

URL: http://cui_www.unige.ch:80/meta-index.html

W3 Search Engines

This documents collects some of the most useful search engines available on the WWW. Omissions are the fault of the maintainer. Suggestions for additions are welcome! **Submit** buttons have now been added to accommodate non-Mosaic browsers.

NB: If you find this page especially useful, why not install a local copy on your machine? It will work from anywhere. You may also be interested in trying out Martijn Koster's **CUSI** (Configurable Unified Search Interface), and the External Info page at Twente University.

Looking for:

- Information servers
- Software
- People
- Publications
- News/FAQs
- Documentation
- Other Interesting Things (Jargon, Acronyms, WIRED...)

Last update on November 16, 1994.

Information Servers

Figure 11-14
Search Engines

2. Scroll down to reveal Information Servers as shown in Figure 11-15.

WebSurfer - W3 Search Engines

File Retrieve Settings Help

Information Servers

List-based WWW Catalogs

submit CUI World Wide Web Catalog

submit Global Network Academy Meta-Library

submit Aliweb (Archie-like Indexing for the Web)

See also:

Aliweb at Nexor

Spider-based WWW Catalogs

submit WebCrawler (Search WWW document content)

submit RBSE's URL database (Search WWW document full text)

submit NIKOS Gateway (Nomad search)

submit JumpStation (Search WWW document title or header)

submit NorthStar (Search WWW document headers)

submit WWW Worm 1. Search titles of documents

Figure 11-15
Information Servers

Let's do a sample search to illustrate how search works. We will pick the WebCrawler as our example and use the search word "commerce."

3. Click on the box to the left of WebCrawler and type in the word `commerce`
4. Click on the **submit button**

If all goes well, you will receive a page similar to Figure 11-16.

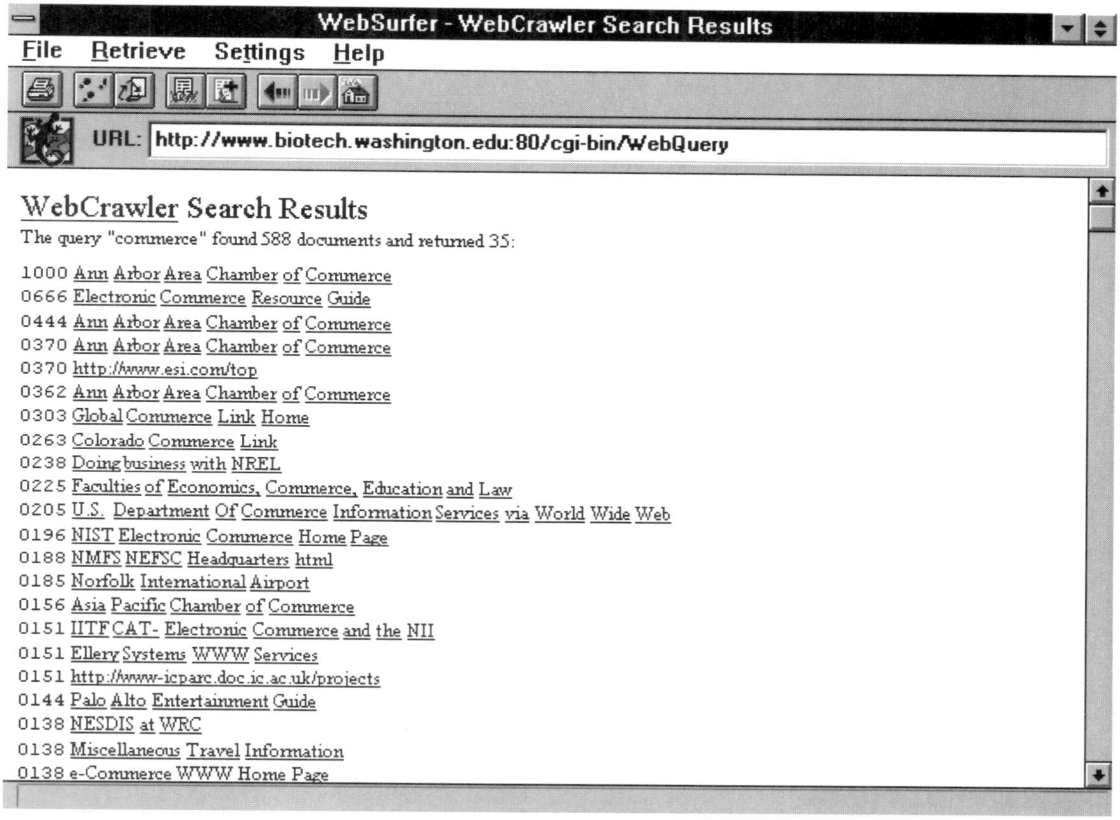

WebSurfer - WebCrawler Search Results

File Retrieve Settings Help

URL: http://www.biotech.washington.edu:80/cgi-bin/WebQuery

WebCrawler Search Results

The query "commerce" found 588 documents and returned 35:

1000 Ann Arbor Area Chamber of Commerce
0666 Electronic Commerce Resource Guide
0444 Ann Arbor Area Chamber of Commerce
0370 Ann Arbor Area Chamber of Commerce
0370 http://www.esi.com/top
0362 Ann Arbor Area Chamber of Commerce
0303 Global Commerce Link Home
0263 Colorado Commerce Link
0238 Doing business with NREL
0225 Faculties of Economics, Commerce, Education and Law
0205 U.S. Department Of Commerce Information Services via World Wide Web
0196 NIST Electronic Commerce Home Page
0188 NMFS NEFSC Headquarters html
0185 Norfolk International Airport
0156 Asia Pacific Chamber of Commerce
0151 IITF CAT- Electronic Commerce and the NII
0151 Ellery Systems WWW Services
0151 http://www-icparc.doc.ic.ac.uk/projects
0144 Palo Alto Entertainment Guide
0138 NESDIS at WRC
0138 Miscellaneous Travel Information
0138 e-Commerce WWW Home Page

Figure 11-16
Search Results

In our example, we have brought back a large number of results. Notice that each is in the form of a hyperlink allowing you to go directly to each result by clicking on the result line. We will let you do this now if you wish or you may choose to navigate back to try another search.

Next, we will briefly introduce you to several other information sources that demonstrate the increasing commercial nature of the World-Wide Web. Each of these locations may be reached by clicking on the **Go to URL button** or by clicking on **Menu Bar - Retrieve** and **Go to URL**

Yellow Pages

THREE

1. Type the URL `http://www.yellow.com`

This will take you to a page similar to Figure 11-17.

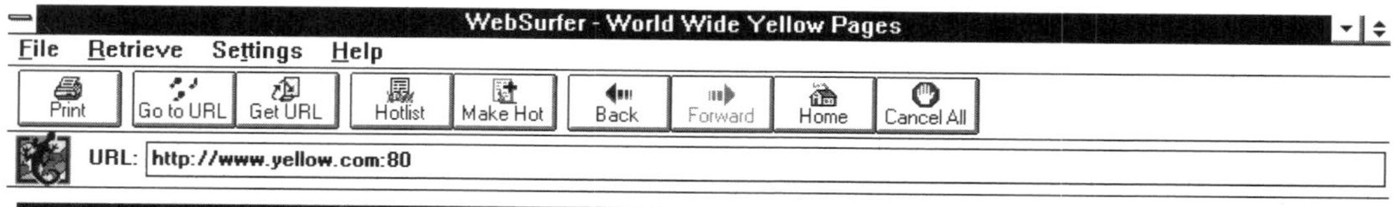

Welcome to the WorldWide YellowPages. Startwithus to findtheworld.

We arejust settingup shop,so mostofourcontentis morelocalthanworldwide, but thatis changingrapidly!

- Lookupa businesswiththeonline**searchpage**.
- Check outnew entrie.
- We realizethattheWWYPis farfromcomplete.
  Pleasetake a secondandadd yourfavoritbusiness.

Information:

- Youcan**be herenow!**Check out our**freepromotioforon-linbusinesse**!:
- Becomingpartofthe WorldWide YellowPages(tm).
- About theWorld Wide YellowPages (tm)

TheWorld Wide YellowPages is a productofHomePages, Inc.

- About the World Wide Yellow Pages (tm)

The World Wide Yellow Pages is a product of Home Pages, Inc.

Allcontent:Copyright© 1994 HomePages, Inc. AllRightsReserved.
Suggestionsand feedback are welcomedat feedback@HomePages.co.n

Figure 11-17
World Wide Yellow Pages

2. Scroll down until you see a search page that resembles Figure 11-18.

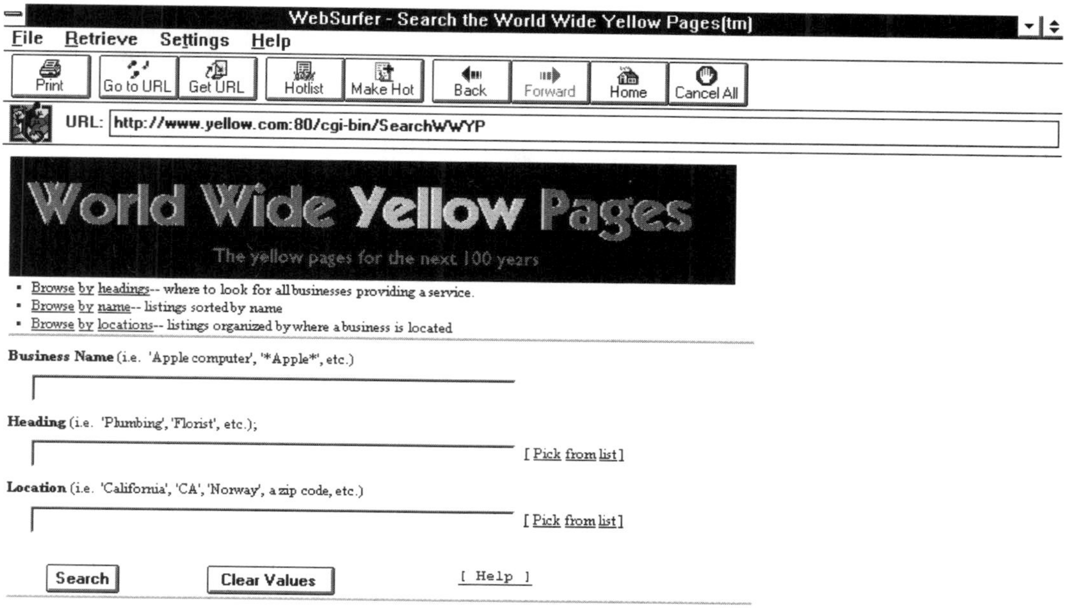

WebSurfer - Search the World Wide Yellow Pages(tm)

File Retrieve Settings Help

Print | Go to URL | Get URL | Hotlist | Make Hot | Back | Forward | Home | Cancel All

URL: http://www.yellow.com:80/cgi-bin/SearchWWYP

World Wide Yellow Pages

The yellow pages for the next 100 years

- Browse by headings-- where to look for all businesses providing a service.
- Browse by name-- listings sorted by name
- Browse by locations-- listings organized by where a business is located

Business Name (i.e. 'Apple computer', '*Apple*', etc.)

Heading (i.e. 'Plumbing', 'Florist', etc.); [Pick from list]

Location (i.e. 'California', 'CA', 'Norway', a zip code, etc.) [Pick from list]

Search | Clear Values | [Help]

Figure 11-18
Search the World Wide Yellow Pages™

3. Select one of the categories, type in a search word of your choice, and click on the **Search button**

You have now embarked on a search on your own. We can't predict (or illustrate) the results of your search, but you now have several tools to explore the World-Wide Web by yourself.

What you have been doing is following a freeform series of hyperlinks. That is, you found an interesting link to another topic, clicked on it, and were off. This process is what the World-Wide Web is all about—following hyperlinks to locate what you may want. It is also quite addictive in that you keep finding things that were not in your original search.

Markets on the World-Wide Web—Open Market

To complete our tour of information searching on the Web, we will visit two of the Web's newest markets. There are many markets now on the Web and more joining every day. These two are very good examples.

1. Type the URL `http://www.openmarket.com:80`

   You will be taken to a page similar to Figure 11-19.

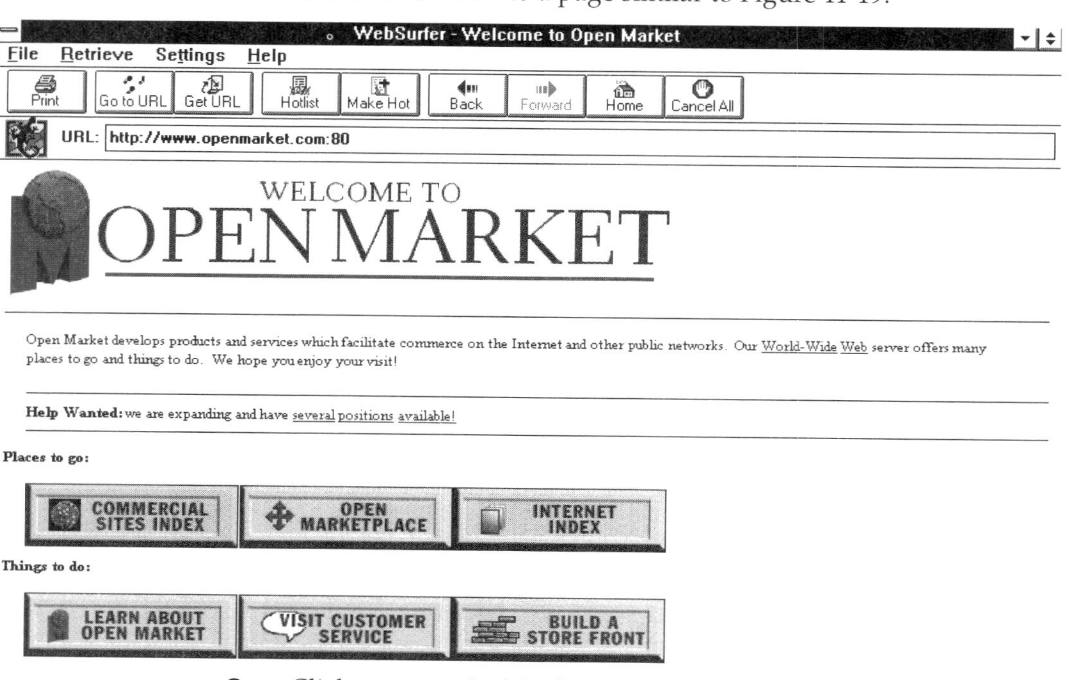

Figure 11-19 Welcome to Open Market

2. Click on several of the buttons to explore this expanding array of products and services.

Markets on the World-Wide Web—Shopping2000

FIVE

Instant Activity

For our last example, we will visit the latest word in catalog shopping on the World-Wide Web—Shopping2000. Shopping2000 bills itself as an interactive shopping guide to products and services of direct merchants. It's a very colorful and attractive place to visit.

1. Type the URL `http://www.shopping2000.com:80/`

You will arrive at a page similar to Figure 11-20.

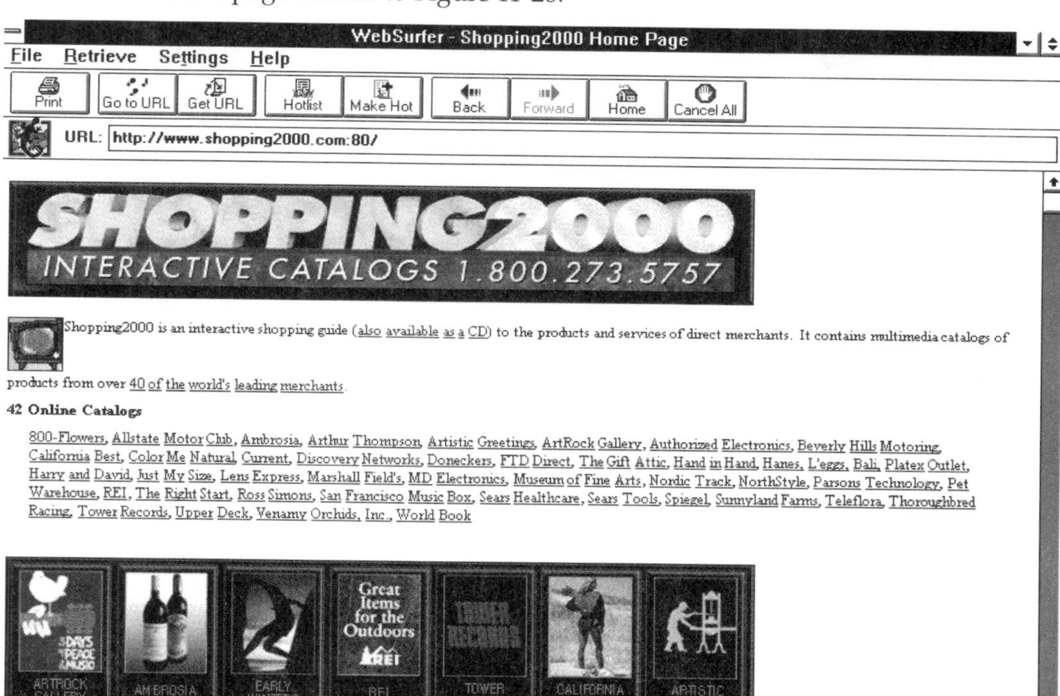

Figure 11-20
Shopping2000 Home Page

Here you can browse in the colorful, multimedia catalogs of many well-known direct marketing merchants. Many more are shown in Figure 11-21.

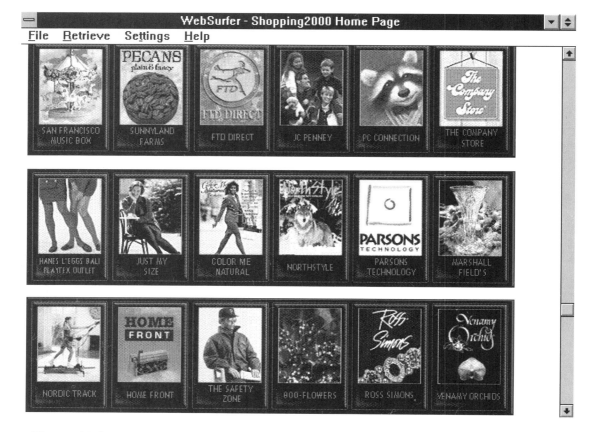

Figure 11-21
Shopping2000 Home Page, continued

We will leave you here to shop, browse, search, and explore the World-Wide Web and its growing resources. Happy Hunting!

Session Summary

As you have seen from the activities in this session, there are many varied ways to search for information on the World-Wide Web. In addition, there are many commercial ventures beginning to appear, whose intent is to help you to find more quickly and effectively the goods and services you may desire. In our next session, we will show you how to add multimedia capabilities to WebSurfer. With these software programs correctly installed, you will be able to view not only text and still images but also sound and moving pictures.

SESSION 12

Activity 1 The NCSA Demo Document

Activity 2 Getting the PC Speaker Driver

Activity 3 Getting a JPEG Viewer

Activity 4 Showing a JPEG Picture

Activity 5 PostScript Viewers

Activity 6 Finding Music, Images, and Multimedia

Using Multimedia with WebSurfer

Session Overview

WebSurfer's power to bring you text and images only begins to show you the power of the Internet and the World-Wide Web. We will now introduce you to WebSurfer's ability to work collaboratively with other software programs to produce sound, brilliant images, and even video clips. These multimedia capabilities will allow you to access, view, and listen to information from all around the globe.

You can listen while corporate chief executives tell you about their companies. You can watch, in near-realtime, as space telescopes bring back planetary images. You can, with some patience, bring in film and animation clips to view at your leisure. You can look at some of the world's finest art treasures on your own PC.

As we write this, the range of sounds, images, and video clips is astounding. We can be sure that when you read this the range will have expanded tremendously! Let's look quickly at how WebSurfer can get and show you all these things.

A Brief Multimedia Vocabulary Lesson

Before learning how to configure WebSurfer so you will be able to hear sounds and see pictures, we will take a moment to introduce you to the vocabulary you will encounter while doing so. It will also be helpful for you to understand the logic of what is taking place. There are vari-

ous types of multimedia files that are available on the World-Wide Web. In this session, we will focus on audio files, postscript files, and image files.

Each one of these files may have one of several possible extensions. In addition, in order for you to be able to see or hear these multimedia files, you must have some additional software programs, known as viewers, players, or sound-playing programs. (We will refer to them as viewers.)

It is important to understand that several activities are required in order for these viewers to work effectively with your copy of WebSurfer. You must

1. Obtain the required viewer.
2. Install the viewer on your hard drive.
3. "Teach" WebSurfer where to find the viewer once it has been installed.

For each one of the files we download, we must make certain associations between WebSurfer and the files, so that WebSurfer will know where to find the files when it needs to use them. In each of the following activities, we will walk you through all of these steps.

Table 12-1 provides you with a listing of the files, their extensions, and the required viewers or players.

Table 12-1 Multimedia Files, Extensions, and Required Viewers/Players

File Type	Extension(s)	Viewer/Player
audio	.wav	speaker
audio	.au	wplany
image	.gif	lview
image	.jpeg, .jpe, .jpg	lview
postscript	.ps, .eps, .ai	ghostview

PostScript and JPEG

We will talk about playing sounds in a moment. Before that, we will focus on the viewers that are needed so we will be able to see either postscript or image files. To do this we will need to download and install two programs known as ghostview and lview31.

ghostview

The first program, ghostview, is a PostScript viewer. *PostScript* is a text and image language that allows very complex documents to be described in plain ASCII text. Here is a sample of the first few lines of a PostScript file. (You are not going to have to create anything like this file; it is provided here only to give you a sense of what a PostScript file looks like!)

```
%!PS-Adobe-3.0
%%Title: (genbbb/wwww US)
%%Creator: (Microsoft Word: LaserWriter 8 8.1.1)
%%CreationDate: (10:47 AM Tuesday, April 26, 1994)
%%For: (Oliver McBryan)
%%Pages: 15
%%DocumentFonts: Palatino-Bold Palatino-Roman Palatino-Italic Courier
%%DocumentNeededFonts: Palatino-Bold Palatino-Roman Palatino-Italic Courier
%%DocumentSuppliedFonts:
%%DocumentData: Clean7Bit
%%PageOrder: Ascend
%%Orientation: Portrait
%ADO_PaperArea: -31 -31 761 581
%ADO_ImageableArea: 0 0 730 552
%%EndComments
```

lview31

The extensions .jpeg, .jpe, and .jpg tell WebSurfer to look for files that have been created in adherence to a standard called JPEG. *JPEG* stands for the Joint Photographic Experts Group. The key word *Photographic* might give you a hint that some of these images will be like photos. In addition, you might expect to find paintings, and so on.

That's enough tutorial for now. Let's play some sounds.

NOTE: If you already have a multimedia PC (or at least a soundboard such as SoundBlaster), you can play sounds right off of the Internet. Our first activity will do just that.

If you do not have a soundboard or multimedia PC, you can download a Microsoft Windows driver to send sounds to your PC speaker. If your computer presently has no sound capability, you may wish to skip ahead to Activity 2, Getting the PC Speaker Driver.

The NCSA Demo Document

Figure 12-1 shows a portion of the NCSA Mosaic Demo Document (Document Title: NCSA Mosaic Demo Document; Document URL: www.ncsa.uiuc.edu/demoweb/demo.html). As explained by the screen text, the clicking on the Loudspeaker Icon will send a sound clip to your PC. With your soundboard and speakers, you should then hear a clear, crisp audio clip.

We are venturing into tricky waters here, as there are many variations in PCs equipped with soundboards. The following activity may work flawlessly, or you may hear nothing.

1. Connect to your Internet service provider and open WebSurfer
2. Click on **Go to URL** In the WebSurfer - Go To Document box, enter the URL
   `http://www.ncsa.uiuc.edu/demoweb/demo.html`
3. When the NCSA Mosaic Demo Document comes up, scroll down to show a screen similar to the one shown in Figure 12-1. Be sure you are showing the bordered Loudspeaker Icon.

4. Click on the Loudspeaker Icon labeled ***What is NCSA Mosaic?*** (If that icon is no longer there, find the nearest Loudspeaker Icon.)
5. On the status bar at the bottom of your WebSurfer screen, you should see a file coming in with the file extension .au The file is many tens of thousands of bytes, but when the transfer has been completed, you should hear the audio clip.

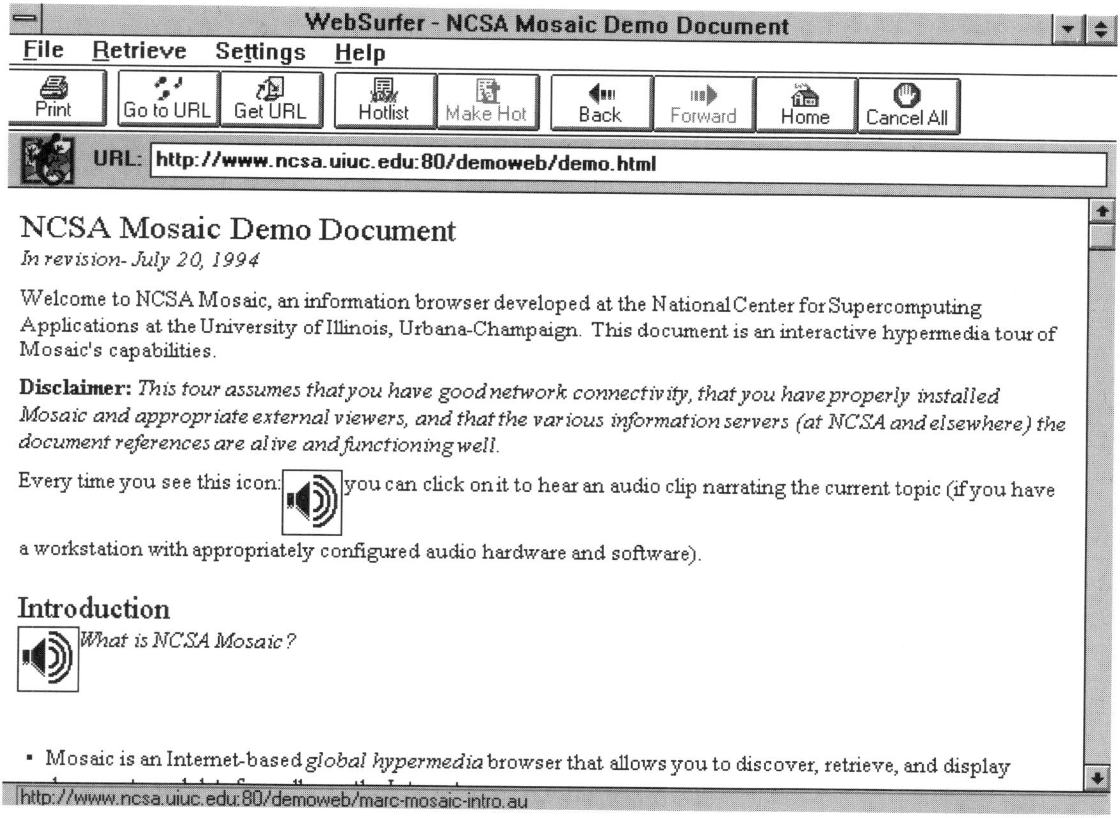

WebSurfer - NCSA Mosaic Demo Document

File Retrieve Settings Help

Print | Go to URL | Get URL | Hotlist | Make Hot | Back | Forward | Home | Cancel All

URL: http://www.ncsa.uiuc.edu:80/demoweb/demo.html

NCSA Mosaic Demo Document

In revision- July 20, 1994

Welcome to NCSA Mosaic, an information browser developed at the National Center for Supercomputing Applications at the University of Illinois, Urbana-Champaign. This document is an interactive hypermedia tour of Mosaic's capabilities.

Disclaimer: *This tour assumes that you have good network connectivity, that you have properly installed Mosaic and appropriate external viewers, and that the various information servers (at NCSA and elsewhere) the document references are alive and functioning well.*

Every time you see this icon: you can click on it to hear an audio clip narrating the current topic (if you have a workstation with appropriately configured audio hardware and software).

Introduction

What is NCSA Mosaic?

- Mosaic is an Internet-based *global hypermedia* browser that allows you to discover, retrieve, and display

http://www.ncsa.uiuc.edu:80/demoweb/marc-mosaic-intro.au

Figure 12-1
NCSA Mosaic Demo Document

PC Speaker Driver

If you do not have sound capabilities on your PC, you may wish to try the PC speaker as a sound driver. Although it will not produce very good sound, you will be able to get some sense of the sound clip.

Getting the PC Speaker Driver

1. Connect to your Internet service provider and open WebSurfer. We wish to go to the document whose title is External Viewer Information and whose URL is
http://www.ncsa.uiuc.edu/SDG/Software/WinMosaic/viewers.html

2. Click once on **Retrieve** and then click on **Go To URL...**

3. In the WebSurfer - Go To Document box, type the URL given in step 1. Your screen should resemble the one shown in Figure 12-2.

WebSurfer - External Viewer Information

File Retrieve Settings Help

Print | Go to URL | Get URL | Hotlist | Make Hot | Back | Forward | Home | Cancel All

URL: http://www.ncsa.uiuc.edu:80/SDG/Software/WinMosaic/viewers.html

Installing viewers and mosaic.ini

Each file sent from a Web Server is associated with a MIME type and Mosaic can't handle some of these file types internally. For example,.ps (PostScript),.mpeg(movie),.jpg (image),.doc (Word documents), etc... However, Mosaic can send these files to an external application(a viewer) if you properly associate the MIME type to an application in the mosaic.ini file. After you have made the necessary changes to your mosaic.ini file, Mosaic will launch the defined viewer and all you have to do is sit back and view the file.

Below an example of the information that needs to be edited in the mosaic.ini file for an.mpeg movie file. You can edit the mosaic.ini file using any ascii editor. For example, Window's Notepad. You can find it in the Accessories program group.

Edit the mosaic.ini

In the **[Viewers]** section of the mosaic.ini file add or edit this information.

TYPEn="video/mpeg"

where n is a unique integer.

video/mpeg="c:\the\directory\path\ExecutableName.exe %ls"

For example: video/mpeg="c:\winapps\mpeg\mpegplay.exe %ls"

In the **[Suffixes]** section define the extensions that Mosaic needs to associate with this MIME type. The last

For Help, press F1

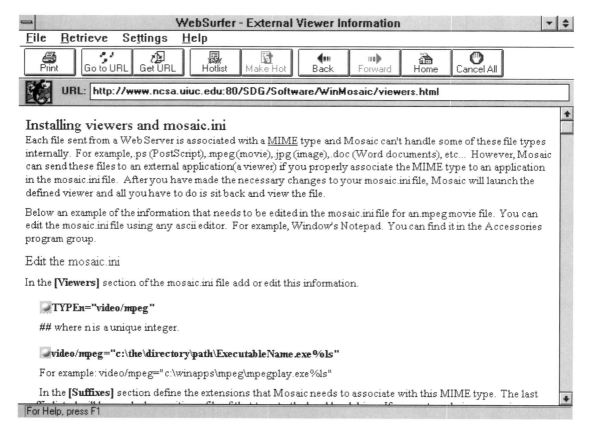

Figure 12-2
External Viewer Information

4. Click on the **down arrow** on the scroll bar until you come to Other Utilities. Your screen should be similar to Figure 12-3.

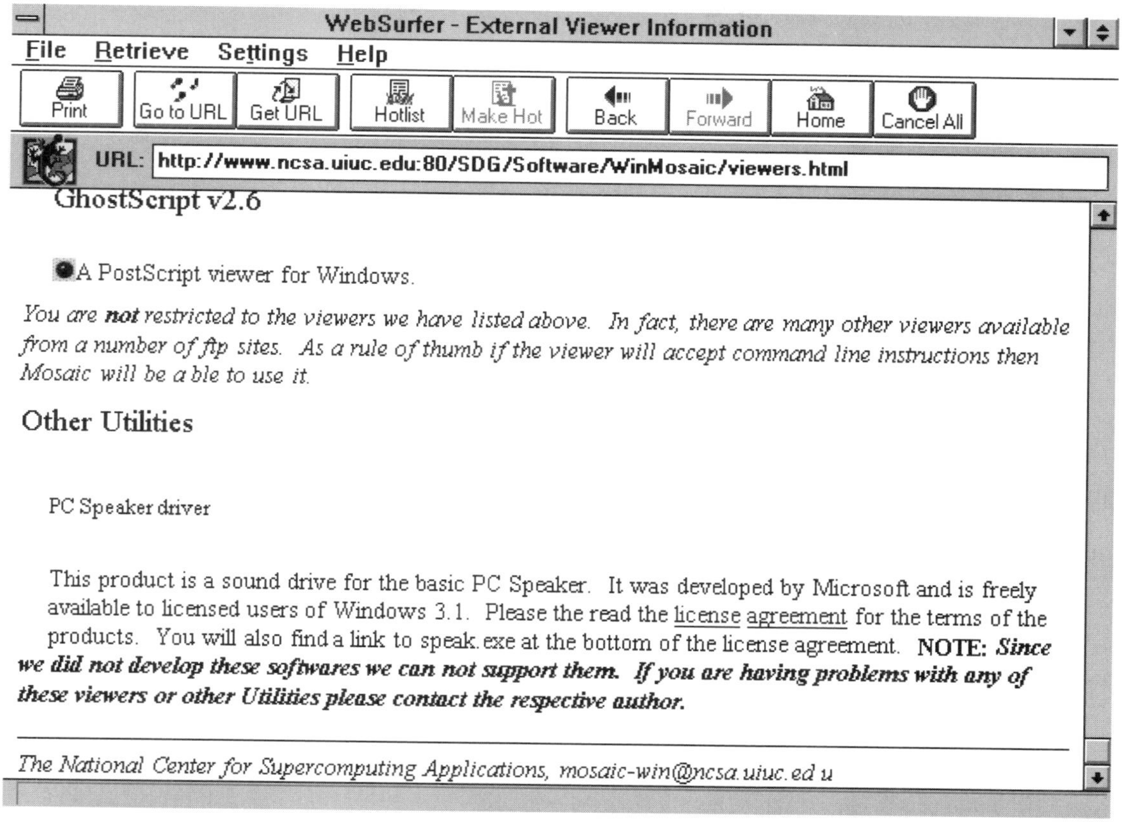

WebSurfer - External Viewer Information

File Retrieve Settings Help

Print | Go to URL | Get URL | Hotlist | Make Hot | Back | Forward | Home | Cancel All

URL: http://www.ncsa.uiuc.edu:80/SDG/Software/WinMosaic/viewers.html

GhostScript v2.6

- A PostScript viewer for Windows.

*You are **not** restricted to the viewers we have listed above. In fact, there are many other viewers available from a number of ftp sites. As a rule of thumb if the viewer will accept command line instructions then Mosaic will be a ble to use it.*

Other Utilities

PC Speaker driver

This product is a sound drive for the basic PC Speaker. It was developed by Microsoft and is freely available to licensed users of Windows 3.1. Please the read the license agreement for the terms of the products. You will also find a link to speak.exe at the bottom of the license agreement. **NOTE:** ***Since we did not develop these softwares we can not support them. If you are having problems with any of these viewers or other Utilities please contact the respective author.***

The National Center for Supercomputing Applications, mosaic-win@ncsa.uiuc.ed u

Figure 12-3
External Viewer Information/Other Utilities

HINT: You may wish to add this URL to your Hotlist, since it contains a wealth of useful information and is one to which you may wish to return often.

5. Under PC Speaker driver find the hyperlink license agreement and click on it. You will receive a long license agreement document. As you read it, you will reach a single large here hyperlink at the bottom of the document.

Note the URL for the file speak.exe. It is ftp.ncsa.uiuc.edu/Mosaic/Windows/viewers/speak.exe

6. We will use FTP to download this file. Since this particular location is a useful source of viewers, you may wish to take a moment to enter this information in your FTP Connection Profile. Here it is:

Description:	`NCSA Viewers`
Host:	`ftp.ncsa.uiuc.edu`
User:	`anonymous`
Password:	your actual Internet address, such as mine, `dsachs@panix.com`
System:	`Auto`
Account:	
Remote Dir:	`Mosaic/Windows/viewers`

If you have done this correctly, your Connection Profile should look like Figure 12-4.

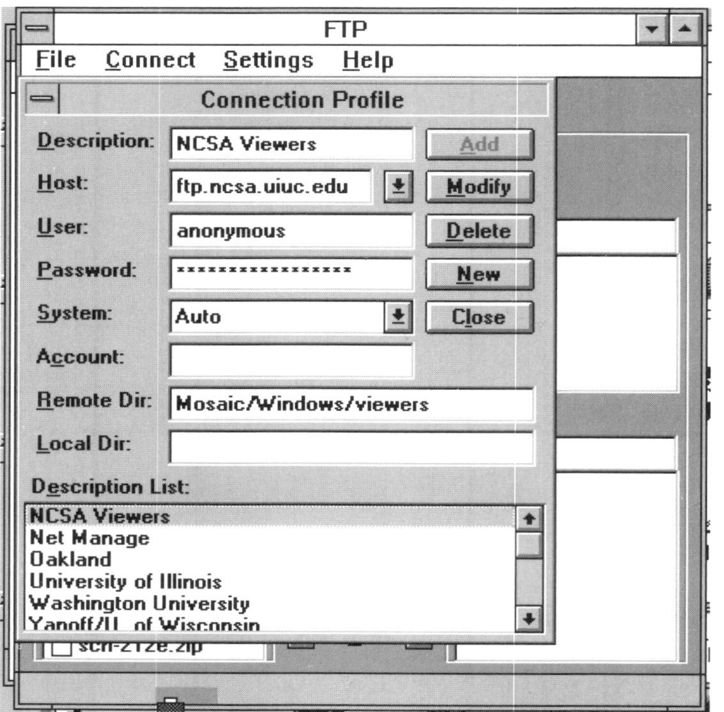

Figure 12-4
Connection Profile for NCSA Viewers

7. Connect to the NCSA Viewers site.
8. Once you locate the file called speak.exe in the Remote Files box, copy it to your local incoming directory.
9. Click on the **down arrow** on the Remote Files scroll bar until you come to two files: wplany.doc and wplny09b.zip. Download both of these to your incoming directory.

You have just downloaded three files, speak.exe, wplany.doc, and wplny09b.zip. Disconnect from your Internet service provider. We will now prepare these files for use.

Installing the PC Speaker Driver

1. Create a directory for your PC Speaker Driver. For example, we created one called speaker (md speaker)

2. Copy the file speak.exe to this directory.

3. Change to the directory called speaker (cd\speaker) and type `speak`

   speak.exe will self-extract all of the PC Speaker Driver files into this directory.

4. Using your favorite word processor, you should print copies of two files: audio.txt and speaker.txt.

   These files will provide you with the information you will need to correctly install the PC Speaker Driver.

5. We will follow the directions given by Microsoft to install the PC Speaker Driver:

   a. In the Main Group, double-click on the **Control Panel Icon**

   b. In the Control Panel, double-click on **Drivers**

   c. In the Drivers dialog box, click on **Add...**

   d. In the List of Drivers box, click on **Unlisted** or **Updated Driver.** Then, choose **OK**

   e. The Install Driver box will appear. If you have installed the files into a subdirectory called speaker, then type

      `c:\speaker`

      Then, click on **OK**

   f. The Add Unlisted or Undated Driver box will appear. You will be told that the name for your file is Sound Driver for PC-Speaker

   g. Since this is correct, click on **OK**

      You should hear a sound emanating from your PC!

IMPORTANT: When you install the SPEAKER.DRV, you will be shown a PC-Speaker Setup box. Change the Seconds to limit playback from its default to No Limit (right end of the bar). Then, click on **OK**

  h. Try hearing the sound by clicking on **Test**

6. When you have finished installing your PC Speaker Driver, you should click on **OK** and then **Cancel** to return to the Control Panel.

Installing and Associating the Windows Play Any File (WPLANY)

1. Create a directory on your hard drive entitled wplayany by typing `md wplayany`

2. Copy the file wplny09b.zip to the wplayany directory

3. Copy the file pkunzip.exe to the wplayany directory

   For example, type
   `copy c:\pkware\pkunzip.exe c:\wplayany`

4. Use pkunzip to unzip wplny09b.zip by typing
   `pkunzip wplny09b.zip`

5. Two files will be created: WPLANY.DOC and WPLANY.EXE

6. Using your favorite word processor, print out WPLANY.DOC

7. Copy WPLANY.EXE to your Windows directory. Type
   `c:\wplayany\wplany.exe c:\windows`

8. In the Main Group, double-click on **File Manager**

9. Click once on **File** and then on **Associate**

10. In the box Files with Extension, enter `au`

11. Tab to the Associate With box, and enter
    `c:\WPLAYANY\WPLANY.EXE`

IMPORTANT: Repeat for the following file extensions: voc and snd

Running the Windows Play Any File (WPLANY)

You can run WPLANY in either of two ways:

1. You can capture sound files (files which typically end in .au) from the World-Wide Web as you encounter them. Then, using Window's Program Manager - File - Run, you can type in `WPLANY filename.au`

   Be patient. The sound won't begin until the file has been loaded completely into the computer's memory.

2. Or, you can associate particular extensions such as au with the particular viewer wplany as we have just finished doing. Once this has been done successfully, the next time you open WebSurfer, you should be able to listen to sound clips from the NCSA Mosaic Demo Page or other locations that contain sound clips.

HINT: If you find that you are receiving other audio types (file extensions) from the Internet, use File Manager, File, and Associate to handle them. Remember that the file must be fully received before it can play. For long sound bites, this may take many seconds.

Playing a Sound

An interesting example of how sound files are being put to use on the World-Wide Web is provided in this next exercise. We will go to the White House to hear a welcome message from President Clinton. To do this,

1. Click on **Retrieve** and then **Go To URL...**

2. In the WebSurfer - Go To Document box, type `http://www.whitehouse.gov`

   The Welcome to the White House Home Page will be downloaded to your computer. It should resemble Figure 12-5.

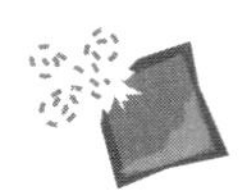

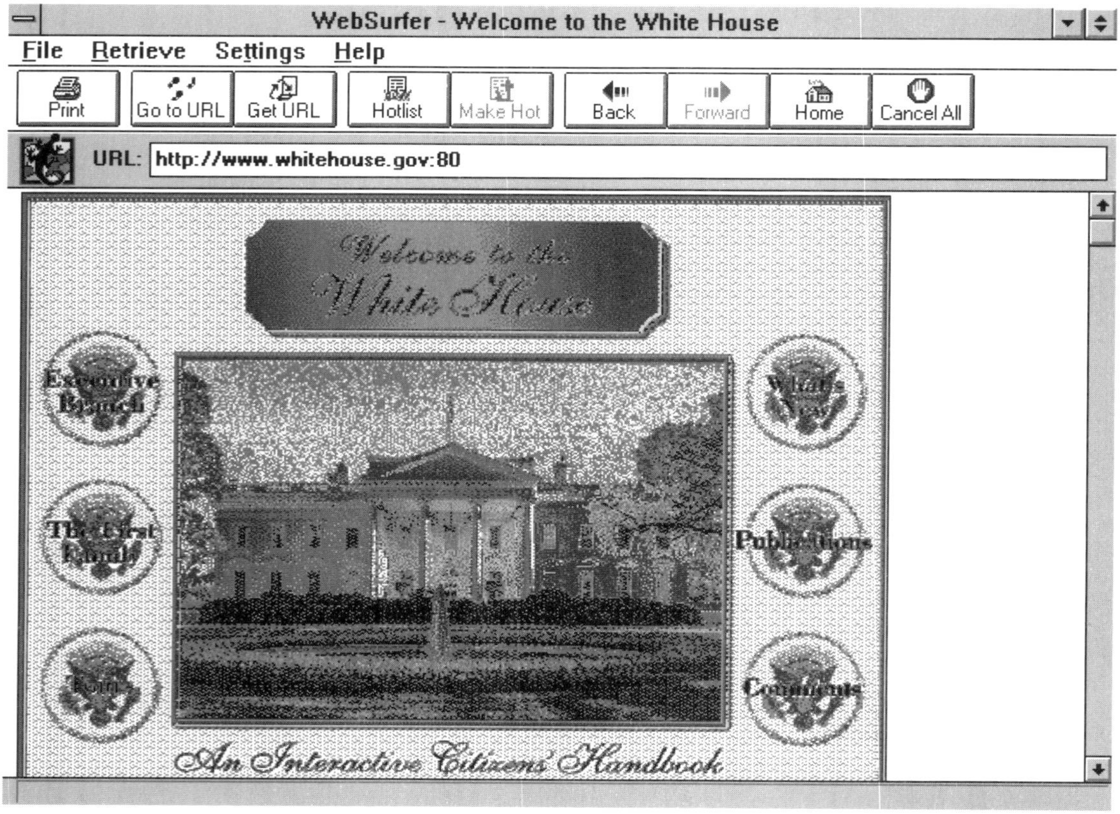

WebSurfer - Welcome to the White House
File Retrieve Settings Help
Print
Go to URL
Get URL
Hotlist
Make Hot
Back
Forward
Home
Cancel All
URL: http://www.whitehouse.gov:80
Welcome to the White House
Executive Branch
What's New
Publications
Comments
An Interactive Citizens' Handbook

Figure 12-5
Welcome to the White House Home Page

3. Click on the hyperlink for **President's Welcome Message**

4. A window labeled Redirection will appear. Slide your cursor over the hyperlink elsewhere. Note the URL that appears on your status bar:

http://www.whitehouse.gov:80/White_House/audio/potus5.au

HEADS UP!

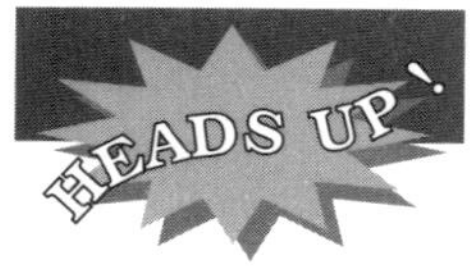

Because of their size, most audio files will take some time to download to your computer, even with a relatively fast modem. Be patient.

Congratulations! If all has gone according to plan, you should now be listening to a welcome message from the President of the United States.

Let's take a break. When we return, we will learn about the many graphics images that WebSurfer permits us to see.

Viewers to See the Pictures

On the worldwide Internet, you can find a marvelous variety of images and video clips that are freely available. For example, space photos from NASA, art from museums, photos of all descriptions, and near-realtime weather satellite views are all available.

Some of the "art" available on the Internet may be objectionable to some people and some of it may be objectionable to almost everyone. To prevent this material from being shown to children, always exercise care and supervision in the use of the Internet.

GIF, JPEG, and PostScript Images

Many formats and standards have evolved for the PC presentation and storage of images and documents. A few have become quite popular and are more commonly found than are others. These more common formats are supported by WebSurfer.

One of them called GIF (and pronounced jiff) is supported directly by WebSurfer. In fact, you have already seen WebSurfer receiving GIF images and then converting them for presentation on your PC's screen. Others, however, require additional software before we are able to see them. Earlier, we mentioned JPEG. GIF and JPEG have become the most common formats for images found around the Internet.

In addition, documents will often be found in PostScript format. If you have a PostScript printer, you can print these files directly. However, even if you have a PostScript printer, you may want to preview these documents before printing. For those without PostScript printers, viewing is the only option. Some viewers are available from the NCSA Mosaic viewers' repository that we visited earlier. We will now get these viewers and help you install them.

Getting a JPEG Viewer

THREE

1. Once again, connect to your Internet service provider and open WebSurfer. As we did earlier in this session, we will use FTP to go to the viewers' repository maintained by NCSA. Make the FTP

Icon active and then click once on **Connect** to connect to NCSA Viewers.

2. Click on the **down arrow** in the Remote Files scroll bar until you come to lview.txt and lview31.zip.
3. Copy both files to your incoming directory. Given its size (224,269 bytes), it may take a few minutes before lview31.zip is loaded to your disk.
4. Close your session with your Internet provider.

Preparing lview for Use

1. Change to the Windows directory
2. Create a subdirectory called apps
3. Create a sub-subdirectory called lview
4. Then, copy LVIEW31.ZIP to the sub-subdirectory called lview
5. Copy pkunzip to the sub-sub-subdirectory called lview
6. Use PKUNZIP.EXE to unzip it as we have done before

   If all goes according to plan, you should wind up with the file called LVIEW31.EXE in a sub-subdirectory called lview.
7. You will need to associate LVIEW31.EXE with the extensions gif and jpeg as we did earlier for the viewer WPLANY and the extension au. Here is how to do so:
   - **a.** Click once on **Main**
   - **b.** Start File Manager
   - **c.** Select **File** and **Associate**
   - **d.** In the Files with Extension box, enter `gif`
   - **e.** Tab to the Associate With box, and enter `c:\WINDOWS\APPS\LVIEW\LVIEW31.EXE`
   - **f.** Click once on **OK**
   - **g.** In the Files With Extension box, enter `jpeg`
   - **h.** Tab to the Associate With box and enter `c:\WINDOWS\APPS\LVIEW\LVIEW31.EXE`
   - **i.** Click once on **OK**
   - **j.** In the Files With Extension box, enter `jpg`
   - **k.** Tab to the Associate With box and enter `c:\WINDOWS\APPS\LVIEW\LVIEW31.EXE`

Showing a JPEG Picture

After putting all of the file associations into place, we connected to San Francisco's Exploratorium and got the photo of a giant bubble, as shown in Figure 12-6.

W0074.JPG: 733x406x256 - LView 3.1
File Edit Retouch Options Help
© 1994, The Exploratorium
http://www.exploratorium.edu:80/imagery/stills/Hand_bubble.jpg

Figure 12-6
Hand Bubble

Here's how you can do it.

1. Connect to your Internet service provider and start WebSurfer
2. Click once on **Retrieve** and then on **Go To URL...** and then type `http://www.exploratorium.edu`
3. Following hyperlinks, we reach the area where images are to be found:
   a. Click on **Digital Library**
   b. Click on **Other Interesting Images**

c. Click on **just use your hands!**

If you do this, the image called HAND_BUB.JPG will be transferred to your computer.

By clicking on a series of hyperlinks, we received the photo shown in Figure 12-6. If all is configured properly, WebSurfer will use lview to display this (or any other GIF or JPEG) image.

NOTE: You may now transfer other images and view them online. Or, you may use the File Save or File Save As feature of LVIEW to save the files for later viewing.

To view files that have been loaded to a file, you have several options:

a. You can use WebSurfer's Retrieve - Open Local File.

b. You can use lview directly from Program Manager - File - Run.

c. You can choose to install lview with its own icon in Windows.

PostScript Documents and Images

To view PostScript documents, you need two tools: Ghostscript and Ghostview. Both are available using WebSurfer and both are needed to display PostScript files. *Ghostscript* is a PostScript interpreter and *Ghostview* is a Windows-based viewer for Ghostscript. The following activity will help you to get, install, and test both programs.

FIVE

PostScript Viewers

1. Once again, connect to your Internet service provider and open WebSurfer. As we did earlier in this session, we will use FTP to retrieve some files from the NCSA viewers' repository.

2. We would like to download a file whose actual file name is gs261exe.zip which is known as GhostScript v2.6 (or whatever the current version is called). This will be our PostScript viewer for Windows. You should see a screen resembling the one in Figure 12-7.

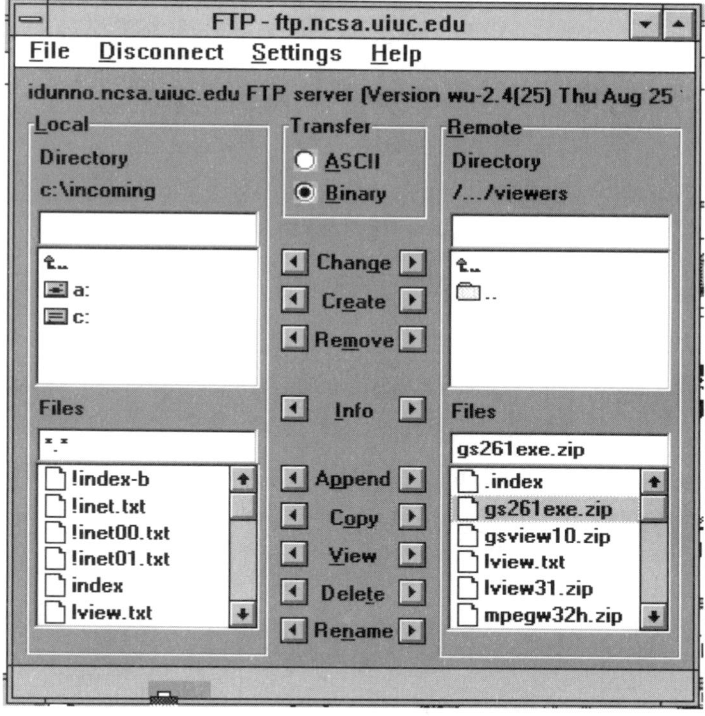

Figure 12-7
GhostScript

gs261exe.zip is another very large file—over a million bytes. Be patient or decide to come back later. To view PostScript files, you will need this program.

3. Be sure that you are prepared to download this file as a binary file to your incoming directory. Highlight `gs261exe.zip` in the Remote Files directory and then click once on the **left-hand copy button.**

4. Now, it is time to download the file whose actual name as of this writing is gsview10.zip. It is known as Ghostview. As before, be sure that you are prepared to download a binary file to your incoming directory. Then, highlight `gsview10.zip` in the Remote Files directory and click once on the **left-hand copy button.**

5. When Ghostview has been downloaded, disconnect from your Internet service provider.

Now we will create a directory called GS and place these files in that directory one at a time. This sequence should be followed carefully to ensure that all of the programs work together.

1. To create the directory GS,
    a. At a DOS prompt, type `c:\mkdir gs`
    b. Now, move to the directory cd\gs
2. Copy gs261exe.zip to the GS directory

NOTE: We are using gs261exe.zip, but you may get a later version. It will be indicated by a number differing from 261.

---

3. Copy pkunzip.exe to the GS directory.
4. Use pkunzip.exe to unzip gs261exe.zip Read the files readme and use.doc
5. Now, copy gsview10.zip to the GS directory and unzip it. (Again, you may get a later version than the number 10 which we found.)
6. Open Windows and use File - New - Program Item to add the GSVIEW program to a group of your choice. You may wish to add it to the Internet Chameleon Group or you may first wish to create a new viewers' group. Figure 12-8 shows an example.

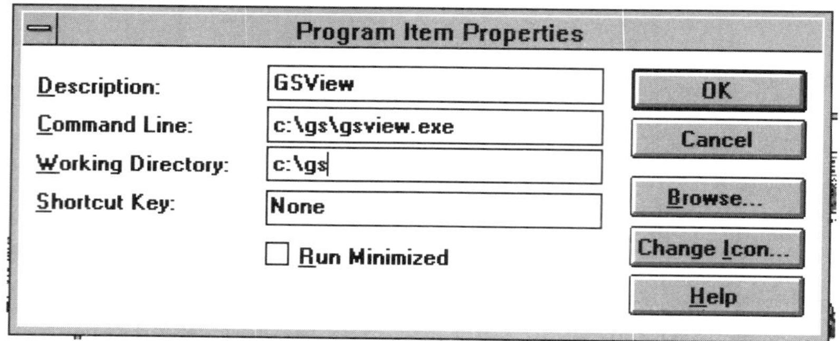

Figure 12-8
Installing Ghostview

7. Click on **OK** and double-click on the new **GSView Ghost Icon**

Before attempting to read any files, there is one more step. We have to tell Ghostview how to talk to both GhostScript and to Windows.

8. With GSView open, click on **Options**

9. Click on **Ghostscript Command...**

10. Type in the following exactly: `C:\GS\GSWIN.EXE -IC:\GS` Now, click on **OK**

GSView should now be operational. You can test this with a PostScript image that comes with Ghostscript.

11. Click on **File - Open** and find GOLFER.PS in the GS directory. Double-click on this file and you should be rewarded with the image shown in Figure 12-9.

Figure 12-9
Golfer

As we have done earlier in this session, you should associate the file extensions that are typically affiliated with PostScript files with the viewer GSView. Here is how to do so:

1. Start File Manager
2. Select **File** and **Associate**
3. In the box Files with Extension, enter `ps`
4. Tab to the Associate With box and enter `c:\GS\GSVIEW.EXE`
5. Repeat these steps for the extensions eps and ai

Here is a quick way to test if this has been successful.

1. Open WebSurfer and click on **Retrieve** and then on **Open Local File...**
2. Go to the GS directory and open GOLFER.PS

You should again see the figure of the golfer that was shown in Figure 12-9.

Congratulations! Your copy of WebSurfer is now capable of receiving and displaying JPEG and PostScript files.

SIX

Finding Music, Images, and Multimedia

Figures 12-10 through 12-13 are included to give you some ideas about where to go next for sounds and images. In each figure, the document name and document URL are shown by WebSurfer. To explore these, we will just show you the figures and not give you our usual step-by-step instructions. By now, we believe, you know how to do this on your own. Happy exploring!

Music, Images, and Multimedia

Document
Title: Internet Resources List

Document
URL: http://www.eit.com/web/netservices.html

Once the Internet Resources Home Page appears, just click on the hyperlink **Music, Images, and Multimedia** to see the screen shown in Figure 12-10.

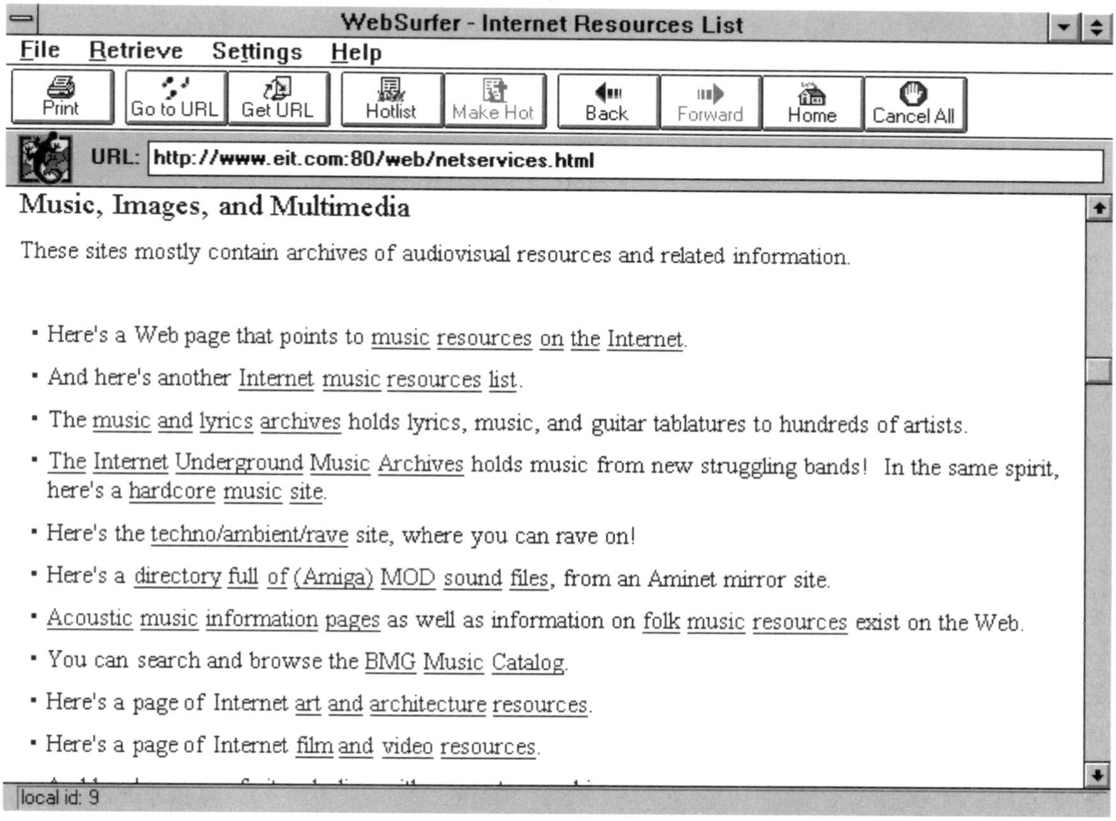

WebSurfer - Internet Resources List

File Retrieve Settings Help

Print | Go to URL | Get URL | Hotlist | Make Hot | Back | Forward | Home | Cancel All

URL: http://www.eit.com:80/web/netservices.html

Music, Images, and Multimedia

These sites mostly contain archives of audiovisual resources and related information.

- Here's a Web page that points to music resources on the Internet.
- And here's another Internet music resources list.
- The music and lyrics archives holds lyrics, music, and guitar tablatures to hundreds of artists.
- The Internet Underground Music Archives holds music from new struggling bands! In the same spirit, here's a hardcore music site.
- Here's the techno/ambient/rave site, where you can rave on!
- Here's a directory full of (Amiga) MOD sound files, from an Aminet mirror site.
- Acoustic music information pages as well as information on folk music resources exist on the Web.
- You can search and browse the BMG Music Catalog.
- Here's a page of Internet art and architecture resources.
- Here's a page of Internet film and video resources.

local id: 9

Figure 12-10
Internet Resources List

Guide to Film and Video

Document
Title: Film and Video Resources

Document
URL: http://http2.sils.umich.edu/Public/fvl/film.html

Click on **Retrieve** and then on **Go To URL...** Type in the URL and then click. The Film and Video Resources Home Page shown in Figure 12-11 will appear.

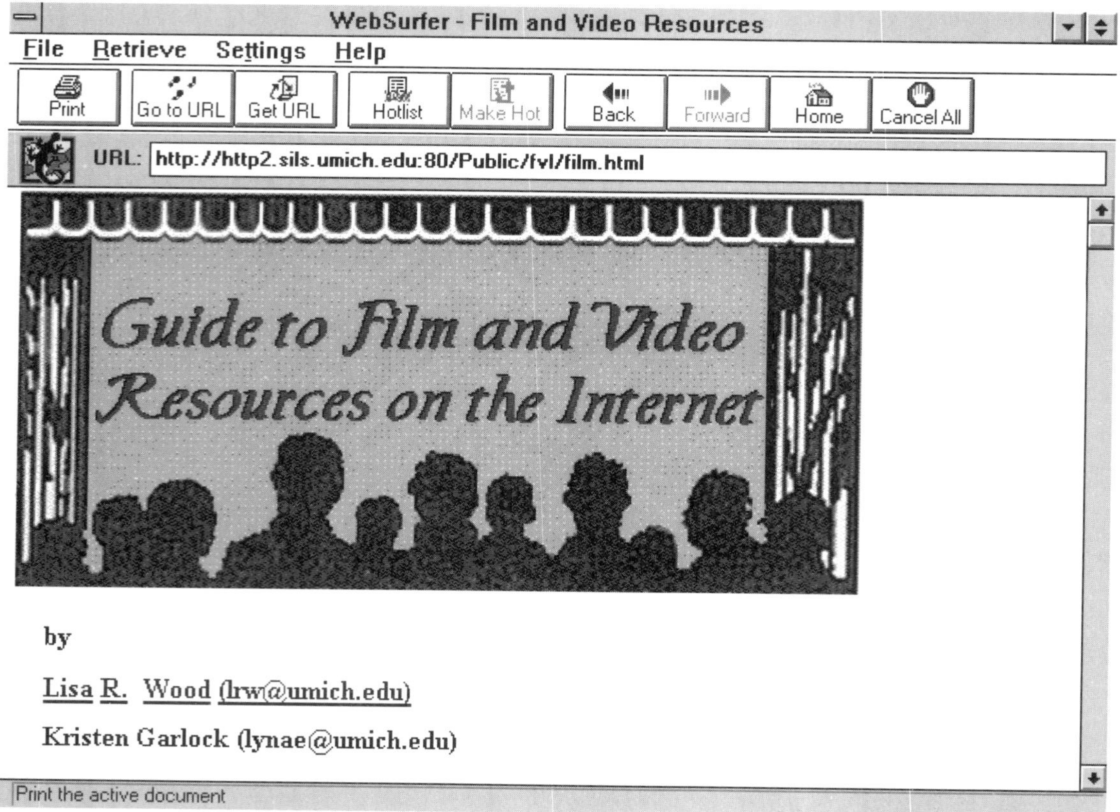

Figure 12-11
Film and Video Resources

USG Current Weather Maps/Movies

Document
Title: Current Weather Maps/Movies

Document
URL: http://clunix.cl.msu.edu:80/weather/

To see the screen in Figure 12-12, click on **Retrieve** and then on **Go To URL...** Type the URL and then click on **OK**.

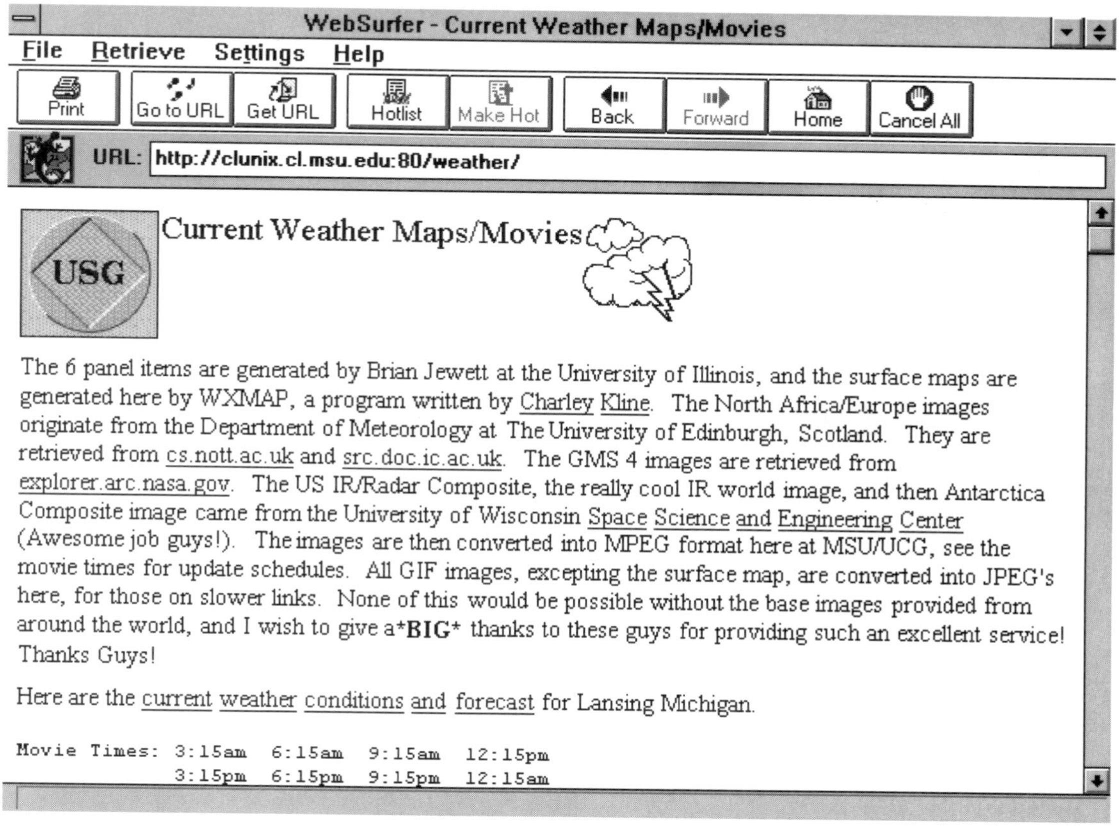

WebSurfer - Current Weather Maps/Movies

File Retrieve Settings Help

Print | Go to URL | Get URL | Hotlist | Make Hot | Back | Forward | Home | Cancel All

URL: http://clunix.cl.msu.edu:80/weather/

USG Current Weather Maps/Movies

The 6 panel items are generated by Brian Jewett at the University of Illinois, and the surface maps are generated here by WXMAP, a program written by Charley Kline. The North Africa/Europe images originate from the Department of Meteorology at The University of Edinburgh, Scotland. They are retrieved from cs.nott.ac.uk and src.doc.ic.ac.uk. The GMS 4 images are retrieved from explorer.arc.nasa.gov. The US IR/Radar Composite, the really cool IR world image, and then Antarctica Composite image came from the University of Wisconsin Space Science and Engineering Center (Awesome job guys!). The images are then converted into MPEG format here at MSU/UCG, see the movie times for update schedules. All GIF images, excepting the surface map, are converted into JPEG's here, for those on slower links. None of this would be possible without the base images provided from around the world, and I wish to give a***BIG*** thanks to these guys for providing such an excellent service! Thanks Guys!

Here are the current weather conditions and forecast for Lansing Michigan.

```
Movie Times: 3:15am  6:15am  9:15am  12:15pm
             3:15pm  6:15pm  9:15pm  12:15am
```

Figure 12-12
Current Weather Maps/Movies

Krannert Art Museum, UIUC

Document
Title: Krannert Art Museum
Document URL:
`http://www.ncsa.uiuc.edu/General/UIUC/KrannertArtMuseum/KrannertArtHome.html`

Click on **File** and **Open URL** Then type in the URL and click on **OK** to see the screen in Figure 12-13.

Figure 12-13
Krannert Art Museum

Session Summary

In this session, you have begun to experience the multimedia aspects of WebSurfer and the World-Wide Web. You have installed software that permits you to hear many of the audio sounds that are available on the World-Wide Web. The viewers you have installed make it possible for you to see an amazing array of images on your PC. In addition, you can now preview PostScript files before printing them. As the last activity in this session illustrated, the array of sights and sounds on the World-Wide Web is limitless. We hope you will enjoy many pleasurable hours exploring the multimedia universe that WebSurfer and these new software programs make available to you!

Index

A

B

C

I

J

S

T

U

V

W

Y

Z

LICENSE AGREEMENT AND LIMITED WARRANTY

READ THE FOLLOWING TERMS AND CONDITIONS CAREFULLY BEFORE OPENING THE DISK PACKAGE. THIS IS AN AGREEMENT BETWEEN YOU AND PRENTICE HALL PTR (THE "COMPANY"). BY OPENING THIS SEALED PACKAGE, YOU ARE AGREEING TO BE BOUND BY THESE TERMS AND CONDITIONS. IF YOU DO NOT AGREE, WITH THESE TERMS AND CONDITIONS, DO NOT OPEN THE DISK PACKAGE.

1. GRANT OF LICENSE: In consideration of your purchase of this book, and your agreement to abide by the terms and conditions of this Agreement, the Company grants to you a nonexclusive right to use and display the copy of the enclosed software program (hereinafter the "SOFTWARE") so long as you comply with the terms of this Agreement. The Company reserves all rights not expressly granted to you under this Agreement. This license is <u>not</u> a sale of the original SOFTWARE or any copy to you.

2. USE RESTRICTIONS: You may <u>not</u> sell or license copies of the SOFTWARE or the Documentation to others. You may <u>not</u> reverse engineer, disassemble, decompile, modify, adapt, translate or create derivative works based on the SOFTWARE or the Documentation without the prior written consent of the Company and the software developer.

3. LIMITED WARRANTY AND DISCLAIMER OF WARRANTY: BECAUSE THIS SOFTWARE IS BEING GIVEN TO YOU WITHOUT CHARGE, THE COMPANY MAKES NO WARRANTIES ABOUT THE SOFTWARE, WHICH IS PROVIDED "AS-IS." THE COMPANY DISCLAIMS ALL WARRANTIES, EXPRESS OR IMPLIED, INCLUDING WITHOUT LIMITATION, THE IMPLIED WARRANTIES OF MERCHANTABILITY AND FITNESS FOR A PARTICULAR PURPOSE. THE COMPANY DOES NOT WARRANT, GUARANTEE OR MAKE ANY REPRESENTATION REGARDING THE USE OR THE RESULTS OF THE USE OF THE SOFTWARE. IN NO EVENT, SHALL THE COMPANY OR ITS EMPLOYEES, AGENTS, SUPPLIERS OR CONTRACTORS BE LIABLE FOR ANY INCIDENTAL, INDIRECT, SPECIAL OR CONSEQUENTIAL DAMAGES ARISING OUT OF OR IN CONNECTION WITH THE LICENSE GRANTED UNDER THIS AGREEMENT, NOR FOR LOSS OF USE, LOSS OF DATA, LOSS OF INCOME OR PROFIT, OR OTHER LOSSES, SUSTAINED AS A RESULT OF INJURY TO ANY PERSON, OR LOSS OF OR DAMAGE TO PROPERTY, OR CLAIMS OF THIRD PARTIES, EVEN IF THE COMPANY HAS BEEN ADVISED OF THE POSSIBILITY OF SUCH DAMAGES.

SOME JURISDICITIONS DO NOT ALLOW THE LIMITATION OF IMPLIED WARRANTIES OR LIABILITY FOR INCIDENTAL, INDIRECT, SPECIAL OR CONSEQUENTIAL DAMAGES. SO THE ABOVE LIMITATIONS MAY NOT ALWAYS APPLY. THE WARRANTIES IN THIS AGREEEMENT GIVE YOU SPECIFIC LEGAL RIGHTS AND YOU MAY ALSO HAVE OTHER RIGHTS WHICH VARY IN ACCORDANCE WITH LOCAL LAW.

Should you have any questions concerning this agreement or if you wish to contact the Company for any reason, please contact in writing:

Mary Franz
Prentice Hall PTR
113 Sylvan Ave.
Englewood Cliffs, NJ 07632